Destroying to Replace

Settler Genocides of Indigenous Peoples

Mohamed Adhikari

Hackett Publishing Company, Inc.
Indianapolis/Cambridge

25 24 23 22   1 2 3 4 5 6 7

For further information, please address
    Hackett Publishing Company, Inc.
    P.O. Box 44937
    Indianapolis, Indiana 46244-0937

    www.hackettpublishing.com

Cover design by Rick Todhunter
Interior design by E. L. Wilson
Composition by Aptara, Inc.
Maps by Liezel Bohdanowics. Copyright © Hackett Publishing Company, Inc.

Cataloging-in-Publication data can be accessed via the Library of Congress
Online Catalog.
Library of Congress Control Number: 2021946131

ISBN-13: 978-1-64792-054-8 (cloth)
ISBN-13: 978-1-64792-049-4 (pbk.)
ISBN-13: 978-1-64792-055-5 (PDF ebook)

The paper used in this publication meets the minimum requirements of American
National Standard for Information Sciences—Permanence of Paper for Printed
Library Materials, ANSI Z39.48–1984.

∞

CONTENTS

For Rafiq and Zaheer

and in loving memory of Marie Maud

ABOUT THE SERIES

Critical Themes in World History focuses on phenomena that have had a profound impact on the course of world history. The first two books in the series, *Shackles of Iron: Slavery Beyond the Atlantic* and *Protests in the Streets: 1968 Across the Globe*, respectively consider, within a global context, human bondage over the past four thousand years and mid-twentieth-century efforts to break the bonds of institutional subordination. Each book, including this newest addition to the series, employs a combination of narrative and primary sources aimed at helping students and general readers alike discover and analyze how the phenomenon under consideration has played a critical role in the unfolding of human history through time and across the globe.

Driving this series is the philosophy that analysis of data and an unconstrained commitment to follow wherever that analysis leads are key elements in any meaningful study of the past. For this reason, the authors of each book have labored to raise as many questions as possible and offer select packages of visual and documentary sources, thereby challenging readers to take an active role in exploring the issue under consideration. Current pedagogical research stresses the benefits of active learning—learning that leads to the sharpening of one's critical faculties. The publisher, this editor, and all authors contributing to the series are committed to offering books that encourage readers to probe, in a meaningful way, the events, institutions, and ways of thought and action that have contributed to the shaping of our world.

Alfred J. Andrea
Series Editor

ACKNOWLEDGMENTS

In a work of this sort, one's intellectual debts are legion. While they are acknowledged in the referencing and in the Further Reading section, there are a few that deserve special mention. In the Introduction, the theorizing of Patrick Wolfe and Lorenzo Veracini around settler colonialism provided the foundation for much of my discussion on the subject; with the Canaries chapter, John Mercer's *The Canary Islanders* first sparked my interest in this case and provided a good deal of the necessary context; in the Queensland case study Raymond Evans's decades-long work on frontier violence in that colony was essential to my inquiry; Benjamin Madley's comprehensive *An American Genocide* was indispensable for the analysis on California; and with the Herero genocide, the work of Jüergen Zimmerer and Henning Melber were key.

Of the many book projects I have worked on, this one has by some measure been the most enjoyable. Importantly, this is the first time I have had the opportunity of combining the writing of a book so integrally with my teaching of the subject matter. Research and writing have always enriched my teaching, but never have I had the benefit of the two feeding off each other in this direct way. For this privilege I thank Rick Todhunter, senior editor at Hackett Publishing, and Al Andrea, series editor of Critical Themes in World History, not only for commissioning this work, but also for allowing me the freedom to choose the case studies I wanted to cover and to develop the content as I saw fit. They nonetheless interrogated my choices and together we explored alternatives, forcing me to think through the options with care. I am also extremely grateful to all the students who unwittingly contributed to the project through class discussion where some challenged my ideas as well as those presented in course readings. By offering fresh perspectives, they often caused me to see matters in a different light, or at times even to rethink my approach to a particular topic altogether. Teaching is indeed a very effective way of learning.

Also, working with Al Andrea was an absolute delight. Never have I had an editor who read my drafts so closely and provided such incisive commentary. The final product benefited enormously from his input. Nor have I ever had an editor whose razor-sharp wit made me laugh so often or so loudly; nor one who brightened my day so much with ongoing email banter. And when for copyright reasons we were unable to use a key primary source for the Canaries chapter, he in an act of uncommon generosity, volunteered to translate the original from medieval French into English. I have said this before, and I will say it again: Al, you are a true mensch!

I am immeasurably appreciative of the congeniality and proficiency of the rest of the team that collaborated in the creation of this book. Rick Todhunter kept a steady hand on the tiller and, while contributing throughout to the three-way email banter, ensured that the process went smoothly from start to finish. Liz Wilson did a sterling job of guiding the manuscript through the production phase. My thanks to Liezel Bohdanowicz for the superb maps she produced from the crude sketches and descriptions I provided. I am also deeply indebted to the anonymous peer reviewers for their thorough scrutiny of the book proposal as well as the draft manuscript, and for their many useful suggestions for improvement. For me this will always be the book project I did during the COVID pandemic. Dealing with such genial and collegial people made this dark time so much more bearable.

I would, in addition, like to acknowledge generous research funding from the National Research Foundation of South Africa and the University Research Committee of the University of Cape Town (UCT), without which this project would not have been possible.

Given that this book is aimed primarily at senior undergraduate students, it is fitting that I dedicate it to an inspired teacher, Marie Maud, one of the history lecturers during my undergraduate years at UCT. Late 1970s apartheid-era UCT was a rather hostile environment for black students; Marie stood out, however, not simply as someone who welcomed social and cultural diversity, but also as one who understood the sense of alienation and other challenges students such as myself faced. Because of Marie's outstanding teaching in the first-year course—considerably enhanced by her flamboyant, melodramatic, and chain-smoking style—I switched from the law program, in which History I was an elective, to a Bachelor of Arts degree majoring in history and African history—and never looked back.

Although her assertively proclaimed liberalism stood awkwardly against my muddled Marxism, she went out of her way to include an initially very reluctant Adhikari in the group of students she gathered around her and that gravitated toward her charismatic presence. This was a group she sought to mentor academically and educate politically—in a decidedly anti-apartheid but moderately activist fashion. For her, peaceful change through intercommunal dialogue and understanding was the only viable option for South Africa, while I at the time was convinced that nothing short of sustained violence would topple the apartheid establishment. Because of her persistent overtures and despite my reservations about her politics, we became firm friends and I, half unwittingly, the object of her informal mentoring. Were it not for her little nudges, sidelong advice, and oblique guidance I would not be an academic today. Thank you, Marie!

An indefatigable activist, Marie tragically died in a car accident in mid-1981, a few months after my BA graduation, while organizing anti-apartheid activity, as a member of the Women's Movement for Peace, in Gugulethu, one of the city's major African townships.[1]

As always, my books are dedicated to my loving sons Rafiq and Zaheer. While poor Mr. Kakles is no more, Mr. Max runs the show. And all I have to say to Skipper and Junior is "long may you run my boys, long may you run"—pace Neil Young.

---

1. Under apartheid, townships were racially segregated dormitory ghettos for black people usually located on the periphery of cities and towns. African people required passes to live and work in urban areas that were regarded as exclusively part of the white, settler homeland and were barred from owning land there. Today the racial composition of these "locations"—a colloquial synonym for townships—has barely changed.

PREFACE

In early January 2009, while passing through Heathrow Airport on my way to the first international conference on genocide organized by the International Network of Genocide Scholars at Sheffield University, a somewhat aggressive immigration officer checking my passport asked me rather abruptly why I was visiting the UK. I told him that I was attending a conference. He asked on what; I replied, "On genocide." His body stiffened and a look of disgust permeated his face. His response: "Why would anyone want to hold a conference *on that?*" Having encountered this attitude before, I could have given him a detailed answer. But not wanting to tangle with an immigration officer I left it at a mildly sarcastic: "Well, should we rather ignore the problem?" Why indeed, organize a conference on genocide or study the subject?

Firstly, genocide is a major historical phenomenon that has played an integral part in the development of human society and to suggest, for whatever reason, that it should not be studied is fatuous. Every aspect of human experience is open to scholarly inquiry. Secondly, and importantly, genocide and mass violence are continuing blights on contemporary life, and I believe that a necessary step in dealing with problems of this kind effectively is to understand their historical, social, and psychological dynamics. Thirdly, on a daily basis, I encounter such appalling ignorance about, and willful distortions of, our violent and compromised pasts that there is clearly an urgent and continuing need to educate, inform, and dispel misperceptions—or at the very least, make relevant information and lines of reasoning publicly available. Finally, my experience has been that survivors of genocide and their descendants overwhelmingly want to tell their stories and want their experiences to be made known and understood. That such voices and communities have on the whole been marginalized in narratives that predominate in public discourses, national mythologies, school curricula, and frequently in academia itself, is further incentive to counter it. There are, of course, other reasons for studying genocide.

Also, it needs to be understood that judgments regarding Western colonial practice, be it genocidal violence, racism, or the exploitation of conquered peoples, do not necessarily imply Western exceptionalism in these respects. Genocide is a human failing and needs to be analyzed as such. Westerners are not any more prone to violence or genocide than any other human group with the power, incentive, and opportunity to commit such atrocities. This is not, however, to deny the intensified destruction that flowed from unique aspects of the Western historical experience—most notably, its lead in developing the global capitalist system, as well as the advantages it gained from being the first to industrialize and develop an extensive range of technologies[1] that aided conquest and the perpetration of mass violence.

Because genocide and settler colonialism, viewed within the context of world history, are both exceptionally broad subjects, I have limited this study to their role in the making of Western global dominance. All-inclusive coverage would have resulted in an analysis that is patchy and conclusions that are diffuse given the constraints presented by the format of this series, especially the limitation to four case studies. The focus on Western expansion, though in itself global in scope, nonetheless allows for a high degree of coherence in the treatment of the subject because of a wide range of common factors at play, as elaborated in the Epilogue, "Reflections and Conclusions."

While the methodology of this study is primarily historical, its scope is necessarily interdisciplinary as both genocide and settler colonial studies are interdisciplinary fields. And although chapters focus on specific cases, the overall approach is comparative. Key themes that run through all case studies include the means, both formal and informal, whereby settlers gained control of the land; patterns in the perpetration of murder and massacre, especially the ways in which settler civilians organized themselves to commit mass violence against Indigenes; how settlers' need for, and attitudes toward, Indigenous labor impacted their behavior; gendered and generational aspects of the violence, including the treatment of captives and conquered both during the lethal frontier phase and afterward; settler relations with metropolitan and colonial governments in the making of these colonial orders, and how they influenced processes of land confiscation and violence toward Indigenes; the role of law and legal regimes in regulating relations between settler and Indigene; the impact of global forces of industrialization, competing imperialisms, and mass migration, among others; the repercussions that specific forms of settler economic activity and commodity production such as pastoralism, crop growing, and mining held for Indigenous societies; and the environmental impacts of settler invasions including those of disease and the destruction of flora and fauna on Indigenous communities. Although the focus of this book is necessarily on the genocide of Indigenous peoples, we should guard against reducing their histories to their destruction.

Popular understandings of genocide are heavily influenced by the Holocaust and the tendency to equate it with mass killing. This predisposition is strongly mirrored in academia in that the field of genocide studies has been too inclined

---

1. Technology is not used in the narrow material sense of guns, transportation, and steelmaking, but in its broader sense of including nonmaterial elements such as legal, landholding, and accounting systems as well.

to use the Holocaust as a yardstick for genocide and too susceptible to focusing on the more recent mass killings, such as the excesses of the Nazi and Stalinist regimes, or those that befell Armenians, Cambodians, and Rwandan Tutsi. The result is that colonial genocides have generally been overlooked within the discipline. It is only in the last two decades that significant attention has been paid to the relationship between colonialism and genocide, and more pertinently, settler colonialism and genocide. This book seeks to subvert this hegemonic understanding of genocide by setting it within a conceptual frame that establishes its ancient roots and emphasizes the very wide range of socially destructive practices, besides killing, that perpetrators have deployed. It also explores the relationship between settler colonialism and genocide in ways that challenge the elaborate mythologies that settler societies have propagated about their histories and claims to the land.

Just as settler establishments around the world have sought to disavow the foundational violence of colonial conquest, dispossession, and in many cases, genocide, so has an abiding sense of historic injustice remained with surviving Indigenous peoples. This is most certainly the case in my native South Africa where the aboriginal Cape San communities were hunted to near extinction by white settler militia known as commandos during the eighteenth and nineteenth centuries. In response to a request in the late 1990s for advice on restitution to be demanded from the South African government, one San elder responded: "Land, water and truth."[2]

---

2. Roger Chennels and Aymone du Toit, "The Rights of Indigenous Peoples in South Africa," in *Indigenous Peoples' Rights in Southern Africa*, eds. Robert Hitchcock and Diana Vinding (Copenhagen: IWGIA, 2004), 98.

SERIES EDITOR'S FOREWORD

On May 15, 2021, a small band of Pomo Native Americans and sympathetic associates held a Sunrise Ceremony of Forgiveness at the base of a hill known variously as Bo-no-po-ti (Old Island) and Badon-napo-ti (Island Village), but more popularly called Bloody Island.[1] Once an island in northern California's Clear Lake, today it is a low hill surrounded by reclaimed land. Moreover, a private agricultural corporation that owns the hill has fenced it off, with signs prohibiting entry. Outside the fence, along a seldom-traveled road, is a marker laid down by the Native Sons of the Golden West on May 20, 1942, and dedicated that day by one of its distinguished members, Earl Warren, then state attorney general and later an icon of progressivism when he served as chief justice of the US Supreme Court. It is at that marker, which commemorates a supposed battle that took place on the island/hill in 1850, that the Pomo and friends gather annually in May to conduct a ceremonial dance of forgiveness and reconciliation and to deposit small memorial tokens.

The plaque mentions a *battle* between soldiers commanded by Captain *Lyons* and Indians *under Chief Augustine* that took place on *April 14*, 1850. Wrong, wrong, wrong. Brevet Captain Nathaniel Lyon commanded a cavalry force that, on May 15, massacred unknown numbers of Pomo, largely women and children, who had peacefully assembled for the spring fish spawn. In his report of May 22, Lyon noted that his men pursued and shot "Indians" fleeing into the water and thick aquatic vegetation that surrounded the island and claimed sixty confirmed dead but estimated "a hundred and upwards" had been slain. He further noted that there had been no effective return fire, and his unit suffered no casualties. Nowhere does he mention Chief Augustine, who apparently was not on the island.[2]

We should not expect the Native Sons of the Golden West to be critical historians or sympathetic to any Native American people. Founded in 1875, the organization limited membership to "native-born" white California males.

---

1. For an account of the 2021 ceremony, see "'We Always Have Our Ancestors within US'": Scenes from Bloody Island's Sunrise Ceremony," KQED, accessed June 5, 2011, https://www.kqed.org/news/11874585/we-always-have-our-ancestors-within-us-scenes-from-bloody-islands-sunrise-ceremony.

2. Report of Brevet Captain Nathaniel Lyon, in *Collected Documents of the Causes and Events in the Bloody Island Massacre of 1850*, ed. Robert F. Heizer (Berkeley, CA: Department of Anthropology, University of California, 1973), 10, accessed June 12, 2021, https://digitalassets.lib.berkeley.edu/anthpubs/ucb/text/arfs010-001.pdf.

The 1942 plaque. Memorial offerings, left on May 15, 2021, include a carved eagle, a block of obsidian, a local volcanic glass from which the Pomo once crafted arrowheads, spear points, and knives, and a shell, an ancient native symbol of renewal. Remains of the blood-red paint tossed onto the plaque in 2002 remain. Photo by A. J. Andrea.

In their worldview, California's history began with the arrival of the Gold Rush '49ers, and the organization's purpose was "to perpetuate in the minds of all native Californians the memories of the days of '49."[3] These so-called native sons were likewise a strident voice calling for the internment of Japanese and Japanese American citizens in the wake of Pearl Harbor. In their view, American Indians and native-born Japanese Americans were equally not true natives.

A short distance away at a large turnout on State Route 20, Historical Landmark 427 presents a more accurate description of what occurred nearby on May 15, 1850. Rightly calling it a "massacre" of largely women and children, it also notes that this was a reprisal for the killing of two white settlers, Andrew Kelsey (after whom nearby Kelseyville and Kelsey Creek are named) and Charles Stone,

---

3. Constitution of the Native Sons of the Golden West, Project Gutenberg Self-Publishing Press, accessed June 11, 2021, http://www.self.gutenberg.org/articles/eng/Native_Sons_and_Daughters_of_the_Golden_West.

Historical Landmark 427. Bloody Island is in the background. Photo by A. J. Andrea.

"who had long enslaved, brutalized, and starved indigenous people in the area." But that is not the entire story.

The two men, the first white American settlers in Lake County, were cold-blooded killers who were an integral part of the genocide visited upon California's Indigenous peoples by settlers, in large part who arrived in the wake of James Marshall's discovery of gold at Sutter's Mill in 1848—a mill that had been built by enslaved Native American labor. Indeed, Chief Augustine, who killed Stone (ironically with a rock), was avenging his wife, whom the men had reduced to sexual slavery. Moreover, the roughly 100 Natives killed on Bloody Island were more than a quarter of the estimated fewer-than-400 Pomo who lived in the Clear Lake Basin in 1850, whereas it is further estimated that about 3,000 had lived there fifty years earlier. Again, estimates place California's entire Native population at about 300,000 in 1800, around 100,000 in 1848, possibly as low as 30,000 by 1870, and as few as 15,000 in 1900.

To be sure, many factors combined to create this tragic near-annihilation of California's Native Americans. As Mohamed Adhikari brilliantly demonstrates, however, this virtual extermination was a direct consequence of the actions of settlers who considered California's Native peoples to be either a disposable resource to be exploited or an obstruction to be eliminated.

In like manner, Professor Adhikari examines in detail similar settler-generated genocides in the Canary Islands during the fifteenth century, in Queensland, Australia during the nineteenth century, and in German South West Africa (present-day Namibia) in the early twentieth century. The stories are horrifying, but they must be read, especially by those of us who live in lands settled at the expense of Indigenous peoples.

All too often the story of settlement has been viewed through the prism of collective amnesia and overlain with romance. A poster on the wall of the Lakeport Historic Courthouse Museum, which stands only a few miles from Bloody Island, tells the following tale of Clear Lake:

> 7,500 years ago, when the Pomo people were firmly established here, they lived in a wonderful and hospitable place. The climate was mild, there were plenty of fish and game, and lots of acorns and other foods to make life here at the lake very comfortable. When the white settlers arrived, they found the same qualities that the earlier Native Americans had discovered. People came from all over to farm, raise cattle, and mine borax, sulfur, and mercury. Today the same lake, the same climate, and the same relaxed way of life continues.

According to this narrative, the only change that took place in the Eden of Lake County was the settlers' wise use of the region's natural resources that allowed them to farm, raise cattle, and mine and, thereby, enjoy "the same relaxed way of life" as the Pomo. And apparently the Pomo still enjoy that lifestyle. After all, an entire gallery celebrates Pomo culture, especially their basket weaving, in which the few hundred who live on the county's five small reservations, or rancherias, still excel.

Not only is there no mention of genocide, ecocide is also neglected. Today Clear Lake is toxic, with an unacceptably high concentration of mercury, much of it apparently a consequence of the settlers' mining activities that began in 1860 and ended in 1957. Sad to say, that mercury poisoning has a direct impact on the Elem Indian Colony, one of the county's Pomo rancherias.

Yes, this book should be required reading by every student of world history, but especially by those who enjoy the fruits of lands wrested at great human expense from Indigenous peoples.

Alfred J. Andrea
Series Editor

INTRODUCTION

Settler Genocides of Indigenous Peoples:
Contestations around Key Concepts

This study sits at the confluence of two historical phenomena of global significance, namely, settler colonialism and genocide. Settler destruction of Indigenous societies has shaped human history in profound ways. It has resulted in the extinction of many ancient cultures and the introduction of new ways of life over large swathes of the earth's surface. Settler invasion of Indigenous lands currently accounts, among other things, for the demographic characteristics of populations across continents, enduring inequalities of wealth and power between communities, as well as far-reaching ecological change in many parts of the world. In a number of instances settler violence on frontiers escalated into genocidal campaigns. The social reality we contend with today, especially for those of us living in settler societies such as the United States, Canada, and Australia, has fundamentally been fashioned by the intertwined plot lines of these two historical forces. The subject demands our attention if we are to understand the making of the modern world.

Of the various forms that Western imperialism has taken over the last six centuries, settler colonialism has been the most violent and prone to genocidal destruction of Indigenous peoples. Because dispossession threatened the very existence of Indigenous peoples it was bound to provoke fierce resistance, and this, in turn, to incite mass violence on the part of the colonial establishment. Much of this violence was driven by settlers themselves rather than by colonial governments or their metropoles, the parent states of colonies. Our four case studies—the genocidal destruction of the aboriginal inhabitants of the Canary Islands in the fifteenth century, that of the Indigenous peoples of Queensland and California in the latter half of the nineteenth century, and the annihilation of Herero society in German South West Africa in the first decade of the twentieth century—span broad geographical and temporal reaches, extensive social and political diversities, and a wide spectrum of settler strategies for perpetrating mass violence against Indigenes. Despite this diversity, it is their common and complementary features that are most significant and striking. This should come as little surprise given that the case studies are part of the same broad historical development—the making of Western global dominance.

Spanish colonization of the Canaries and the obliteration of their Indigenous peoples have a significance beyond the modest size of the archipelago and what its general neglect in world history might suggest. As the earliest of the genocides perpetrated in Europe's expansion across the Atlantic and driven to a large extent by civilian rather than state initiative, it exhibits significant features present in subsequent settler annihilations of Indigenous societies. This was most conspicuously the case with Spanish depredations in the Americas, especially the Caribbean, but also with other Western settler conquests. Both Queensland and California were offshoots of industrializing imperial powers—Great Britain and the United States, respectively—and integral to the rapid globalization of commercial markets and commodity production generated by industrial capitalism. Besides providing outlets for restless, land-hungry emigrants seeking economic opportunity and often greater political freedom, they became major exporters of raw materials critical to the economic development of their metropoles. The destruction of Indigenous societies in headlong rushes to seize land and resources in both settler colonies was bloody and swift, and effected through shifting combinations of civilian-driven and state-directed violence. In contrast, the specifically genocidal aspects of the annihilation of the Herero people in German South West Africa—present-day Namibia—were almost entirely orchestrated by the metropolitan state and informed by European political considerations, despite the governor of the colony seeking a negotiated solution to the conflict. The use of the latest industrial technology, racial science, and concentration camps in the perpetration of cataclysmic violence against an entire social group signaled the arrival of a more modern variant of exterminatory warfare that would scar the twentieth century, often characterized as the "century of genocide."

Despite the comprehensive downplaying, even denial, of colonial violence in mainstream Western societies, Indigenous victims of genocidal violence in settler colonial situations have nonetheless expressed prescient insight into the nature of the beast they were facing—firstly, of the utter devastation wrought on their communities by genocidal violence; and secondly, of the unconditional claims settler establishments made on the lives and territories of their people. To illustrate the former, one might quote Dawid Kruiper, a leader of the ≠Khomani San people, who today endure abject lives in the Kalahari Desert in the farthest reaches of South Africa's Northern Cape province. Kruiper articulated the sense of social desolation that reverberated to him down the generations when in 1998, he lamented of his people that: ". . . we have been made into nothing."[1] The ≠Khomani San are a tiny remnant of the hunter-gatherer communities that

---

1. Jennifer Crwys-Williams, comp., *Penguin Dictionary of South African Quotations* (Sandton: Penguin, 1999), 62.

once inhabited most of the land that currently constitutes South Africa. Whereas Kruiper was voicing concern about the utter marginalization of the ≠Khomani San, even after the ending of apartheid, his judgment applies in a very literal sense to the fate of foraging societies of the Cape Colony that were dispossessed, slaughtered, enslaved, and abused to the point of near extinction by invading European settlers during the eighteenth and nineteenth centuries. Kruiper's words spotlight the essence of genocide—social groups "being made into nothing"—or what might be termed social death.

Hendrik Witbooi, leader and charismatic prophet-warrior of the Nama people, provides a good example of the latter, nine months after going into revolt against the colonial administration of German South West Africa. During the remarkably brutal colonial wars between 1904 and 1908, German forces killed about 80 percent of Herero and 50 percent of Nama people in the first genocides of the twentieth century. In response to a false overture of peace and a call for the Nama to surrender in late July 1905 by General Lothar von Trotha, supreme commander of the German army in the colony, Witbooi declined with the words: "Peace will spell death for me and my nation for I know there is no place for me in your midst ... in your peace I can see nothing but a desire to destroy us to the last man. After all, we have known each other for a lifetime."[2] The casual yet pointed sarcasm of the seventy-five-year-old Witbooi's last sentence—after all, von Trotha had been in the colony for only about a year—was meant to signify the intimacy with which he grasped the annihilatory impetus at the heart of German settler colonialism. Also, "I know there is no place for me in your midst" spotlights an awareness of the essence of settler colonialism—of invaders striving to establish new homelands on expropriated land from which all Indigenous claims are extinguished. Witbooi's acumen came from generations of Nama having to contend with colonial incursion—grappling that included cultural borrowing, collaboration, and resistance. Long before Germany laid formal claim to Namibia in 1884, the Nama had to adapt to the presence of missionaries in their midst and inroads made into their territories by settlers from the Cape Colony.

Raphael Lemkin and the Origins of Genocide

People often confuse genocide with mass killing largely because of widespread popular association of genocide with the Holocaust and a few of the largest twentieth-century mass atrocities. If genocide consisted only of mass killing, then the term

---

2. Quoted in Horst Drechsler, *Let Us Die Fighting: The Struggle of the Herero and Nama People against German Imperialism, 1884–1915* (London: Zed Press, 1980), 189–90.

would be redundant. In simple terms, the key difference between the two is that mass killing is precisely that; killing large numbers of people. At the core of genocide, however, is the intent to destroy an entire social group; and killing is not the only means of such destruction as our case studies will confirm, even though it is usually the most significant. Sociologist Martin Shaw pithily described the role of killing in genocide as "a means, not the meaning of group destruction."[3]

The term "genocide" is unusual in that its origin is relatively recent, can be attributed to a specific individual, and its entry into the public domain can be precisely dated. The Polish jurist and life-long campaigner against exterminatory violence, Raphael Lemkin, coined the word in his 1944 book, *Axis Rule in Occupied Europe*.[4] Lemkin created it by combining the Greek noun *genos*, a people of common descent or culture, with the Latin verb *caedere*, "to kill." Genocide in its most literal sense thus means to kill people of a particular kind. The idea of destroying an entire human collectivity is probably as old as intercommunal conflict in human society itself.

Lemkin, who was born in 1900 and raised within a Jewish family, from a young age exhibited a talent for learning languages and developed a consuming interest in mass atrocities committed throughout history. Together these qualities kindled in him a sensitivity to the richness of the world's cultures and the irreparable loss to humanity when any of them was obliterated, as well as a deep aversion to exterminatory violence. The destructiveness of World War I and the accompanying wholesale massacre of Armenians in Turkey had a deep impact on his thinking, as did ongoing persecution of Jews in eastern Europe. By the time Lemkin was at university, and later a young lawyer, his cherishing of human cultural diversity, together with his abhorrence of the impunity with which the powerful so often committed mass violence against the weak, aroused within him a passion to put an end to such depravity and bring perpetrators to book. Most of these abuses came from states killing their own citizens and subjects, often ethnic minorities. They were able to do so without qualms because the primacy placed on national sovereignty in international relations effectively prevented outside intervention. Lemkin recognized this as a deficiency in international law and made it his mission to remedy the failing. By the early 1930s he advanced the twin concepts he called "barbarity" and "vandalism"—the former referring to the annihilation of ethno-national groups and the latter to the eradication of their cultures—as part of a crusade to rally international support for outlawing mass violence of this kind. Although Lemkin campaigned in legal forums throughout

---

3. Martin Shaw, *What Is Genocide?* (Cambridge: Polity Press, 2015), 50.
4. Raphael Lemkin, *Axis Rule in Occupied Europe: Laws of Occupation, Analysis of Government, Proposals for Redress* (New York: Columbia University Press, 1944).

Europe during the 1930s his cause found little resonance before it was overtaken by events in 1939.

With the onset of the Nazi invasion of Poland in September of that year, Lemkin, having failed to persuade family members to join him, fled to neutral Sweden. There he taught at the University of Stockholm for some months before resolving to go to the United States, where he hoped his ideals would find fertile ground. In April 1941, after a circuitous journey of 14,000 miles across Eurasia, he arrived in the United States, where he secured a post teaching international law at Duke University. Once in the United States, he spent much of the wartime years researching and writing *Axis Rule in Occupied Europe*, and reformulating his ideas and strategies for outlawing exterminatory violence in ways that were to prove remarkably successful.

More than simply coining the term, Lemkin played a key role in having genocide recognized as a crime in international law by indefatigably campaigning for this ideal in the immediate aftermath of World War II. He grasped a unique opportunity to pursue his goal in a world still coming to terms with shocking revelations around Nazi depredations in eastern Europe and pondering the sheer scale of wartime destruction. The global response of setting up the United Nations Organization (UN) in the hope of collectively maintaining international peace more effectively, provided Lemkin with the means for doing so. Sensing from the rhetoric of Western leaders the possibility of the newly founded UN adopting a convention criminalizing genocide, he sprang into action, launching a ceaseless crusade to have genocide outlawed as an international crime.

Lemkin relentlessly lobbied delegates to the UN, first managing to persuade representatives from India, Cuba, and Panama to propose a draft resolution criminalizing genocide, and then petitioning others to support the motion. He wrote hundreds of letters to interested parties, promoted his ideas through the media, and button-holed anyone of influence he could find who might advance his cause. Often disheveled, exhausted, undernourished, in ill-health, and surviving off the charity of sympathizers, he cut a lonely and eccentric figure in the halls and corridors of the UN headquarters, campaigning with single-minded tenacity to realize his mission. It was largely through Lemkin's persistence that the UN General Assembly on December 11, 1946 unanimously passed a resolution to criminalize genocide, setting in motion a two-year-long process of negotiation and horse-trading among the leading powers to draft the genocide convention. Lemkin's crowning achievement came on December 9, 1948 with the unanimous adoption of the Convention on the Prevention and Punishment of the Crime of Genocide (UNCG) by the UN General Assembly. This was nonetheless a bittersweet moment for Lemkin as he had been driven in this quest by the unbearably

Raphael Lemkin. Between 1945 and 1947, Raphael Lemkin was employed as adviser on foreign affairs by the United States War Department.

distressing knowledge that nearly his entire extended family—at least forty-nine people, including his parents—had died in the Holocaust. Only his brother's nuclear family of four survived. He referred to the convention as an "epitaph on his mother's grave" and confirmation that "many millions did not die in vain."[5]

Unremitting stress over the previous years and continued exertion over the next decade to entrench the UNCG by persuading as many governments as possible to become signatories took a toll on Lemkin's health, no doubt contributing to his premature death from a heart attack on August 28, 1959. He was particularly distressed by the United States' refusal to ratify the convention, a step it eventually took in 1988. Lemkin's activism and scholarship promoted international awareness of the growing scourge of systematic violence targeted at civilian populations and initiated a global movement for the eradication of such atrocities. His reformulation of exterminatory violence as genocide produced a new framework for the interpretation of a major historical and social phenomenon that in time spawned a distinct field of academic inquiry, genocide studies.

Genocide: Definitional Disputations

The meaning of the term genocide is intensely contested, and more so than in most fields, genocide studies pivots on disputes around the definition of its

---

5. Quoted in Samantha Power, *"A Problem from Hell": America and the Age of Genocide* (New York: Basic Books, 2002), 60.

foundational concept. There is thus a large number of contending approaches to the subject and a proliferation of competing definitions. This is hardly surprising given the inherently contentious nature of academic inquiry. Moreover, genocide is inherently a highly complex as well as an unusually emotive issue for both perpetrator and victim groups, their respective sympathizers, and anyone who takes a moral or political stand on the matter. While inflamed emotions are integral to all episodes of mass violence, passions are further amplified in the case of genocide because it is generally regarded as the most heinous of all crimes. Allegations of genocide, denials, and demands for reparations have become part of the cut-and-thrust of world politics. Also, potentially serious political, legal, and financial consequences flow from genocide being a crime in international law. Then there is, in addition, abuse of the term—obfuscation by both academic and nonacademic parties with dubious agendas seeking to exploit its cachet as the crime of all crimes.

For Lemkin, genocide did not simply mean the physical annihilation of a population but the deliberate destruction of a social group's ability to sustain a communal existence. He defined genocide in the following terms:

> By "genocide" we mean the destruction of a nation or an ethnic group. . . . Generally speaking, genocide does not necessarily mean the immediate destruction of a nation, except when accomplished by mass killings of all members of the nation. It is intended rather to signify a co-ordinated plan of different actions aiming at the essential foundations of the life of national groups, with the aim of annihilating the groups themselves.[6]

I am highly sympathetic to Lemkin's definition particularly because of its emphasis on the myriad of ways in which social destruction can occur, rather than focusing mainly on killing. It also closely follows the general contours of settler genocides. I do, however, have one serious criticism of Lemkin's definition, namely, that he limits possible victim groups of genocide too narrowly to culture-bearing entities, especially national and ethnic ones, although he elsewhere includes those defined by race or religion. Also, Lemkin construes culture as elite culture rather than a group's way of life or as encompassing folk culture. He has thus been censured for placing greater value on the lives of elite strata—politicians, painters, and poets—over the lives of peasants and proletarians. The reality, however, is that the elimination of those responsible for key functions in any social group, such as its political, spiritual, military, intellectual, and cultural leadership, will have a disproportionate impact on its viability. The common

---

6. Lemkin, *Axis Rule*, 79.

perpetrator strategy of targeting such leaders, often from the outset, bears this out.

While Lemkin had a major influence on the content of the UNCG and its definition of genocide, not least by being allowed to participate in the drafting process, key elements of his thought were disregarded. To his chagrin, cultural destruction was omitted as a specified act of genocide from its definition outlined in article 2 of the convention:

> In the present Convention, genocide means any of the following acts committed with intent to destroy, in whole or in part, a national, ethnical, racial or religious group, as such:
> (a) Killing members of the group;
> (b) Causing serious bodily or mental harm to members of the group;
> (c) Deliberately inflicting on the group conditions of life calculated to bring about its physical destruction in whole or in part;
> (d) Imposing measures intended to prevent births within the group;
> (e) Forcibly transferring children of the group to another group.[7]

In academic inquiries the UNCG definition has tended to take precedence over Lemkin's more coherent and compact characterization because of its canonical status as the definition used in one of the bulwarks of international human rights covenants. While the UNCG definition has much to commend it, it has serious deficiencies for use in academic studies.

This definition's main strength, like Lemkin's rendering, is that it stresses the importance of a wide range of harms other than killing in the making of genocides. Indeed, it does not even require killing for genocide to occur. Its weaknesses, though, are critical. Firstly, it shares with Lemkin's version the flaw of privileging culture-bearing groups for protection. In this respect, the UNCG definition is often regarded as being too narrow. Critics contend that there have been many instances in which other social groups, such as those defined by class or political ideology, for example, have been targeted for genocidal destruction. Some scholars have pointed to vagueness around what "serious bodily or mental harm" might entail; question why child removal has been singled out when the transfer of adults, especially women, can be equally detrimental to victimized societies; and a failure to mention such important and consistent aspects of genocide as sexual violence, enslavement, and forced removals. Case law has to some extent, and will in time, resolve some uncertainties and fill lacunae.

---

7. For the text of the convention, see https://www.un.org/en/genocideprevention/documents/atrocity-crimes/Doc.1_Convention%20on%20the%20Prevention%20and%20Punishment%20of%20the%20Crime%20of%20Genocide.pdf.

Most importantly, however, by defining the degree of social destruction necessary for genocide in an exceptionally broad way, the UNCG effectively renders the concept meaningless. The key problem lies in its characterization of genocide as being "committed with intent to destroy [a designated group], in whole or *in part.*" While "in whole" is fine, the "in part" segment is highly problematic as it introduces unacceptable levels of ambiguity and vagueness. Almost any conflict involving the four-named groups that results in fatalities—even a single death—can be characterized as genocidal as these hostile acts can be interpreted as having been "committed with intent to destroy" a designated group "*in part.*" There has hardly been a war or intercommunal massacre that is not genocidal in terms of a literal reading of the UNCG definition. Taken to its logical extreme, even in cases where there were no deaths, but fatalities were intended, the UNCG definition implies genocide. To say that the intended meaning was "in *substantial* part" hardly helps as the question of what the threshold for "substantial" might be replicates the uncertainty and imprecision.

The UNCG definition illustrates the axiom that the broader the definition of genocide, the less meaningful it is bound to be. There is also the opposite danger of making the definition overly restrictive, as that diminishes its relevance and if taken to extremes will also result in meaninglessness. This is demonstrated by the group of scholars who, seeking to privilege the Holocaust, absurdly tried to argue that it was the only true genocide ever committed.[8] Both extremes lead to the trivialization of the concept.

Recognizing that definitions of genocide operate in two distinct, yet overlapping, contexts can go a long way toward avoiding much of the confusion that bedevils the concept. On the one hand, the UNCG's conception is first and foremost a legal definition that delineates a specific crime in international law, and as such, is an extremely important formulation. It operates in the factious worlds of international relations, civil strife, and armed conflict where the prevention and punishment of genocide are its paramount concerns. The scholarly enterprise, on the other hand, operates primarily in the realm of ideas, truth seeking, and knowledge creation, not that academia cannot be as cutthroat in its own ways. Here the primary aim is to understand and explain a particular historical and social phenomenon, namely, the intentional destruction of social groups. Of course, the two interests converge, at the very least to the extent that most scholars of genocide have a desire for their work to contribute to the prevention,

---

8. For perspectives on the subject see Alan Rosenbaum, *Is the Holocaust Unique? Perspectives on Comparative Genocide* (Boulder: Westview Press, 2001). See especially chapter 4 by Steven Katz, the preeminent proponent of Holocaust uniqueness, and chapter 13 by David Stannard for a blistering critique of this proposition.

punishment, and recognition of genocidal violence, and some may even regard themselves as activists first and academics second. On the other hand, jurists might wish to help clarify conceptual uncertainties and contribute to intellectual debate around the term. While the vagueness of the UNCG definition may well be useful in the legal and political realms concerned with deterrence, prosecution, armed intervention, humanitarian relief, reparation, and memorialization, it is decidedly problematic in academic inquiry where a greater degree of analytical precision and a more rigorously bounded conceptualization of genocide is needed.

It is also useful to recognize that the UNCG definition is not some neutral, best-practice product that fits all needs and is above the menial squabbles of disputatious academics as is sometimes assumed. It is, on the contrary, the outcome of great power rivalry and compromise in the emergent Cold War environment of heightened suspicion and discord. This definition was, moreover, devised by lawyers, politicians, and diplomats, who can hardly be described as having untarnished reputations for altruism, integrity, and pursuit of truth. This is not to suggest that academics are necessarily of a morally superior bent, but that they need to devise definitions that better suit their purposes.

Partly because of the shortcomings of the UNCG definition and partly because of the inherently adversarial nature of academic inquiry, many scholars have formulated their own definitions of genocide. Inevitably, this has resulted in a great deal of contention around the concept, and there has also been a discernible evolution of meanings and approaches attached to it as genocide studies and the context in which it operates have evolved over the decades. A brief survey of, and my commentary on, some of the controversies around specific elements that feature in most definitions of genocide will help to clarify the definition that is to be used in this book.[9]

One area of contention among academics revolves around whether the state or its structures are necessarily the perpetrators of genocide. It is worth noting that neither Lemkin nor the UNCG mentions the state as perpetrator. The emphasis on state action arose early on in academic inquiries and has remained a major focus as most research concentrates on the iconic twentieth-century mass killings, where the role of the state was completely dominant. I do not agree that states or their agents are necessarily the perpetrators of genocide as it is perfectly possible for non-state actors, such as corporations or civilian bodies acting independently of the state, to commit acts of genocide. There is also no imperative that

---

9. Although it comes to materially different conclusions on several issues, the structuring of the discussion that follows owes much to Adam Jones's approach in *Genocide: A Comprehensive Introduction* (Abingdon: Routledge, 2nd ed., 2011), 20–25.

genocidal violence be centrally directed. This book will present several examples where civilian groupings, both independently and in collusion with state
structures, organized themselves to perpetrate genocidal violence, a common
occurrence in settler colonial situations.

A second set of debates centers on which victim groups qualify for consideration in determining genocide. As already indicated, I take a capacious view on
this aspect of genocide and would prefer not to restrict it to particular kinds of
social groups as Lemkin and the UNCG have done. I would extend the definition to include any substantive social group that has a collective sense of identity
to the extent that members recognize distinct social markers of group membership, share basic norms, form institutions through which they give expression to
their affinities, and through which adhesion to group membership is reinforced
and reproduced. The target group can thus be defined in terms, or in any combination, of racial, ethnic, national, religious, class, political, gender, or other socially
relevant criteria. Case law decisively moved in this direction when the International Criminal Tribunal for Rwanda in the Akayesu judgment of September
1998 extended protection under the UNCG to include "stable" and "permanent"
groups.

While victims usually identify with or as a community, they do not necessarily have to do so because such membership can be imputed by perpetrators irrespective of it having any basis in reality. During the Holocaust, for example, many
people who did not regard themselves as Jewish were killed as Jews because Nazi
authorities regarded them as such; and in mass killings in the Soviet Union under
Stalin, many people were arbitrarily assigned to targeted class-based or politically
defined groupings to which they had, or felt, no affiliation. Since the initiative lies
with perpetrators, it is their perceptions of persecuted groups and persons that
are most relevant. This is not to deny the agency of victims but to recognize the
asymmetry of power relations in genocidal situations, where perpetrators often
have unfettered capacity to define social groups and assign individual membership. In settler genocides of Indigenous peoples, differences have been so stark as
to avoid all uncertainty about group membership, except perhaps for a very tiny
proportion of people of mixed descent.

Thirdly, issues of scale can be quite problematic as genocide cannot be defined
in terms of numerical thresholds of deaths, whether proportionate (as in a given
percentage) or absolute (as in a given number). Because the extent of social
destruction or slaughter necessary for genocide is a subjective matter, a specified percentage or numerical standard will always be open to legitimate challenge.
If anyone stipulated, say, 50 percent, one could justifiably ask, why not 49 percent? It is the dynamic and the intent behind the violence, rather than simply

the scale, that is significant. Relatively small bloodbaths may be far more geno-cidal in nature than much larger atrocities where intent to destroy an entire social group is absent. Thus, killing 80 percent of the Herero, about 65,000 people, as happened in German South West Africa, was much more clearly genocidal than would be randomly killing 1 percent of the Chinese population, amounting to perhaps 13,500,000 people. This, despite the latter resulting in more than 200 times the number of casualties. Similarly, the effective extermination of about 5,000 Aboriginal Tasmanians and the killing of 6,000,000 Jews, roughly two-thirds of European Jewry, are both clearly genocidal despite the latter being over 1,000 times larger.

Specifications among academics regarding the extent of social destruction necessary for genocide cover a wide spectrum. Some academics require extermi-nation or near physical eradication, while others might not even require killing, or yet others resort to some indefinite prescription, such as a "substantial" num-ber or proportion of casualties. My own view is that since the objective of geno-cide is the destruction of a social group, the minimum requirement is that the targeted group be crippled to the extent that it is no longer able to function as a social entity. The key requirement for functionality is that social groups be able to reproduce their communal lives, not only because so much of any social group's energy goes into biological and cultural reproduction, but also because the inabil-ity to do so will in time result in social death.

Some scholars require that genocides necessarily consist of exceptional out-bursts of intense violence within a concentrated period of time. This misconcep-tion generally arises from Holocaust-centric thinking and equating genocide with mass killing. Genocide is a process that can take many different forms, and social destruction numerous guises—and no time limit can be imposed on it. As will be seen in our case studies, genocides can happen incrementally over lengthy peri-ods of time and with a repetitive dynamic, as when an invading settler population takes piecemeal control of what can sometimes be vast territories. Indeed, it can be argued that consistently exterminatory behavior by settler establishments over decades is a good indicator of genocidal intent.

Finally, for some, genocide is essentially a modern phenomenon. Adherents to this idea argue that it is only relatively recently, especially with the dawn of the industrial era, that human society developed the capacity for killing on a scale large enough to justify being called genocide. Such arguments are untenable, as there is a great deal of evidence of exterminatory thinking and practice stretching back to ancient times and beyond recorded history. It is worth noting that many explicit references to genocidal behavior occur in the founding texts of Western civilization, most notably the Hebrew Bible and Homer's *Iliad*. While Lemkin developed the concept of genocide in the context of Nazi exterminatory violence during World War II, he applied the term retrospectively and indicated that the word was meant "to denote an old practice in its modern development."[10] Prior to this, genocide was referred to as extermination, extirpation, eradication, or similar phrasing. Indeed, in his draft of the world history of genocide, incomplete at the time of his death, Lemkin cites many examples of genocide from ancient, medieval, and colonial times. Leo Kuper, one of the pioneers of genocide studies, framed the matter succinctly: "The word is new, the crime ancient."[11] Similarly, the preamble to the UNCG document recognizes "that at all periods of history genocide has inflicted great losses on humanity." What is clear though, is that throughout history technological advancement—the agricultural revolution and the rise of industrial society being key landmarks—has enhanced human capacity for mass violence. Modern genocides thus tend to be larger, more systematic, and more efficiently executed than earlier ones.

The Issue of Intent

Amid the cacophony of disputation that is genocide studies, there is one issue on which there is broad agreement, namely, that genocide cannot arise accidentally. There needs to be a degree of purposeful action—what is generally referred to as "intent." The UNCG definition hinges on intent, which is expressly articulated in one form or another in most other formulations as well. This consensus, of course, does not mean that the issue of intent is free of controversy or misconception, nor deny the existence of the occasional eccentric voice claiming that intent is not necessary. A fair degree of misunderstanding has arisen from confusion of motive with intent. While in everyday speech motive and intent can generally be used interchangeably without problem, in both juridical contexts and genocide studies they have distinct meanings. It is not inappropriate to apply juridical understandings of terms to genocide studies as genocide is, after all, a crime in international law. There is, however, no single definition of intent that can be offered, as its use differs in legal regimes across geographies, time, and different branches of law. There are also distinct variants of intent in legal discourse.

I suggest that the key distinction between motive and intent is that with motive there is premeditation and a consciously desired outcome to actions, whereas with intent there only needs to be an awareness of possible or probable consequences of one's actions—of what may reasonably be expected. While the

---

10. Lemkin, *Axis Rule*, 79.
11. Leo Kuper, *Genocide: Its Political Use in the Twentieth Century* (New Haven: Yale University Press, 1981), 11.

two concepts are closely related, with motive implying the presence of intent, the latter represents a lower burden of proof. Put in these rather abstract terms, the distinction between the two may not be very clear. A concrete example should dispel uncertainty. Assume that I plan to rob a bank. I take a gun, go to the bank, point the firearm at the teller, and demand money. At that point, a security guard walks in through a side door; I wheel around, shoot, and kill the guard. In this example, my motive very clearly was to rob the bank and not to kill anyone. But under most legal jurisdictions, I will be charged with murder and will be held to have had intent to kill, as any reasonable person should foresee that robbing a bank with a firearm could result in the death of innocent people. Intent is not synonymous with motive and, importantly, does not require premeditation.

This logic is eminently applicable to episodes of mass violence to determine whether perpetrators had intent to commit genocide and is decidedly relevant to settler colonial situations where Indigenous societies were violently destroyed. Typically, in such instances it may be said that the motive of the metropolitan power was to establish a colony for the purposes of economic exploitation, national aggrandizement, or whatever other premeditated reason it had, and the motive of settlers was to create a new homeland for themselves, and that neither set out specifically to destroy Indigenous peoples. However, if in the process of conquest, dispossession, and exploitation the settler establishment effectively eradicated Indigenous societies by killing large numbers of natives, laying waste to their sources of food, capturing and enslaving large numbers, sexually exploiting the women, removing their children, segregating survivors in conditions resulting in high mortality rates, and suppressing their cultures, among other abuses, could the perpetrators be said to have had intent to commit genocide? For me, it would be an unequivocal yes. There can be no gainsaying this conclusion if colonists or the colonial state articulated the realization that their actions were destroying Indigenous societies, or they developed exterminatory attitudes toward Indigenes.

Intent need not be explicitly declared and may be inferred from the actions of perpetrators or their exterminatory attitudes. Failure to act, such as state authorities refusing to rein in civilian perpetrators, provide life-saving sustenance, or medical treatment in the face of preventable disease, can be construed as genocidal behavior. Opposition to the killing from within the perpetrators' society, such as the church or even government, does not invalidate such intent. It is sufficient that perpetrators exhibit genocidal intent, for it is the intent of the perpetrators—not the state, government, national leader, or any other entity—that counts. Genocidal intent does not have to be present at the start of the violence as objectives can, and very often do, change; genocides are usually not planned far ahead of their commission but are generally born of perpetrators' escalating responses to dynamic situations. This process, generally referred to as cumulative radicalization, is common in settler colonial situations as frontier land confiscations fueled intensifying resistance by increasingly desperate Indigenes, which in turn served as a major driver of exterminatory violence on the part of the settler establishment. Once their socially destructive actions are recognized, or should be recognized, by perpetrators as possibly leading to the destruction of the targeted group, to persist in these actions is to display genocidal intent. It does not matter whether these acts were perpetrated in an uncoordinated or incremental fashion, or as part of a centrally directed campaign of concentrated mass violence. If perpetrators could reasonably be expected to foresee the genocidal consequences of their actions, the criterion of intent is fulfilled.[12]

The Definition of Genocide Used in This Book

Because the concept of genocide is beset by so many definitional conundrums, confusions, and deep controversy, it is necessary to define the meaning of genocide used in this book. It is that **genocide is the intentional physical destruction of a social group, or the intentional annihilation of such a significant part of the social relationships that constitute its communal life, that it is no longer able to reproduce itself biologically or culturally.** This definition covers both fatal and nonlethal forms of social destruction, such as large-scale child removal, enslavement, deportation, and sexual exploitation. A corollary applicable specifically to settler genocides of Indigenous peoples is that after the closure of settler frontiers, remnant populations are subject to ongoing violence and social harm with a view to the elimination of an Indigenous presence in the newly consolidated settler homeland. Such survivors are usually reduced to forced labor or utter destitution on reservations, sometimes to the point of starvation. This represents a relatively "hard" definition in that it sets a comparatively high threshold for episodes of mass violence to count as genocide, as opposed to a "soft" framing such as that of the UNCG.

In terms of this definition, coerced cultural assimilation without overt mass violence, such as using administrative coercion to pressure a nomadic people to become sedentary or inducing hunter-gatherer societies to practice stock farming, does not constitute genocide, even though their communal lives are irrevocably changed and they experience psychological trauma. Ethnocide, crime against

---

12. There are several kinds of intent in legal discourse. This is what is generally referred to as general intent.

humanity, and cultural suppression are more appropriate terms to denote this sort of abuse. Similarly, mass displacement or deportation on their own do not necessarily amount to genocide—neither do conquest or suppression of resistance—without genocidal intent and consequences. The degree of social destruction necessary for genocide would include precipitous population decline, collapse of the institutions and practices central to reproducing Indigenous group identity, and survivors being reduced to a state of social anomie. While it might have been the intention of perpetrators that the destruction or crippling of the enemy be permanent, the social lives of groups who have suffered genocide may over time be revitalized, though necessarily on a very different basis to that prior to the genocide.

In conclusion, it bears repeating that genocide is not equivalent to extermination, although it may well result in it as Hendrik Witbooi appreciated. And genocide is not just about mass killing—it is about much more than that. Genocide is about the destruction of the intricate skein of relationships that constitute the communal lives of social groups to the extent that they are "made into nothing" as Dawid Kruiper intuited. One might add that survivors are made into nonentities.

Imperialism, Colonialism, and Settler Colonialism

The meanings of these three terms denoting foreign control or the dependency status of territories are deeply controversial. Definitions vary, sometimes radically so, depending on the user's ideological, political, and disciplinary dispositions. Since there are no consensual definitions to fall back on, it is sensible to explain how these concepts will be used here.

Of the various terms signifying external domination of territories, "imperialism" is the most general. By imperialism I mean any form of foreign subjection, whether formal or informal. Formal empire—generally referred to as colonialism—entails the imposition of political control, in whatever form, over foreign or peripheral societies, usually as a result of conquest or cession. Informal empire, on the contrary, resorts to control by less obvious or concealed means. This could include economic domination, covert or explicit threats of violence, promises of protection or other benefits, or regime change, among others, while the subordinate territory maintains formal political independence. Examples of informal empire include British influence over Egypt, China, and much of Latin America during the nineteenth century; the manner in which the United States maintains ascendancy over certain strategically located or resource rich countries, especially where it maintains military bases; and Soviet domination over much of eastern Europe during the Cold War era.

Over the decades, scholars have proposed many typologies of colonialism. My experience of these attempts at categorization has been that the more complex their breakdown, the less useful they tend to be, as there are in effect two types of colonial domination, namely, resource exploitation and settlement. Colonies of resource exploitation—where resources are defined broadly to include natural, human, and strategic assets—are also referred to as colonies of occupation or franchise colonies. It does not make much sense to see colonies of settlement and colonies of resource exploitation in binary terms—where cases are rigidly separated into either category—because virtually all colonies display both forms of dominance to varying degrees, the relative significance of which is likely to change materially over time. It is much more helpful to see colonies as fitting—and shifting—along a continuum between poles of unadulterated resource exploitation on the one extreme, and purely settler domination on the other. While settler colonialism is commonly assumed to be a subtype of colonialism, in my opinion, colonialism and settler colonialism are better understood as distinct phenomena. As Lorenzo Veracini, one of the leading theorists of settler colonialism has explained, the two: "routinely co-exist and reciprocally define each other" and "constantly interpenetrate . . . and overlap." He goes on to describe the two as "not merely different" but "in some ways antithetical formations."[13] Scholars often use the phrase "settler colonial situation" to take into account the reality that the phenomenon does not occur in isolation from resource exploitation.

It is important to distinguish between the two types of colony as their fundamental characteristics determine clear propensities for different kinds of violence toward Indigenes. In the case of colonies dominated by resource exploitation—prime examples being India, Nigeria, and Indonesia—there is generally a distinct incentive for colonial powers to limit overt and mass violence to what is necessary to achieve Indigenous compliance, whereas in settler colonial situations, there is a decidedly greater proclivity for exterminatory violence. The most obvious reason for this difference is that in colonies of resource exploitation the benefits sought are likely to be compromised by excessive or gratuitous violence, as the labor and cooperation of Indigenes are required. Exceptions are rare and may occur in situations where, for example, the main value of a colony lay in its strategic location or, as transpired in late nineteenth-century Congo Free State, where a closing window of opportunity to extract wild rubber at exorbitantly profitable rates fueled violence on a genocidal scale. In the case of settler colonies—prime examples in addition to those already mentioned being Brazil, Argentina, New Zealand, and Israel—where the expropriation of Indigenous land is central to the

---

13. Lorenzo Veracini, *Settler Colonialism: A Theoretical Overview* (Houndmills: Palgrave Macmillan, 2010), 2–4, 12.

colonial project, violence is likely to be more intense. Because the very existence of Indigenous societies is usually at stake, they are likely to resist much more forcefully, and settlers in turn, to respond with greater ferocity and at times with exterminatory violence.

Other striking differences between the two forms of colonialism are that in colonies of exploitation, colonizers are relatively few in number and are mainly sojourners, such as soldiers, administrators, traders, adventurers, and the like, who eventually return home; Indigenes meanwhile remain a clear majority of the population. In settler colonies, however, colonizers migrate in much larger numbers, come to stay, and often become a large majority of the population, while Indigenes usually become a tiny remnant or in some cases are effectively exterminated. Whereas in the former, indirect rule in collaboration with Indigenous elites is common, in the latter, settlers deny Indigenous peoples sovereignty and strive for political autonomy. Finally, whereas nearly all colonies of exploitation have been extinguished through a process of decolonization, successful settler colonies are much more enduring and decolonization hardly imaginable. It is only in failed settler colonies, such as South Africa, Algeria, and Zimbabwe, where colonists were relatively few and Indigenous societies and economies robust, that Indigenes have regained political independence.

Settler Colonial Orders and Indigenous Societies

Settler colonial situations arise when colonists from a metropolitan center or associated societies migrate to a foreign territory with the intention of making it their new home and founding a new sociopolitical order in the image of the metropolitan society. Although settler societies to varying degrees replicate the cultures and institutions of their metropoles, they are also necessarily distinct in most ways. Not only does geographical distancing ensure that they are discreet communities, but where transoceanic travel was involved, strikingly different natural, social, and demographic environments contributed to these differences.

Settlers, moreover, often consciously wish to create societies that are free of what they regard as pernicious aspects of metropolitan society—the inequalities, lack of freedoms, rigid social hierarchies, shortage of land, and lack of economic opportunities, among others—suffered by those who were not part of the elite. Such settlers are generally out to build a model society—a shining city on the hill, as it were.[14] Besides shared participation in the settler colonial enterprise,

---

14. The "city on the hill" metaphor is derived from Jesus's Sermon on the Mount and has animated the efforts of many Western settlers seeking to build model Christian communities in their new homelands.

settler societies have cohered around mutually reinforcing hierarchies of inclusion and exclusion encompassing cultural, religious, and racial affiliations; and from the nineteenth century onward, with the rise of nationalist ideologies, through the pursuit of nation-building projects as well. That settler colonial worldviews were strongly gendered meant that much of the violence against Indigenes was also gendered, as will be evident from the patterns of killing and sexual violence in the case studies that follow.

The establishment of settler colonial societies entails the migration of a wide variety of individuals to the colony. Sojourners, who come and go, form an important category of migrant, are usually integral to the making of settler colonies, and can be every bit as destructive of Indigenous societies as settlers. There are also likely to be unwilling immigrants, such as refugees and migrant laborers, as well as forced immigrants, such as convicts, slaves, indentured laborers, captives, debt peons, and the like, who may be sourced from diverse parts of the world, including the metropole. Settlers, however, are distinctive in that they have the intention of founding new societies and political orders that replicate those of the metropole. Importantly, Veracini distinguishes settlers as migrants who "carry their sovereignty with them," meaning that they retain their rights and freedoms as citizens of the metropole when they migrate to the colony. It is through these rights that they regard themselves as being capable, and even having the prerogative, of establishing separate political orders.[15] It is through these entitlements, which they tend to claim as inherent, that settlers develop and assert ideas around freedom, equality, popular sovereignty, democracy, representative government, and the like in the settler colony, and through which they make claims to self-rule.

This categorization of immigrant groups of course recognizes the fluidity of relations on the ground in that intended sojourners can become settlers and vice versa, while other migrants can selectively be co-opted into the settler community. Also, the wide range of outsiders that settlers import to meet their labor and security needs adds layers of complexity to settler social systems. Settler perceptions of Indigenes and their status within the social hierarchy can vary or change quite radically depending particularly on the levels of resistance they offer and their evolving demographic relevance to colonial imperatives.

Settler colonial intrusions on Indigenous land initiate frontiers that become fluid and contested zones of complex and interpenetrating social interaction. Frontiers are borderlands of cultural exchange and political interaction characterized by both conflict and cooperation, not just between settler and Indigene, but importantly within these groupings as well. Historically, settler frontiers have

---

15. Veracini, *Settler Colonialism*, 3, chapter 2.

been marked by highly divergent social, racial, economic, and technological disparities, all of which contributed to the intensity of conflict. By their very nature, frontiers are spaces that are not wildernesses but in which state authority is either absent or insubstantial. This lack of state control has usually been seen by settlers—ranging from politically influential larger landholders to penurious squatters—as an opportunity for substantial economic advancement, principally for those who are proactive in their acquisition of land. This engendered a rapacious mindset that promoted ongoing frontier conflict by prompting individual acts of violence as well as vigilante action on the part of settlers. James Belich justifiably describes settlers as "dangerous people, especially when in full-frothing boom frenzy."[16] Frontiers can be said to close when one side is able to assert unconditional political dominance over the other, the most definitive sign of which on settler frontiers was the ability of the colonial state to monopolize the allocation of land.

Hostilities on frontiers also have provoked intervention by usually distant colonial authorities—sometimes grudgingly but often willingly or even with alacrity. While the colonial state was at times wary of the costs of intervention, it was generally also mindful of economic benefits that would accrue from settler dispossession of Indigenes. Racial and cultural ties, together with political and economic considerations, almost invariably ensured the colonial state's support of encroaching, sometimes even marauding, settlers. Colonial governments tended to intervene forcefully on the side of settlers when their hold on desirable land and the lives of their families were seen to be at risk. Metropolitan governments tended to act in expedient ways which, given their interest in having economically profitable colonies and their distance from frontiers, greatly favored settler welfare over that of Indigenes. For the most part metropolitan states ignored settler depredations, and at their most pernicious, directly participated in military action against Indigenes. Very seldom did they intervene decisively to protect Indigenes.

While Patrick Wolfe, an eminent theorist of settler colonialism, is correct to point out that: "rather than something separate from or running counter to the colonial state, the murderous activities of the frontier rabble constitute its principle means of expansion,"[17] it would be counterproductive to conflate metropolitan and settler aspirations, outlooks, values, protocols, and actions as simply "colonial." The colonial state embodied a fluctuating balance of metropolitan and settler influences and interests that tended to favor settler demands for political

---

16. James Belich, *Replenishing the Earth: The Settler Revolution and the Rise of the Anglo-World, 1783–1939* (Oxford: Oxford University Press, 2009), 558.
17. Patrick Wolfe, "Settler Colonialism and the Elimination of the Native," *Journal of Genocide Research* 8, no. 4 (2006): 392.

autonomy over time in the more successful settler colonial ventures. Their interests were, from the outset, rarely aligned, and settlers were seldom compliant with metropolitan expectations and demands. Settlers tended to display an independence and an insurgent disregard for metropolitan sovereignty, policies, and restraints from the outset, despite usually being highly dependent on colonial and metropolitan states in various ways and regularly appealing for their help. Settlers on frontiers tended to be highly mobile and routinely operated beyond colonial jurisdictions with the colonial state belatedly seeking to extend the reach of its authority in a game of ongoing catch-up. And the more viable settler societies and economies became, the more their interests tended to diverge from those of the metropole. This resulted in growing demands for political autonomy, and in extreme cases rebellion, warfare, and revolutionary breaks with the metropole as occurred throughout the Americas from the latter part of the eighteenth century onward. It can be taken as almost axiomatic that the greater control settlers gained over the colonial state, the more rapid land alienation, and the more intense violence against Indigenous societies became. Settler colonial societies thus display a dual character in that they tend to be decidedly anti-imperial in relation to metropolitan power but strongly imperial in relation to Indigenous societies.

A decisive challenge, one of existential significance, facing all settler societies is that they need to come to terms with the Indigenous presence in their newly acquired homelands. The displacement, dispossession, and conquest of Indigenous peoples is a basic condition for the viability of settler projects, as there is effectively no room within the settler paradigm for sharing their homeland with autonomous native societies. Bolstered by a range of cultural and racial chauvinisms as well as access to a range of superior technologies, especially of warfare and repression, the settler establishment demanded total security from any Indigenous challenge or claim to sovereignty. As Wolfe notes, for settlers, colonization is a zero-sum game—the most obvious consequences of which has been not only a total denial of Indigenous sovereignty in settler homelands, but also attempts at the complete "elimination of the native" from settler society.[18]

A congruent effect was an ongoing tension between settler identification with metropolitan culture and values, on the one hand, and a deeply rooted compulsion, on the other, for settler collectives to try to gain legitimacy both in the eyes of the world and of the settler collective itself. They did this by striving for autonomy from the metropole and asserting themselves as rightful owners of their new homeland, usually to the point of claiming a special relationship to the

---

18. For one of his many expositions of these ideas, see Wolfe, "Settler Colonialism."

land—even akin to being Indigenous to it. Terry Goldie bluntly summarizes settler thinking in this regard in Newfoundland, where the Beothuk people were effectively exterminated, as: "We had natives. We killed them off. Now we are natives." His observation applies to many settler societies.[19] Given the foundational violence necessary for their establishment and a constant need to legitimate themselves, the ultimate goal of settler societies is thus to supersede themselves—to reach a stage where they are no longer recognized as such.

That the success of settler ventures is dependent on the violent dispossession, and often genocidal destruction of Indigenous societies, is of course not to suggest that frontier relations have historically been a simple drama of relentless violence and unmitigated settler aggression, and that settler and Indigenous societies were never able to adapt to one another, negotiate modes of accommodation, form alliances, acculturate, or display tolerance or empathy toward those from the opposite camp. Nor is it to deny the agency of Indigenous peoples or that there was a degree of cooperation, peaceful exchange, and mediation of differences. Such symbiotic, ambivalent, or hybridizing relations were, however, temporary and generally lasted only for as long as settlers lacked the power to dominate and take control of the land they claimed, or when settler projects failed. Sometimes these compromises were sustained by non-settler intermediaries, such as missionaries or traders. "Middle grounds" or "third spaces," as these transient periods of accommodation in the settler colonial encounter are sometimes called, almost inevitably degenerated into land grabs, race wars, ethnic cleansing offensives, and in a number of cases, escalated into exterminatory campaigns on the part of settlers when the balance of power swung in their favor. The inner drive of settler establishments for exclusive control of their homeland made lasting peaceful coexistence with Indigenous communities all but impossible.

The rise of the global industrial economy and its adjuncts—what Belich has dubbed the settler revolution and explosive colonization—all but put an end to middle grounds. From the late eighteenth century onward and continuing well into the twentieth century, a surge of tens of millions of emigrants from Western societies poured into settler colonies, mostly in temperate regions of the world, propelling Western imperial expansion, sometimes at breakneck speed. Settler colonial claims were backed by unparalleled leaps in technology, most notably in arms, soaring capacities for warfare, and resourcing that included an ability for the demographic swamping of Indigenous societies. At its most rampant, the settler revolution gave rise to explosive colonization, which Belich characterizes as "... allowing huge cities like Chicago or Melbourne to sprout in a single lifetime."

---

19. Terry Goldie, *Fear and Temptation: The Image of the Indigene in Canadian, Australian, and New Zealand Literatures* (Kingston: McGill-Queen's University Press, 1989), 157.

With the industrial and settler revolutions feeding off and amplifying each other, Indigenous societies had no counter to mass migration powered by the industrial revolution with its factories, railways, steamships, and much more deadly firearms.[20]

Settler Colonialism and Racism

Although frontier conflict between settler and Indigene was not primarily about race but fundamentally about incompatible ways of life vying for control of land and resources, settler ideology was nonetheless deeply modulated by ideas of European racial superiority. From the late eighteenth century onward, Enlightenment thought popularized pseudoscientific theories about human differences that made racial distinctions a matter of biology, and thus innate and unchangeable. This represents a definitive hardening of attitudes compared to earlier views that racial diversity was the result of environmental and cultural differences, which in theory at least, could be mitigated by cultural and environmental change. Racist ideologies played a key role in the dehumanization of Indigenous peoples and in that sense was an important enabler of settler violence. Subsequent to acts of violence it played a justificatory role, helping settlers to rationalize their violent actions to themselves and the world. Racism tended to be particularly virulent in settler societies as the ideology carried a heavy burden of representing and vindicating settler violence, especially when it escalated to exterminatory levels.

While political scientist Adam Dahl notes that in settler colonial situations racism finds expression "less through body politics than through the politics of land and space,"[21] Wolfe makes the key point that racism is a highly versatile ideology that racialized subordinate others in ways that suited the purposes of dominant groups. It was able simultaneously to racialize groups in antithetical ways as, for example, when enslaved Africans in the United States retained their enslaved status through the "one drop" of African blood rule, thereby maximizing slave masters' labor supply, whereas Native Americans were subject to "blood quantum" criteria that conveniently diluted their Indigeneity, progressively erasing their claim to the land.[22] Similarly, enslaved Africans in Brazil, Australian Aborigines, European Jewry, and Palestinians in Israel were racialized in different ways depending on the needs and protocols of prevailing settler establishments.

---

20. Belich, *Replenishing the Earth*, 9, 178–79, 183.
21. Adam Dahl, *Empire of the People: Settler Colonialism and the Foundations of Modern Democratic Thought* (Lawrence: University of Kansas Press, 2018), 11.
22. Paul Jentz, *Seven Myths of Native American History* (Indianapolis: Hackett Publishing, 2018), 134–35.

As Wolfe pithily commented: ". . . race cannot be taken as given. It is made in the targeting."[23]

From the 1870s onward, the rise of Social Darwinist theories, premised on the idea that natural selection resulted in the "survival of the fittest"—to use their catchphrase—depicted human history as an epic struggle between the races in which the fittest, naturally the Caucasoid race, would triumph. Because survival of the fittest implied the dying out of the unfit, it gave spurious scientific credence to a wide variety of "vanishing," "dying," and "doomed" race theories that had been applied to Indigenous peoples, especially in settler colonies, for some time. Because Social Darwinists wanted humanity to be rid of the supposed drag inferior peoples placed on progress, it is not surprising that some adherents to these theories who were in a position to do so, took it upon themselves to help eradicate the "unfit." Social Darwinist thinking thus had a decided bias toward exterminatory violence and a powerful self-fulfilling streak to its makeup, as case studies in this volume will demonstrate.

Ideologies espousing one or another form of "civilizing mission" operated as a counterweight, albeit a relatively light one, to the homicidal and exterminatory tendencies within settler establishments, most notably during their bloodstained frontier phases. Most prominent in this category were missionaries who sought not only a spiritual conversion but the complete abandonment of "heathen" ways of life as well. Other progressives who stand out are some higher-ranking colonial officials, usually mindful of the humanitarian appeals of lobby groups in the metropole, and a few newspaper editors and journalists, as well as educationists. Although many missionaries and other progressives held extremely negative views of Indigenes, their ideological frame challenged more extreme racist assumptions in that they deemed the "savage" to be capable of moral and intellectual improvement, even if only to the lowest levels of Western standards. Theirs, being an assimilationist enterprise, was nonetheless very much part of the settler colonial project of the "elimination of the native," which in many instances came into their own after the frontier had closed. At no point did progressive individuals consider withdrawing from the colony, restoring Indigenous sovereignty, or in any way abandoning the settler project. Indeed, seldom did they challenge settler projects in any fundamental way. Progressives did little more than advocate what they regarded as more humane ways of implementing the settler enterprise of dispossessing Indigenes and creating a new society modeled on metropolitan precepts on conquered territory.

---

23. Patrick Wolfe, "Structure and Event: Settler Colonialism, Time and the Question of Genocide," in *Empire, Colony, Genocide: Conquest, Occupation, and Subaltern Resistance in World History*, ed. A. Dirk Moses (New York: Berghahn Books, 2008), 111.

Settler Colonialism and Genocide

As destructive as settler colonialism has been of Indigenous society, it is not inherently genocidal as some scholars have claimed. There are simply too many examples of settler conquests not resulting in genocide for such a view to be tenable. And in parts of the world where settler violence did radicalize into genocide, it did not do so consistently across time and space as Canadian, South African, Australian, and American experiences attest. I do, however, regard ethnic cleansing to be inherent to settler colonialism because gaining unfettered control of their newly claimed homeland, eliminating any Indigenous claims to sovereignty to it, and sometimes even their presence in it, is foundational to the phenomenon. "Elimination of the native" is not equivalent to their extermination, as that can be achieved through a wide variety of means other than killing. Displacement and expulsion beyond settler boundaries is one, while segregation in reserves on land that settlers do not want, is another. Assimilation of remnant Indigenous populations into settler society, which usually occurs during the post-frontier phase, is a third, even though it runs counter to more extreme racist precepts that Indigenes do not have the capacity to adapt to "civilized" life and that miscegenation results in racial degeneration. A wide range of symbolic and discursive strategies of elimination have also been used to disavow an Indigenous presence or loosen their claim to the land.[24]

Most settler genocides of Indigenous peoples experience two distinct stages as our case studies will confirm. The first is a slaughterous frontier phase in which a struggle for control of the land and access to resources escalates to exterminatory levels. Because of an undue focus on killing in many analyses, the frontier phase is often seen as *the genocide* and the continued social destruction that occurred subsequently is neglected. The post-frontier phase, though usually less overtly violent, continues the process of razing Indigenous ways of life and identities by subjecting survivors to a wide range of eliminatory practices such as cultural suppression, forced acculturation, expulsion, segregation, child confiscation, assimilation, and, of course, continued violence, to mention a few of the more obvious means whereby settler regimes have sought to obliterate Indigenous societies or transfer Indigenous individuals into the settler collective. Settler obsession with the elimination of the native has been propelled by the inescapable reality that the very existence of the Indigene challenges the legitimacy of the settler regime. Even when Indigenous society has been completely eliminated, the specter of the Indigene still haunts the settler psyche. This explains continued symbolic disavowal of Indigenous claims long after autonomous native societies have ceased

---

24. For a comprehensive review of such strategies see Veracini, *Settler Colonialism*, 35–50.

to exist in settler homelands, as well as ongoing attempts at the Indigenization of the settler.

Indeed, the near universal use of the term "settler" to describe colonists who have migrated to foreign lands to found new political orders is clearly misleading. Such colonists are more accurately referred to as invaders or conquerors, as one can only legitimately settle empty or unclaimed land.[25] Except for a number of smaller islands, such as the Azores, Mauritius, and Cape Verde Islands, there have been precious few areas of the world that were genuinely uninhabited and that could sustain a settler colony. The pervasive use of "settler" in this euphemistic way reflects vanquishers' power to name themselves—and to a large extent, those they have conquered as the widespread use of terms such as "Indian" in the Americas, "Aborigine" in Australia, and "Bushman" in southern Africa indicate. Besides conquerors being able to propagate mythologies about the founding of their societies and largely control interpretations of its history, victors, in addition, have considerable power to shut down or contain counter-narratives, especially of subjugated Indigenous peoples.[26]

The narrative that successful settler projects across the globe have propagated can be summarized as: "We made the land productive through hard work and enterprise, and the land, in turn, remade us. We are as good as Indigenous." This forms the subtext of the remarkably similar national myths of settler societies such as the United States, Australia, Canada, New Zealand, Israel, and apartheid South Africa. It is not unusual for them to go so far as to claim some form of providential status as well—of having a "manifest destiny" or being a "chosen people." Denying, disavowing, obfuscating, and eliding the foundational violence of colonial conquest and subsequent human rights abuses are integral to settler societies' perceptions of themselves as legitimate and moral, and how they present themselves to the world. The use of "settler" to describe themselves is one such strategy of disavowal—and an important one at that. Despite these observations, I will nonetheless stick with "settler" because alternatives, such as "settler-invader," are clumsy; "invader" is so ideologically and emotionally loaded as to impede communication; and trying to invent a new term is likely to cause confusion and invite controversy. Settlerism's ability to mask its foundational violence is powerful, indeed. Unmasking its subterfuge by using its own terminology has its own efficacy.

---

25. Anna Johnston and Alan Lawson, "Settler Colonies," in *A Companion to Postcolonial Studies*, eds. Henry Schwarz and Sangeeta Roy (Malden, MA: Blackwell Publishers, 2000), 364–66.
26. See, for example, Jentz, *Seven Myths*, 53–83; Timothy Bottoms, *Conspiracy of Silence: Queensland's Frontier Killing Times* (Sydney: Allen & Unwin, 2013), 1–11, 177–208.

Patrick Wolfe observes that: "Territoriality is settler colonialism's irreducible element," and elaborates that "Settler colonialism destroys to replace."[27] How and why settler regimes have sought to destroy and replace Indigenous societies through exterminatory violence in four particular instances during the making of Western global dominance will be examined going forward. In each case it will be argued that the destruction of Indigenous societies was not the inadvertent consequence of colonial conflict and economic competition, but the intentional outcome of settler societies seeking to eliminate an Indigenous presence from their new homeland.

---

27. Wolfe, "Settler Colonialism," 388.

Chapter 1

Conquest, Enslavement, Deportation: The Erasure of Aboriginal Canarian Societies

Western Europe's earliest exploratory and colonizing forays into the eastern Atlantic during the fourteenth and fifteenth centuries culminated in the complete destruction of the Indigenous societies of the Canary Islands situated off the southern coast of Morocco. By the time Christopher Columbus set sail on his celebrated first voyage across the Atlantic in 1492, aboriginal Canarian societies had already been driven to the brink of oblivion by European invaders, the last independent Canarians to resist Spanish colonizers surrendering in September 1496. By the end of the fifteenth century no more than a few hundred native Canarians, nearly all of whom were enslaved, were left alive. After a century-long process of conquest, which included ongoing mass violence, land confiscation, scorched-earth tactics, enslavement, mass deportation, and child removal, it would not be long before continued bloodshed, sexual abuse, exploitation, and cultural suppression obliterated a tangible Indigenous presence in the archipelago.

The reconnaissance and colonization of three island clusters southwest of the Iberian Peninsula—the Azores, Madeira, and Canary Islands—by Spaniards and Portuguese during the two centuries before Columbus's voyages were in part products of advances in ship design and navigation, as well as the extension into the Atlantic Ocean of a long-standing European tradition of conquest, settlement, and empire building in the Mediterranean. Since the Canaries was the only eastern Atlantic archipelago that was inhabited, it was the only one that needed to be conquered, in the process serving as an apprenticeship for Castilian ultra-marine empire. These eastern Atlantic islands functioned as strategic bases for further European exploration westward and would serve as testing grounds for Iberian colonialism in the New World.

The Canary Islands and Their Indigenous Peoples

The Canary Archipelago, which is today part of Spain, consists of seven habitable volcanic islands strung out in a 280 mile latitudinal chain, its closest point slightly over 60 miles off southern Morocco. Although much of the archipelago consists of rugged, mountainous terrain of jagged ridges with alternating ravines, and although there are many rocky outcrops and stone-strewn lava fields, it also

1

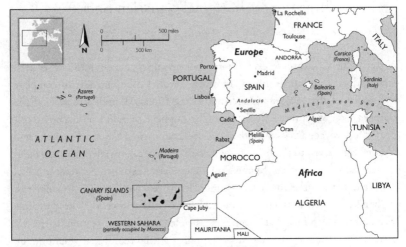

Canary Islands in relation to Europe and north Africa.

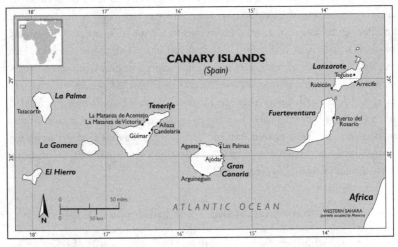

Canary Islands.

has extensive and verdant coastal lowlands. The steep gradient of their topographies means that these islands have a wide range of climatic conditions and natural vegetation within relatively confined areas. This allowed an Indigenous economy based on daily and seasonal movement between croplands and pastures, and made available a diversity of wild foods. There was also no shortage of materials for stone tools or pottery, and vegetable fibers for cords and rough textiles. Extensive forested areas provided an abundant supply of wood, but the lack of metallic ores precluded the development of metalworking.

Indigenous Canarians were derived from Berber-speaking societies of Northwest Africa. This is confirmed by close links between Berber and native Canarian languages, material cultures, blood types, physical appearance, and cosmology. Despite cultural diversity across the islands, Canarian communities nevertheless shared cultural similarities indicative of common origins. Cultural variation arose because island communities developed in isolation of one another over long periods, and immigrants did not spread evenly across the archipelago. Archaeological evidence and folklore indicate that migrants from the African mainland arrived in several waves between the second millennium BCE and the early centuries CE. With prevailing winds and sea currents, it would have been relatively easy for simple vessels to have traveled from the Moroccan coast to the Canaries but nearly impossible for them to have made the return journey. It is also clear that early migrants had the intention of settling there as they came as families and with domesticated animals and seeds. They lived in isolation from the adjacent continent as well as from other islands.

Canarians were agropastoralists. They cultivated crops of barley and in some areas wheat, while also foraging fern roots that were roasted and ground into flour. Beans, peas, fruit trees, and other foods were grown in small-scale horticultural initiatives, while wild fruits, berries, seeds, honey, and yams among other foods were also gathered. On all the islands, shepherds tended substantial herds of goats that provided them with meat, milk, tallow, and hides, as well as bones and tendons for tools. Sheep and pigs were also present on some islands. Shellfish and fish formed an important part of the Canarian diet. Birds, small rodents, and several varieties of lizard were also available. The precontact Canarian economies most likely supported a population of perhaps 80,000, with some estimates as high as 100,000, and about two-thirds lived on the main islands of Gran Canaria and Tenerife.

Their Spartan way of life, to which stock rearing was central, precluded population concentrations any larger than small villages. Canarian society consisted mostly of dispersed settlements, often no larger than the extended family. Gran Canaria, socially and economically the most developed of the island societies, had a few larger settlements. Islanders often lived in caves and constructed simple stone dwellings with thatched roofs. Canarian societies had hierarchical social structures consisting of hereditary ruling families, a small nobility, and common-ers. Caste-like social divisions were reinforced by founding myths, social customs, status markers in dress and grooming styles, as well as the exercise of force where necessary. At the upper end, a small order of high priests had considerable influ-ence, while at the lowest, butchers were a despised, segregated group. Politically, Canarian society was organized into rudimentary, hereditary chiefdoms with a fair degree of fluidity in power relations. On the more populous islands, Canarian chiefs were capable of marshaling substantial fighting forces efficiently in the face of outside threats, as several European expeditions found to their cost.

Although they were limited to weapons of wood and stone, as opposed to the more advanced arms available to Europeans, Canarians proved to be formi-dable adversaries in combat. Island warriors were legendary for the force and accuracy with which they hurled rocks and stones at opponents. They were able not only to break the shields of European soldiers, but often also the arms hold-ing them. Combatants used a variety of fire-hardened wooden lances reinforced with horn tips. Acclimatized to local conditions, Canarians moved swiftly over rocky, rugged terrain in contrast to clumsy European soldiers usually hampered by heavy, inappropriate armor and gear. Many used wooden staves to vault nim-bly down inclines or across rough ground. The craggy, precipitous uplands with deep, narrow gullies, especially when forested, provided many natural fortresses, as well as opportunities for escape or surprise attack—all favoring island defend-ers. Limited by their relatively small ships and medieval weapons, European raid-ers were usually outnumbered and ill-equipped for the unconventional methods of the Canarians. These advantages, together with their adept use of guerrilla tactics, meant that many of the islanders' military successes came in the form of ambushes in rough terrain.

Reconnaissance, Raiding, and Slaving

The Canaries came to the attention of European mariners for the first time since the fall of the Roman Empire when the Genoese navigator Lancelotto Malocello landed on the eastern-most isle, Lanzarote, in 1336. The archipelago became the object of Portuguese, Genoan, Majorcan, Aragonese, Catalan, Norman, and Castilian voyages of exploration and raiding. Trading and proselytization occurred but were completely overshadowed by violent encounters. Between Malocello's landing and the onset of conquest in 1402, European interlopers came to the Canary Islands mainly with the intention to loot and raid for slaves. Plunder-ing expeditions to the Canaries were organized by pirates as well as merchants, aristocrats, and the monarchs of various southern European states. One of the earliest and best documented accounts is that of the 1341 venture sponsored by

Alfonso IV of Portugal and led by Genoese navigator Nicoloso da Recco. Expeditions were disappointed in their quest for urban settlements, precious minerals, spices, fine fabrics, and the other spoils late medieval brigands coveted. Regardless, persistent hopes of finding gold continued for quite some time to motivate adventurers and freebooters to visit the islands.

Rather than gold, the Canaries did offer several commodities that made the voyages profitable. In addition to hides and tallow, the Canaries provided Europeans with sealskins from the two eastern-most islands; orchil, a lichen used in the making of a rare purple dye much in demand in Europe; and dragon's blood, the bright red resin tapped from the dragon tree (*dracaena draco*) and used in dyes, medicines, and varnish for musical instruments. The most valuable commodities obtained from the Canaries, however, were the inhabitants themselves. The presence of Canarian slaves was reported in Majorca already in the early 1340s, and they were subsequently sold in Iberian, Italian, and North African markets. Canarian slaves were also sought after on other eastern Atlantic archipelago colonies. With the onset of conquest, enslaved natives were also used to build the colonial economies of the Canaries themselves, and a few were used as interpreters.

During the latter half of the fourteenth century, redoubtable Canarian warriors in many instances staved off European attacks, but on other occasions slavers, who usually surprised their victims with sneak attacks at night, carried off boatloads of captives. The French conquerors of Lanzarote noted that these raids had depleted that island's population to the extent that there were little more than 300 inhabitants left by the time they invaded in 1402. Three such raids on Lanzarote, in 1385, 1393, and 1399, had resulted in as many as 500 slaves, including the island's ruler and his wife, being captured and sold in Spain. Hierro also suffered continuous raiding which thinned the population markedly. Communities on the larger, more populous islands of Tenerife and Gran Canaria, better able to defend themselves, were generally avoided by slavers but nevertheless experienced periodic raids.

Increased demand for Canarian slaves was created with the Portuguese settlement of Madeira from the 1420s, and the Azores from the late 1430s, onward. The Azores, with its temperate climate and economy based on wheat, stock farming, and the harvesting of timber, had limited demand for slaves, although Canarians were prized for their animal husbandry skills. Madeira had a greater demand for forced labor. Its tropical climate and the availability of water meant that it was suitable for sugarcane cultivation, a highly profitable but labor-intensive undertaking. Insatiable demand from Europe ensured explosive growth of the sugar industry from the mid-fifteenth century onward. Canarians were among the first slaves to be used on Madeira, which conveniently lay on route from the Canaries to Europe. Because of their legendary agility over rocky terrain,

Canarians were in particular demand to cut levadas, the intricate system of water courses that carried precipitation from the mountains to the coastal plains where sugarcane was grown. Their skills as drovers also meant that they were used to look after settlers' flocks in the highlands. By the 1480s, a much larger sugar industry was emerging in the Canaries itself, fueling intensified demand for slaves.

The Conquest of Lanzarote, Fuerteventura, and Hierro

From pillaging and slave raiding in the fourteenth century, the emphasis of European activity in the archipelago swung toward conquest in the fifteenth, though slaving and plunder continued unabated. The subjugation of the Canaries was a slow, fitful process that took the better part of a century. The two main islands of Gran Canaria and Tenerife with their large, doggedly defiant populations and difficult terrain took a long time and great effort to vanquish. In the first phase of conquest, Lanzarote, Fuerteventura, and Hierro were subjugated between 1402 and 1405. Their flatter, more open, and drier terrains made Lanzarote and Fuerteventura easier targets; and Hierro, given its small size and a population considerably thinned by slave raids, was particularly vulnerable.

The expedition to subjugate these islands started as a private Norman enterprise that placed its conquests under Castilian sovereignty. It set sail from La Rochelle on May 1, 1402 with 280 men and was led by Gadifer de La Salle and Jean de Bethencourt, two aristocratic adventurers. The imaginations and cupidity of the two buccaneering knights were captivated by tales of the riches the Canaries had to offer. Bethencourt financed the undertaking by raising a loan against his estate and intended using his political connections to find a royal patron; whereas La Salle, a warrior of some renown and a veteran of many campaigns, provided the ship and military leadership. Whatever chivalrous, crusading, and missionary ideals they espoused, it was clear that their main aims were mercenary—the plunder of any valuable commodities they might find and the establishment of personal fiefdoms.

Things got off to an inauspicious start when the crew mutinied upon reaching Cadiz and most deserted. The sixty-three remaining men pressed on and reached Lanzarote in July 1402, where, because of internal rivalries, they struggled to seize the island from its severely diminished population. Pretending to come in friendship and being well received by islanders, the Normans gained permission from its ruler to construct a fort on the far south of the island in return for protecting them against European raiders. In that same month, another mutiny broke out among the invaders. Bethencourt sailed back to Europe with the mutineers who had commandeered the ship, leaving La Salle with about two dozen men, scant supplies, and a promise that he would soon return with reinforcements and fresh provisions. La Salle and his depleted force nevertheless persevered in their efforts to conquer Lanzarote.

La Salle's aim in subduing Lanzarote, as recorded by the expedition's two chaplains, Pierre Boutier and Jean le Verrier, who accompanied him on the expedition, was to kill all the men of fighting age and to capture, baptize, and enslave the rest of the island population. This was largely accomplished—except that some adult males were taken captive—and represents as clear an indication of genocidal intent as any, especially as enslavement in nearly all instances entailed deportation from the island. It is also an accurate description of the intentions of subsequent conquerors and would-be conquerors.

La Salle first tried the tactic of divide and rule. He befriended Afche, a Lanzarotean leader who disputed the chief's authority, recruiting him as an accomplice on the promise that he would be made ruler. La Salle's plan started off well with the capture of the island chief in a surprise attack on his stronghold but ended badly with the chief's escape and execution of Afche. Open hostilities between the invaders and the islanders ensued. Given the small size of their force, the deprivations they suffered, and the difficult terrain, subsequent fighting consisted of a series of small skirmishes in which the French used the security of the fort and their superior weaponry to capture islanders individually and in small groups, some of whom were exchanged for supplies with passing ships. Those who evaded capture or supported the king in his guerrilla campaign were unable to tend their fields or flocks, and most of their food and seed stores were confiscated by the interlopers. Some died of starvation while most, driven by hunger, gave themselves up to be taken prisoner, baptized, and enslaved. The high death rate reported among prisoners was probably as much due to malnutrition and disease as brutal treatment by their vanquishers. In January 1404, the island chief and about twenty of his followers were among the last of the Lanzaroteans to be captured and enslaved. The surviving population was taken into bondage and most were shipped off for sale in Europe. Lanzarotean society was destroyed. Motivated by chivalric considerations, Bethencourt, upon his return to the archipelago several months later, allowed the chief to return to the island, allotting him a small parcel of land.

Meanwhile, back in Europe, Bethencourt had spent his time soliciting royal support for the venture, as he needed the legitimacy and protection that a sovereign could provide. The erratic French monarch, Charles VI, given to bouts of insanity, was hardly suitable, whereas Henry III of Castile proved to be receptive to Bethencourt's lobbying. He was willing to sponsor the enterprise to preempt Portuguese claims to the islands. Bethencourt also managed to persuade the king to recognize him as "Lord of the Islands," and his conquests in the Canaries as his fiefdom under the sovereignty of the Castilian crown, in the process betraying La Salle. Bethencourt's gambit set the stage for eventual Castilian conquest of the archipelago.

When Bethencourt finally returned to the Canaries with reinforcements and fresh supplies in April 1404, the marauders turned their attention to Fuerteventura. There was great tension between the two leaders and their followers. Besides having left La Salle to fend for himself while he furthered his own interests in Castile, Bethencourt on his return asserted himself as "Lord of the Isles." What is more, Bethencourt kept most of his supplies for his own fresh, well-fed party while the ragged, worn-out group loyal to La Salle remained deprived. The two factions, Bethencourt's by far the larger and better provisioned, built separate forts on Fuerteventura and competed for control of the island. La Salle soon returned to Europe.

Bethencourt, now styling himself "King of the Canaries," headed the offensive to conquer Fuerteventura. Throughout 1404, there were numerous skirmishes, at times daily, between the French and Fuerteventurans. Outnumbered and occasionally outmaneuvered, the French armed some Lanzarotean slaves who fought and died for the Castilian cause. The security of their fort and superior arms nonetheless gave the French major advantages. Islanders taken captive were ferried back to Lanzarote. Worn down by this war of attrition and unable to engage in subsistence activities, the two Fuerteventuran chiefs and their subjects surrendered together in January 1405, marking the fall of the island. The two chiefs were baptized and, in another show of chivalry, were given small land grants and allowed to live on the island. Their subjects, however, were baptized and enslaved, some shipped off for sale in Europe, the rest to Lanzarote. Bethencourt immediately set off for Normandy, where he recruited nearly 200 settlers to repopulate the island. Because most were single men, many took Canarian women as wives or concubines.

Looking to extend his control of the islands, Bethencourt in October 1405 went on an ill-advised sortie to Gran Canaria, in which over twenty of his men were killed. Chastened, he then waged war on La Palma for six weeks, claiming to have killed over a hundred of its inhabitants before turning his attention to tiny Hierro. Here a ruse against trusting Canarians proved successful. Bethencourt persuaded Augeron, brother to the island's leader, to propose a mass meeting to seal a peace agreement between the two groups. The Normans used this gathering of Indigenes to round them up and enslave them. A reported 112 islanders were taken prisoner. Only a small number of Hierroans remained free in the mountains as the island had already been substantially depopulated by slave raids, perhaps as many as 400 taken in 1402 alone. Bethencourt immediately settled some 120 European families on the island. After a fruitless reconnaissance of Gomera,

which did not deter Bethencourt from claiming the island
as part of his fiefdom, he
left the Canaries for good in
December 1405, appointing
his nephew Maciot de Bethencourt as governor of the conquered isles.

Between the end of 1405
and serious incursions into
Gran Canaria in the late
1470s, very little headway was
made in the conquest of independent islands. The situation
was complicated by the entry
of the Portuguese as serious
contenders for control of the
Canaries from the mid-1420s
till about 1480. The Portuguese challenge to Castilian
control was based partly on
the assertion that because
Malocello had been a vassal
of the Portuguese king, who
had also sponsored da Recco's
expedition, Portugal had prior
claim to the archipelago. The
Portuguese launched several
fruitless military expeditions
to the Canaries to give substance to their claims, in the
process obstructing and delay-
ing Spanish conquest.

Illuminated Canarian manuscript. This illuminated
page comes from the Canarian manuscript produced by
Pierre Boutier and Jean le Verrier, and therefore favors
Gadifer de La Salle greatly. The illustration reflects the
tension between La Salle and Bethencourt, the two
seated figures to the right of the mast. La Salle is posi-
tioned so that the crest on his shield features prom-
inently but that of Bethencourt is hidden behind him.
Also, while La Salle's emblems are clearly visible on the
pennants, those of Bethencourt have been erased.

The Subjugation of Gran Canaria

Gran Canaria withstood attempts at European invasion for much of the fifteenth
century, even though its substantial, fertile lowlands and large population of perhaps 25,000 made it an attractive prize. The fierce, well-organized fighting forces

its leaders were able to summon kept intruders at bay. Invading parties, such as those of Bethencourt in 1405 and a 1424 Portuguese expedition, were sent packing under a hail of missiles. Private claimants were also sidelined in 1477 by the ambitious Ferdinand II and Isabella, whose marriage in 1469 unified the kingdoms of Aragon and Castile. They decided that the crown would henceforth take responsibility for conquering the Canary archipelago, marking a new phase in the conquest of the Canaries.

Ever since Henry III had backed Bethencourt's venture in 1403, the Castilian crown had encouraged seigneurial attempts at conquest in the Canaries. These private endeavors by adventurers and minor nobles to establish fiefdoms in the archipelago had made very little progress in nearly three-quarters of a century, and it was clear to Ferdinand and Isabella that decisive intervention by the state was needed to subdue the unconquered islands. The timing of their intervention was in response to Portugal launching a renewed military effort in the archipelago in the midst of its involvement in the War of Castilian Succession (1475–1479).

Despite the considerably greater resources of the Castilian crown, little was available for the Canarian venture as its primary commitments were to fighting for Isabella's right to the throne and then the conquest of Granada, Islam's last foothold in Spain. Conquistadors were thus expected to raise most of their own finances from merchants and noblemen, who were promised a share in the immediate spoils of conquest, such as slaves, orchil harvests, and land grants, as well as privileged access to the colonial economy, of which sugar production was the most attractive prospect. It was mainly Italian, Spanish, and Flemish merchants who provided the necessary capital.

Ferdinand and Isabella thus organized a military expedition for the conquest of Gran Canaria under the leadership of General Juan Rejon. In mid-1478, Rejon set sail with a force of over 600 hundred soldiers and thirty horsemen. He set about establishing a garrison at the present-day site of Las Palmas. Before the fort could be completed the invaders were engaged by a force of 2,000 Canarian fighters. The Europeans narrowly staved off the attack through effective use of cannon and cavalry. In flat, open spaces mounted warriors gained considerable advantage from the height, speed, maneuverability, and shock force provided by their horses. The partially completed fort also afforded protection.

Once the fort was completed, the Spaniards launched raids throughout the fertile northeastern part of the island, destroying crops, confiscating flocks, and taking captives. Gran Canarians were forced to retreat to the mountains. The Spaniards did not have it all their own way, though. One of their sorties into the southern part of the island at Arguineguin was ambushed by Canarian forces while passing through a gorge and completely routed, resulting in twenty-two dead, eighty taken captive, who were later released, and over one hundred wounded. Rejon also had to fight off a Portuguese seaborne attack, and a subsequent naval blockade hampered the delivery of supplies to his garrison. Rejon's inability to pursue the Canarians into their mountain fastnesses led to a stalemate. These and other difficulties resulted in morale-sapping intrigues and conflict among the Spaniards, culminating in Rejon's rash execution of the governor appointed by the Spanish crown. Ferdinand and Isabella deposed Rejon and in August 1480 replaced him with Pedro de Vera, whose reputation for ruthlessness made him an ideal candidate for rescuing their foundering Gran Canarian enterprise.

De Vera's military strategy was to build a second fort on the northwestern coast of the island and to launch a two-pronged campaign against the mountain strongholds of the Gran Canarians, while implementing a comprehensive scorched-earth policy of destroying crops and seizing stock. This plan paid dividends from 1482 onward as Gran Canarians were deprived of food. Most of the fortified mountain refuges in the northern part of the island were taken one by one, often with the help of Gomeran and Lanzarotean fighters. There is also evidence that contagious diseases introduced by Europeans weakened Canarian resistance.

An intriguing feature of the Spanish campaign on Gran Canaria was the strategic use made of collaborators, most notably one of its two chiefs, Tenesor Semidan, who was taken prisoner in 1482. Semidan was immediately sent to Seville and put on public display in his traditional goatskin dress as an example of the Canarian savage. Later, he was attired in the finest European clothes, baptized Fernando Guanarteme, and paraded around the realm. This treatment and the promise that he would be allocated a tract of land on Gran Canaria and allowed to live there with his family and entourage won Semidan's unwavering loyalty. Presumably overawed by the wealth, power, and technological superiority of the Europeans, he henceforth cooperated fully with the Spaniards, even in the most devious and damaging of their tactics and strategies, and played an important role in the final phase of the conquest of Gran Canaria. In the closing stages of the war, Semidan was even allowed to lead an attacking force of 500 baptized islanders. He later also assisted with the occupation of La Palma and the invasion of Tenerife.

With their backs to the wall, most defenders fought to the bitter end. Some preferred ritualized suicide by leaping from cliffs to being taken prisoner. At least one leader, Aytami, a high priest, defected, however, and accepted baptism. The Gran Canarians were not without their successes in the latter stages of the conquest, though. A force of 200 Spaniards suffered near annihilation in a reckless attack on the coastal fortress of Ajodar. The closing encounter in the conquest

Canarian woman statue. This statue of an infuriated Canarian woman hurling a stone was erected in Doramas Park, a small urban green in Las Palmas, Gran Canaria, in 1980 as part of a grouping of sculptures erected to celebrate the 500th anniversary of the founding of the city. Canarians had a widespread reputation for the ferociousness with which they resisted invaders, as well as the accuracy and force with which they were able to hurl stones and rocks at adversaries.

of Gran Canaria came in April 1483 with the siege of the mountain fortress of Ansite, where approximately 600 men, 1,500 women, and a large number of children were forced to surrender. The Spaniards sent Semidan to make empty promises of immunity in return for their surrender. While the defenders opted to submit, their leader, Ben Tegui, and his *faycan* (high priest) flung themselves from the fortress summit, reportedly shouting "*Atis Tirma!*" (for my land!). De Vera saw to it that the bishop of Lanzarote was on hand to oversee the performance of a celebratory Te Deum and the baptism of prisoners, which marked their descent into slavery.

It was decreed that all Canarians be deported from the island for fear of subsequent uprisings. The majority were exiled on conquered islands, where they served as slave laborers. A contingent of several hundred, including many of the island's elite, was shipped off to Castile. Many Gran Canarian children were distributed among settlers on the pretext that they were to be raised as Christians but were used as slaves. Only forty Canarians, who formed part of the household and retinue of Fernando Guanarteme, were allowed to occupy a stretch of poor pasturage along the northwestern coast promised him by King Ferdinand.

The Occupation of Gomera

From the mid-fourteenth century, Gomera had endured slave raids and some attention from missionaries. Despite inhabiting one of the smaller islands, Gomerans were well capable of defending themselves as demonstrated by the ignominious end of a European slaving expedition to the island in 1384, when its members were trapped on a rocky outcrop by an Indigenous fighting force. The raiders had little option but to surrender and were allowed to go free.

Gomera became a significant site of struggle between Castile and Portugal for supremacy in the archipelago for over two decades from the mid-1420s until the Portuguese withdrew in 1448, because it was the easiest of the remaining isles to subdue. Both sides were allied to factions within the Gomeran population, which was split into four chiefdoms. Though divided, and enduring both Portuguese and Spanish presences, the island chiefdoms remained independent, as they could muster significant fighting forces and had ready access to highland refuges. The next four decades witnessed ongoing skirmishes with islanders, alliances being formed with one or another Gomeran faction against others, and a good deal of intrigue all round. The Castilians meanwhile shipped off whatever orchil and captives they could take. The stalemate continued until Pedro de Vera made a concerted effort to subdue the island in the late 1480s after consolidating control of Gran Canaria.

In 1486, de Vera quelled a localized Gomeran uprising after which 200 of its inhabitants were deported into slavery on Gran Canaria, which he governed. Two years later the self-proclaimed governor of Gomera, Hernan Peraza, was killed when surprised in the cave of his Gomeran lover by a small group of insurgents. De Vera's tactic for suppressing this incipient insurrection and subduing the island permanently was to order all Gomerans to attend the funeral of the slain "governor" and to take all of those who complied prisoner. De Vera then used these hostages, together with false promises of amnesty, to persuade a substantial number of fugitives who had taken to the mountains to surrender. All prisoners over the age of fifteen who hailed from the rebellious regions of Agana and Orone were sentenced to death and were either hanged, drowned, impaled, or torn apart by horses. Children were distributed among colonists as slaves. The rest were baptized, enslaved, and deported to Lanzarote, with a good number thrown overboard along the way. De Vera learned that some Gomerans he had deported to Gran Canaria in 1486 had encouraged this later insurrection. His response was to hang all the males in this group. A further hundred Gomerans were sold into slavery in Spain. Being by then in principle against slavery, especially of people who professed Christianity, Ferdinand and Isabella manumitted this contingent and sent them back to the Canaries. In contravention of the crown's intentions, de Vera saw to it that they were detained on Gran Canaria to replace the laborers he had executed the year before. Denuded of Indigenes and occupied by an influx of European settlers, Gomera subsequently developed a productive sugar industry.

The Vanquishing of La Palma

La Palma was subject to slave raids but retained its independence until the early 1490s because its terrain was particularly rugged, and its population had a well-earned reputation for ferocity. The most notable slaving sortie to this island came in 1447, when Palmans successfully defended themselves against a Castilian invasion by 200 European soldiers and 300 Canarian subordinates. Ambushed in rugged terrain in the interior, the invaders had little defense against the rocks hurled at them with pinpoint accuracy and were soon put to flight. From midcentury, slave raids were mounted by settlers from neighboring Hierro and Gomera. Hostilities were punctuated by ephemeral peace pacts, trade agreements, and attempts at evangelization that resulted in several Palman leaders being baptized in 1488. They and their followers were now recognized as *bandos de pazes* (people of peace), who could not be enslaved, while heathens, called *bandos de guerra* (people of war), remained fair game for slavers.

Alonso de Lugo, who had played an active role in the subjugation of Gran Canaria under both Rejon and de Vera, emerged as the foremost conquistador of the Canaries in the 1490s after de Vera had been deployed in 1491 to the siege of Granada. With a mandate from the Spanish crown to conquer the two remaining Canary Islands and with the financial backing of mainly Italian merchants, in 1491–1492, de Lugo mustered a force of nearly 1,000 men for an attack on La Palma. Many were Gran Canarians, among them Semidan.

Landing on the central west coast of La Palma at the end of September 1492, de Lugo set about building a fort at Tazacorte. With this security measure in place, he put an ultimatum to the island leaders representing twelve chiefdoms. Those who accepted Spanish rule and conversion to Christianity were offered peace and freedom as *bandos de pazes*, while those who resisted would be attacked and enslaved. Those amenable to the offer were further lulled into a false sense of security by assurances of fair treatment by Francisca Palmesa, an enslaved Gran Canarian woman used as intermediary by the Spaniards. Roughly half the chiefs, particularly in the vulnerable southern part of the island, accepted the offer. Those who refused were not able to resist for long and were captured and enslaved. The last of the resisters, Chief Tanausu and a few followers who were holed up in the mountain fortress of Ecero, were tricked into submission. Tanausu refused to consider a peace treaty until de Lugo left his territory. De Lugo withdrew, his departure visible from high ground, but left a force of men hidden near the fortress. Lured from his sanctuary, Tanausu was easily overcome and captured. This event on May 3, 1493 symbolized the fall of Palma.

Once in full control of the island, de Lugo immediately shipped off into slavery those he could classify as *bandos de guerra*, including Tanausu's party. Tanausu refused to speak or eat and soon died en route to Spain. It did not take long before de Lugo also started transporting *bandos de pazes* into slavery. The predictable rebellion by Palmans gave de Lugo the excuse he needed to declare all Palmans *bandos de guerra*. He then rounded up the entire surviving population of about 1,200 people, appropriated perhaps 20,000 head of stock, executed the leaders, and sold the rest into slavery. European settlers soon repopulated the island, sugarcane becoming the staple crop.

The Conquest of Tenerife

Tenerife, the last of the Canary Islands to be conquered, had a preconquest population that might have been as high as 30,000. Populous, relatively prosperous, and politically well organized, this island was the one most capable of defending itself against intruders. Tenerife was thus generally avoided by plunderers who sought easier pickings elsewhere. Through much of the fifteenth century, raiding parties who tried their luck were routed, others deterred by the sight of Guanches[1] massing on the shore to fight them, while a few netted a small number of captives.

Meanwhile, during the fifteenth century an Indigenous religious cult around a wooden sculpture of the Virgin Mary carrying the Christ Child had emerged in Guimar, along the east coast of the island. The carving, which probably came from missionaries across the strait at Agaete on the northwestern coast of Gran Canaria, had washed ashore during the 1390s. Believed to have supernatural powers, it was housed in the Guimar chief's cave. A mid-fifteenth-century raid on Tenerife had captured a seven-year-old boy, who was taken back to Lanzarote, christened Anton Guanche, and instructed in Christianity. In his teens, Anton Guanche escaped from a ship stopping off at Tenerife on its way to Gomera. Anton used his knowledge of Christianity to establish himself as priest of this cult centered on the wooden sculpture, which came to be known as "Our Lady of Candelaria." Converted to Christianity as a result of this cult, the leaders and people of Guimar became the foremost collaborators of the Spaniards.

Until the mid-1490s, the logistical problems of mounting an effective campaign against Tenerife, its challenging terrain, and the military prowess of its defenders combined to deter aggressors. In the early 1490s, the prospects for conquest by Spain, by now the only contender for control of the Canaries, improved considerably. The capture of Granada in January 1492 freed resources that could be deployed in the Spanish colonial enterprise, and Columbus's reconnoitering of the Caribbean later that year boosted Spanish colonial ambitions. By this time firearms, though still relatively primitive, were coming into wider circulation and helped swing the balance of power in favor of Europeans. Barely a year after concluding his campaign on La Palma, de Lugo was commissioned by the Spanish crown to conquer Tenerife. De Lugo's quest, which began in April 1494, consisted of two campaigns and was concluded in a little less than two and a half years. The first ended in disaster for the Spaniards. The second resulted in victory, not only because of their superior weaponry and resources, but because they gained considerable advantage from invisible helpers—disease-causing microbes.

Alonso de Lugo landed at Anaza on April 30, 1494, with a force of 1,000 infantry and 120 horsemen funded partly by the sale of his personal assets. Fearing an attack before they could set up fortifications, de Lugo sent Semidan to the chief of Anaga to request that the landing party be left in peace, a mission

---

1. The Indigenous people of Tenerife were known as Guanches, the Spanish corruption of the Indigenous words *guan* (man) and *Chenerche* (Tenerife).

he accomplished. A few days later, when he was ready to venture forth from his Santa Cruz fortress, de Lugo was confronted by a Guanche force under Ben Como, the chief of Taoro located in the northwest. Como emerged as the pre-eminent leader on Tenerife, and Taoro as the epicenter of resistance to Spanish incursions. De Lugo made Como an offer of freedom and peace in return for his adoption of Christianity and acceptance of Spanish rule. Como declined, asked de Lugo to leave and, in a gesture of goodwill, offered him some supplies. A battle was averted, both sides retreating to consider their strategies.

Guanche leaders called a joint council a few days later to plan a course of action. Only eight of the nine chiefs attended, Guimar having thrown in its lot with the Spaniards. Besides the influence of the cult of Candelaria, the Guimar chief Acaymo was involved in an ongoing feud with Ben Como. With Anton Guanche acting as interpreter, Acaymo, together with 600 warriors, visited de Lugo's camp, accepted Spanish authority, cemented a formal alliance with the invaders, and was baptized Añaterve el Bueno (Añaterve the Good). It is likely that Acaymo had ambitions of acting as surrogate ruler for the Spaniards after conquest. The four westerly chiefdoms of Icod, Daute, Adeje, and Abona rejected Como's proposal of united action under his military leadership because of internal rivalries, whereas the chiefs under immediate threat, those of Anaga, Tegueste, and Tacoronte, allied themselves under Como's chieftainship.

Deciding to wait out the winter, which lasts into March, de Lugo resumed his campaign in the spring of 1495. His plan was to confront Como in his own territory. De Lugo marched with 800 men from his base camp at Anaza, toward Taoro. He became suspicious at not encountering any Guanches and decided to call off the attack. Returning through the Acentejo ravine, the Spanish invaders were ambushed by a contingent of 300 Guanches under Tinguaro, brother and lieutenant of Como. The Spaniards were caught completely off guard and had little defense against the boulders and tree trunks that came crashing down and rocks hurled at them. Trapped in the gorge, and in disarray, the Spanish force suffered major casualties and came off second best in the hand-to-hand combat that followed. Two hours into the battle, Como arrived with a large force ensuring the utter defeat of the Europeans. Over 600 Spanish soldiers were killed with scattered bands of survivors fleeing to the Santa Cruz fort. This bloody rout was by far the Spaniards' worst defeat in the Canaries.

Acaymo sent his ally 300 men and supplies to help shore up his depleted garrison. De Lugo, ever in need of funds, reciprocated with a remarkable act of treachery and myopia. He placed the allied islanders in chains and shipped them to Spain to be sold as slaves. An annoyed Spanish crown, which placed higher value on its Guimar confederates, freed the men and sent them back to Tenerife in the hope of saving the alliance. Worn down by harrying attacks on his demoralized garrison, de Lugo in early June 1495 packed up camp and returned to Gran Canaria.

Despite this setback, de Lugo managed to gain the backing of Italian and Castilian merchants and a few Spanish noblemen to sponsor a second campaign in return for a share in the spoils of conquest. De Lugo almost immediately went about reassembling a force of 1,100 men and seventy cavalry for a second invasion of Tenerife. By early November 1495, he had once again landed at Anaza and started rebuilding the fort. This campaign was better equipped with more soldiers carrying firearms.

Shortly after landing, the Spaniards were fortunate to capture a Guanche spying on their camp. From him they extracted information about Ben Como's whereabouts and tactics. De Lugo outmaneuvered Como by marching on his encampment through the night. Taken by surprise, the Guanche army was comprehensively defeated, suffering a reported 1,700 deaths in the ensuing battle. Acaymo, who in the meanwhile had remained on the sidelines, in the wake of this display of military superiority, once again declared his support for the Spaniards and contributed men and supplies to their war effort.

As in the previous year, de Lugo suspended his campaign and dug in for the winter. Although relatively mild, the Canary winter can be wet and uncomfortable with snowfalls in higher lying areas. Forced to abandon the lowlands, the Taoro confederacy clearly had the worst of the weather, which on this occasion was unusually rainy and cold. The Guanches also had to cope with the loss of their croplands and disruption to other subsistence activities. Hunger was widespread, and despair at the imminent destruction of their way of life must have taken a toll. Among the Guanches, the outbreak of an unknown epidemic devastated the population, with several thousand succumbing. There can be little doubt that the plague stemmed from microorganisms introduced by the invaders. Malnutrition, psychological distress, the large number of rotting corpses strewn across the land, and the Guanche practice of eviscerating and embalming the bodies of deceased nobles, contributed to the severity of the outbreak. Spanish parties foraging for supplies reported large numbers of corpses littering the landscape, settlements deserted, and flocks left untended. They nevertheless came under periodic attack from enfeebled Guanche forces.

De Lugo had to contend with a different set of problems during the winter break. Insufficient funding from his backers in Europe meant a large shortfall in provisions. Captured Guanche flocks and food supplied by Acaymo were not sufficient to tide him over the winter. By the end of November 1495, the situation had deteriorated to the point where soldiers were forced to forage for wild foods to supplement their daily rations. An outbreak of disease and growing ill-discipline among the rank and file resulted. The situation was saved by one of de Lugo's lieutenants volunteering to sell two Gran Canarian sugarcane estates, as well as houses, slaves, and stock, to buy provisions. The supplies bought from this fire sale arrived none too soon at the beginning of December 1495.

Revitalized, de Lugo decided to go on the offensive and before the end of that month, marched on the Taoro league. A substantial force of Guanches under Ben Como engaged the invaders only a few miles from the site of their victory the previous year. Once again, learning of their battle-plan from a captured Guanche, de Lugo was able to counter the attack successfully. As many as 2,000 Guanche warriors were reputedly killed while Spanish casualties amounted to sixty-four dead. Preferring not to press home his advantage, de Lugo at the end of May 1496, returned to his Santa Cruz fortress to await the arrival of additional provisions. By early July, he was ready to confront the Taoro alliance head-on and marched into the heart of their territory. Como, observing the strength of the opposing force, and his own army depleted by disease, hunger, and battlefield losses, decided to sue for peace. De Lugo required that they accept Spanish sovereignty, convert to Christianity, and help him subdue the rest of the island. Como agreed, and the two sides joined together in revelry to celebrate their pact and the Guanches' new status as Spanish subjects.

During August and September, de Lugo moved against the four remaining polities. Realizing they had no chance against the forces ranged against them, their chiefs formally submitted to de Lugo on the September 29, 1496. Tenerife had finally been conquered. The obligatory religious ceremony to thank God for this victory followed, and surrendered Guanches were baptized and enslaved. Substantial numbers were immediately shipped off to Spain or other islands, and only a few remained on Tenerife itself. Male slaves were used as shepherds and on sugarcane plantations. A few collaborating nobles were allowed their freedom but were required to carry an official document confirming their free status. A handful with stock of their own were displaced to marginal lands. Women, both slave and free, were exploited in a variety of ways. Some were taken as concubines and domestic servants, while sexual violence seems to have been common and perpetrated with impunity. A small number of Islanders who refused to submit to Spanish rule, together with escaped slaves, lived in the mountains, foraging and preying off settler flocks. From 1499, de Lugo formed squads of settlers to hunt down and kill refugees. By the close of the fifteenth century there were barely a few hundred Indigenes left on the island, their numbers rapidly declining through disease, settler violence, and wretched living conditions.

Cases of Genocide?

Individually and collectively all seven Canarian cases represent clear examples of genocide. Not only were all Indigenous Canarian societies utterly destroyed and their populations removed from their native islands, but this was accomplished with a great deal of violence directed at entire communities. The Castilian conquerors practiced near-total confiscation of the land; and near total enslavement and deportation of survivors from their home isles not simply for immediate profit, but also for the explicit purpose of repopulating the islands with European settlers and establishing completely new economies and ways of life. In the closing decades of the fourteenth century the realization that highly lucrative sugarcane crops could be cultivated in much of the archipelago spurred on this process.

More so than the slaughter of Canarians, the main forms of social destruction were the mass enslavement and deportation of captives, mostly within the archipelago, but also beyond, notably to Europe and Madeira. Socially, this practice was as destructive as killing because the islands were denuded of their aboriginal populations. Individual raids purely for the sake of acquiring slaves, though highly damaging to Canarian society, were not genocidal in themselves. However, in the cases of Lanzarote, Fuerteventura, and Hierro the cumulative impact of slave raiding depleted the population so severely that it would be no exaggeration to describe it as being of genocidal proportions. Much more damaging and unquestionably genocidal were the slaving activities of conquerors for whom captives formed the most lucrative part of the Canarian virgin bonus—resources invaders and conquerors could harvest prior to settlement. For conquistadors, the taking of chattels was counted on to help cover the costs of conquest and as immediate reward for those who both funded and fought on these ventures. Conquerors thus sought to enslave entire surviving communities, by and large succeeding in this endeavor. Deportation was used to realize higher prices for slaves, to channel labor where it was needed most, and as a security measure to subvert resistance. By the end of the fifteenth century, of the few hundred Canarian survivors, very few were free and hardly any lived on their native islands. Especially from the 1480s onward, increasing numbers of slaves were imported from the African mainland to replace the declining Indigenous labor pool and to meet the burgeoning demand from the developing settler economy. Enslavement of entire surviving island communities, compounded by their deportation, formed the lynchpin of the genocidal process not only because it accounted for more victims than any other means of social erasure, but also because it represented intentional and irreparably damaging acts of collective social destruction.

There were other forms of social destruction as well. Scorched-earth tactics severely undermined the subsistence and communal lives of Canarian societies, resulting in malnutrition, starvation, disease, psychological distress, and social dislocation. Child removal, usually into slavery or some form of forced labor, was common. After conquest, cultural suppression was the norm, most consistently and insistently through the imposition of Christian beliefs, values, and customs by settlers, as well as through state and church structures, which were backed by the terror of the Spanish Inquisition. Cultural suppression also came indirectly through Canarians needing to abide by Western standards and modes of behavior to survive under the new order. Both during and after conquest, Canarian men were commonly recruited as fighters and often deliberately used as cannon fodder. It was not unusual for such volunteers and forced conscripts to be deployed in Spanish colonial ventures in the Americas and Africa. While this provided some opportunity for preferment and allowed Canarian genes to be spread into Latin America, Africa, and beyond, it was extremely dangerous work that contributed to the post-conquest extinction of Indigenous Canarian cultures. Communicable diseases introduced by Europeans and poor health due to depressed living conditions continued to take a heavy toll on the vestigial Canarian population after conquest. Adventurer Girolamo Benzoni, who visited the islands in 1541, attested to hardly any Indigenes being alive by then, and Alonso de Espinosa, a Dominican priest who lived on Tenerife and published an influential history of the Canaries in the mid-1590s, claimed that none bar a few of "mixed" descent had survived.

Straddling the late medieval and early modern epochs, the genocidal destruction of aboriginal Canarian societies and their supplanting by European settlers, constituted a crucial initial extension of European colonialism into the Atlantic that had repercussions far beyond the fifteenth century and their modest island cluster. Although the aboriginal peoples of the Canaries were geographically and culturally part of Africa, their annihilation was thematically part of the conquest of the Americas. This episode spearheaded the much larger and much more violent annihilation of Native American societies in the Caribbean and Latin America from the sixteenth century onward. Indeed, Christopher Columbus on all four of his voyages to the Americas first sailed to the Canaries, on the edge of Europe's known world at the time, to rest, refit, and revictual. The Caribbean islands, where the Spaniards established their first American colonies, were called the "New Canaries" for decades, and lessons learned in Canarian campaigns were consciously applied there. The plunder of natural resources, unrestrained violence toward Indigenous populations, widespread use of slave labor, development of plantation economies, and the devastating impact of disease witnessed in the Canaries foreshadowed the holocaust that was to engulf the New World.

Although settler invasions centuries later in locations as far apart as California and Queensland were very different in nature, echoes of Canarian antecedents were detectable—less so in the actual methods of genocidal conquest than the imperatives common to settler colonial projects.

SOURCES

Key Episodes in the Conquest of Lanzarote

There are two surviving accounts of the Norman invasion of Lanzarote. The first, dating from about 1420, was coauthored by Gadifer de La Salle's chaplains, Pierre Boutier and Jean le Verrier, both of whom had accompanied La Salle on his quest. The second was authored about 1490 by Jean de Bethencourt V, a descendant of Jean de Bethencourt. There was a third, now lost, source. While Boutier and le Verrier provide the more credible account, they do favor La Salle. Although based on the Boutier manuscript and the lost source, the Bethencourt manuscript freely—and rather ineptly—distorts the record to present Bethencourt in a positive light. This extract comes from Bethencourt's text.

Questions for Consideration

How do the author's prejudices against Canarians manifest in this extract? Contrast this with his depiction of Europeans. Are these preconceptions more accurately described as racism or as cultural chauvinism? Explain your answer. What evidence can you glean from the document to show that the author is biased against La Salle and favors Bethencourt? How would this affect your use of it as a historical source? What other inaccuracies, distortions, or fabrications are you able to detect in this document?

Jean de Bethencourt, *The Canarian, or Book of the Conquest and Conversion of the Canarians in the Year 1402*[2]

How Asche, one of the most important men of the Isle of Lancerote, prepared to betray the King. CHAPTER XXX.

---

2. Manuscript B, Bibliothèque Municipale de Rouen, France, *Le Canarien: Manuscritos, Transcripción y Traducción*, eds. Berta Pico, Eduardo Aznar, and Dolores Corbella (Santa Cruz de Tenerife: Institutio de Estudios Canarios, 2003), 228–40. English translation from Middle French by Alfred J. Andrea.

While all of this was happening,[3] a pagan islander called Asche wanted to be King of the Isle of Lancerote. And Monseigneur Gadifer and he discussed this matter at length, and then Asche departed. And after a few days, he sent his nephew, whom Monseigneur de Bethencourt had brought from France to serve as his interpreter. He told him that the King so deeply hated our religion that as long as he lived, we would have little success in getting anything from them and that he was totally responsible for the deaths of these people. If, however, he wished, Asche would find a way of apprehending the King and all the others who had participated in the murder of his companions. Gadifer was delighted with respect to this and commissioned him to carefully take care of everything and let him know the time and the hour. And so it was done.

How Asche betrayed his master in hope of betraying Gadifer and his company. CHAPTER XXXI.

Now this was double treachery. For he wished to betray the King, his lord, and he also proposed and intended to betray Gadifer and all his men with the help of his nephew Alphonse, who was constantly with them. He knew that we were few in numbers and thought that it would not be a difficult matter to annihilate us, given that we had only very few surviving men for our defense. But we shall see in the sequel how he succeeded. Now you will hear what happened when Asche saw his opportunity to turn against the King. He told Gadifer to come and that the King was in one of his homes in a village near Arrecife, and he had fifty of his people with him.

Gadifer immediately departed, taking with him twenty of his company. This was on the eve of [the Feast of] Saint Catharine, 1402.[4] Marching throughout the night, he arrived where they were before dawn. They were gathered together in a house plotting against us. He thought he could fall upon them, but they were guarding the entrance to the house, offered a stiff defense, and wounded several of our men. Five of those who had killed our companions rushed out, three of whom received terrible wounds, one with a sword and the others by arrows. Our people forced their way in and took captives, but since Gadifer found that they were not guilty of the death of his men, he set them free at the insistence of Asche. He retained the King and another named Alby and chained them around the neck. . . .

---

3. Immediately prior to this, while relations between islanders were amicable, the mutineers who had seized Gadifer's ship had taken over twenty Canarians prisoner, raped the women, and sailed off with their hostages. In revenge, Canarians had turned on Gadifer's unsuspecting followers, killing several.

4. November 24.

They then all returned together to the castle of Rubicon, and the King was put into two sets of shackles. After a few days, he freed himself because the shackles were poorly fitted and too large. When Gadifer saw this, he had the King put in chains, and removed a pair of shackles, which troubled him greatly.

How Asche pressed upon Gadifer that he should be made King. CHAPTER XXXII.

A few days after Asche arrived at the castle of Rubicon, they agreed that he should be made King on condition that he, along with all of his supporters, should be baptized. When the King saw him, he looked at him with great contempt, exclaiming, *"fore troncqueuay,"* that is to say, "wicked traitor." With this, Asche left Gadifer and invested himself as King. A few days later, Gadifer sent some of his men in search of barley, because we had only a little bit of bread. They collected a huge quantity of barley, and . . . set out toward Rubicon seeking people to carry the barley. While on the way, this Asche, who had named himself the new King, came out to meet them with twenty-three others. Feigning friendship, they walked with them some distance. But Jean le Courtois and his companions began to experience a sense of mistrust. Everyone kept close together and kept these others from joining them; except Guillaume d'Andrac walked with them and suspected nothing. When they had walked a bit, they saw their opportunity. They then assaulted the aforementioned Guillaume, dragging him to the ground and inflicting on him thirteen wounds. And they were about to finish him off when the aforementioned Jean and his companions heard the noise, turned vigorously upon them, rescued him with great difficulty, and carried him back to the castle of Rubicon.

How the King escaped from Gadifer's prison and how he had Asche put to death. Chapter XXXIII.

Now it happened that during the night of this same day the former King escaped from the prison at Rubicon and carried away with him the fetters and chains with which he was bound. And as soon as he reached his own house, he seized the aforementioned Asche who had made himself King and also betrayed him, and had him stoned and afterwards incinerated. Two days later, the garrison of the old castle learned how the new King had attacked Jean le Courtois, d'Andrac and their companions. They took a Canarian whom they held, led him to the summit of a mountain for decapitation, and stuck the head on a very high pole so that everyone could see it clearly. Following that, they commenced war against the natives. They captured great numbers of them—men, women, and children. The rest were in such a state that they hid themselves in caves and did not dare approach anyone. The majority [of the Europeans] continuously patrolled the open countryside, while the others remained at home to guard the castle and the prisoners. They put all the effort they could at capturing people, for it was their only consolation until the arrival of Monseigneur de Bethencourt, who shortly would send help, as you will hear. . . .

How Gadifer decided to kill all the fighting men of the Isle of Lancerote. Chapter XXXIV.

Gadifer and his companions decided, if there were no other solution, to kill all the men of the country who bore arms, and to save the women and children and have them baptized; and to remain there until God should provide otherwise for them. And so at Pentecost,[5] counting men, women, and children, more than eighty were baptized. By the grace of God, they will be confirmed in our faith so that they will be a good example to all lands round about. There is no reason to doubt that if Monseigneur de Bethencourt had been able to return, and if he had had a bit of help from some prince, he would have conquered not only the Canary Islands, but many other great countries which were then very little mentioned, but as fine as the best in the world and well populated with unbelievers of many different laws and languages. Had Gadifer and his companions desired to sell off their prisoners, they would have easily recovered the cost of the expedition. But God forbid that they did not so desire, because most were baptized.

◆◆◆◆◆

Closing Encounters in the Subjugation of Gran Canaria

This extract comes from an account of the history of the Canary Islands written by Spanish poet and historian Gonzalo Argote de Molina in the first half of the 1590s. The manuscript was amended and augmented by an anonymous copyist who published it in 1632 under the pseudonym of Juan Abreu de Galindo. The manuscript was then translated into English and published in 1764 by Scottish merchant ship's captain and adventurer George Glas, a frequent visitor to the islands. The extract recounts the capitulation of the Gran Canarian resisters— but not before they were able to hand the invaders a stinging defeat.

Questions for Consideration

What are you able to deduce about the military tactics of both sides from this excerpt? What were the advantages and challenges that each side faced? Why was an eventual Spanish victory a near certainty? Consider the significance of Canarian collaborators in this episode and whether Tenesor Semidan should be seen as a traitor or as a pragmatist who tried to shield his people from utter destruction.

---

5. June 3, 1403.

George Glas, *The History of the Discovery and
the Conquest of the Canary Islands*[6]

CHAP XX   *The Sequel of the Conquest*

Pedro de Vera, after having made some stay at Palmas to refresh his troops and
recover those that were wounded, mustered his forces, consisting of Castillians,
the natives of Lancerota, Fuerteventura, and the other islands, with the Companies of the Holy Brotherhood,[7] as also some of the reduced Canarians, amounting in the whole to about a thousand men. These completely furnished with arms
and all other necessaries, determining to make an end of the conquest before he
returned to Palmas.

Finding by his spies, that all the Canarians were assembled at Ansite, a
place deemed impregnable, together with their wives and children, he marched
thither, and pitched his camp at the bottom of the mountain. Don Fernando of
Galdar, knowing that his countrymen were determined to die rather than surrender to the Spaniards, went, with the consent of the Governor, to try what
he could do with them by means of persuasion. So soon as they beheld their
old Guanarteme, they crowded about him with loud acclamations, and everyone present wept a long time before they were able to utter a word: the Guanarteme wept also in sympathy, and observed a profound silence. The number of
the natives then assembled was about six hundred fighting men, and a thousand
women and children, among whom were all the nobles, with the Faycag, and the
young Guanarteme of Telde.[8] This youth was on the point of being married to
the King of Galdar's daughter, then present, by which marriage he purposed to
make himself King of the whole island. After their grief began to find vent in
words, Don Fernando, in an eloquent speech accompanied with tears, conjured
them to have compassion on their wives and children, and to lay aside all thoughts
of resistance, which would only end in their own destruction; adding, that he
would take upon himself to be answerable for the Spaniards, that they should
treat them well; protect them in the possession of their liberties and effects, and
that especial regard should be had to the rank and dignity of the nobles, which

---

6. George Glas, *The History of the Discovery and Conquest of the Canary Islands* (London:
Adamantine Media Corporation, 2006), 129–32.

7. The Holy Brotherhoods, or Santa Hermandad, were associations of armed civilians sanctioned by the medieval kings of Spain to maintain public order in various municipalities.
Ferdinand and Isabella used the Brotherhoods to bolster monarchical power and to support
royal projects such as the conquest of the Canaries.

8. The *Faycag* (*faycan*) was a spiritual leader, and the Guanarteme (king) of Telde, Ben Tegui,
led the resistance movement.

should in nowise suffer. With these and the like soothing speeches, he at length prevailed on the natives to surrender, which they did by throwing down their arms, and at the same time setting up a dismal howling and crying. The young Guanarteme of Telde, feeling his hopes thus blasted, went to the brow of a precipice, accompanied by his old Faycag, where embracing each other, and crying out Atirtisma![9] they threw themselves down and perished together. When the tumult and weeping were a little subsided, Don Fernando brought the Canarians down to the camp (among whom were his own daughter Teneshoia) and presented them to Pedro de Vera, by whom they were courteously received and entertained: he felt no small satisfaction to see the natives so easily brought in, being sensible, that, if they had resolved not to hearken to the persuasions of Don Fernando to surrender, he could not have made himself master of the place without much bloodshed. The Bishop, Don Juan de Frias, who was then present, having a few days before arrived from Lancerota, sung Te Deum[10] on the occasion. This event happened on the 29th of April 1483, being seventy-seven years after the first attempt upon the island by John de Betancour.

◆◆◆◆◆

Spain's Worst Defeat in the Canaries

Alonso de Espinosa was a Dominican friar born in Spain in 1534 and raised in Guatemala, where he was ordained. He settled in Tenerife in 1579, drawn there by his keen interest in the Candelarian legend. While in Guatemala he was strongly influenced by the ideas and writing of Bartholomé de las Casas, the leading sixteenth-century critic of Spanish abuses of Native Americans and the chief advocate for reform of Spanish colonial practices. Both in Guatemala and while traveling through Latin America, de Espinosa witnessed the oppression of Native Americans firsthand. He published his book on the Candelarian phenomenon in Seville in 1594. The volume also contained an ethnographic account of the Guanche people and of the Spanish conquest. This extract describes the decisive episode in Alonso de Lugo's ill-fated first campaign to conquer Tenerife.

Questions for Consideration

How does the author differ in his attitude toward Indigenous Canarians compared to conventional settler views? What evidence is there that, in addition to narrating events relating to the conquest of Tenerife, de Espinosa also wanted

---

9. "For my land!"
10. "Te Deum laudamus" (God, we praise you), a hymn of celebration.

to impart some degree of instruction? What kind of instruction was this and to what extent does it, and other attempts to dramatize the account, compromise the value of his account as historical evidence?

Alonso de Espinosa, *The Guanches of Tenerife: The Holy Image of Our Lady of Candelaria and the Spanish Conquest and Settlement*[11]

CHAPTER V. *Of the Battle between the Spaniards and the Guanches at Centejo, and the slaughter which took place*

It is an acknowledged fact, both as regards divine and human right, that the wars waged by the Spaniards against the natives of these islands, as well as the Indians of the western regions, were unjust and without any reason to support them. For the natives had not taken the lands of Christians, nor had they gone beyond their own frontier to molest or invade their neighbours. If it is said that the Spaniards brought the Gospel, this should have been done by admonition and preaching—not by drum and banner; not by force.

... The Governor of the Conquest, Alonso de Lugo, thinking less of the power of the natives than he should have done, and seeing that the Overlord of Taoro would not submit, but was resolved to await and resist him, without further deliberation commenced his march towards the Lordship of Taoro. He thought that when this Overlord was conquered and subdued, being the most powerful, the others would come to terms and surrender. But "he who despises his enemy falls by his hands." The Lords of Anaga, Tacaronte, and Tegueste, through whose territories the Spaniards had passed, offered no resistance with all their power, though they made some feints and attacks. They either saw our numbers and power, or they left us to advance farther to await further opportunities for their own ends. So the forces continued to march to Orotava without meeting any resistance. There they found a great multitude of flocks. They collected a large number of sheep, and began to return with their spoils, thinking that the Guanches did not dare attack them. But Bencomo, the Overlord of Taoro, was on the watch, and neglected nothing. He waited for an opportunity to strike a blow. Seeing that the enemies believed that they were returning victorious, he quickly assembled 300 of his bravest men under the command of his brother,

---

11. Alonso de Espinosa, *The Guanches of Tenerife: The Holy Image of Our Lady of Candelaria and the Spanish Conquest and Settlement*, trans. Clement Markham (London: Hakluyt Society, 1907), 91–94.

(his name Tinguaro) a daring and spirited leader, with orders to keep in line with the Spaniards on the heights above them, and to attack them in a rugged pass, while he followed them with the rest of his force. The Overlord's brother was not negligent in carrying out his orders. Taking the higher slopes, he waited for the Governor and his people to arrive at a point where they would not be able to make use of their cavalry. It was the mounted soldiers that the natives most feared, and this was the main strength of their enemies. The locality chosen was a place thickly overgrown with trees, on ascending ground, and much broken by rocks and ravines. From this point they made an outcry, and whistled to their flocks which our men were carrying off. When the Spaniards saw themselves in such a dangerous place, where the knights could not avail themselves of their arms, nor make use of their horses, that the natives held the passes, and that to turn back would be to deliver themselves into the hands of their enemies, pushed forward the vanguard well in front. The main body was broken and thrown into confusion, because the flocks, hearing the whistle, had got loose. The rear-guard pressed forward to join the main body. . . .

The Christians, thus forced into a conflict, did not know what counsel to take. Some blamed the Governor, who had been advised by the Canarians[12] not to go so far into the country without securing his retreat, because the Gaunches could take advantage of the bad passes, but he held them too cheap; or else God saw fit that, as a punishment, he should not take the advice. Others say that the blasphemy of certain soldiers was the reason that God allowed this loss and punishment of the Spaniards. For some said that, although the place was dangerous, yet the enemies were few and unarmed, and that, fighting as they ought, they would conquer with the help of God. They spoke like Christian knights, but one answered unlike a Christian. He said: "I swear to God that I think we shall conquer without His aid, for with such wretched people and so few of them, we do not need His aid." But this knight was not saved, nor did he gain a victory, trusting in his own strength and valour. The contrary happened.

The Guanches fell upon the Spaniards in this difficult pass when they were tired, and unable to join forces or to use their arms with dexterity, although they did their duty and fought valiantly—the position being against them, so was their fortune. They were defeated, and there was a great slaughter among them. Hence the name of the place is "La Matanza de Centejo" [The slaughter of Acentejo].[13] . . .

---

12. Their allies from Guimar.

13. Today the eponymous town near the site of the battle commemorates the event, whereas the neighboring town of La Victoria de Acentejo (the Victory of Acentejo) celebrates de Lugo's subsequent triumph over Como's forces.

A remarkable thing happened in this battle, which was that the blasphemous soldier who made that wicked speech, when the natives began to fall on our people, came to the front with arms and horse, a little apart from the squadron, which was in disorder owing to the flight of the sheep. A Guanche came along the road to him and, throwing a dart which wounded the horse, it fell to the ground. The Guanche then stood over the knight, and put an end to him ignominiously in payment for his blasphemy. He was the first that they killed. Thus God punishes those who do not put their trust in him.

◆◆◆◆◆

A Settler Colonial Perspective on the Conquest of the Canaries

This book was published in Spanish as *Las Islas Canarias a Traves de la Historia* in Madrid in 1971, before being translated into English in 1978 as *The Canary Islands through History*. Aimed at a popular readership, the volume was clearly meant to flatter Spanish nationalist sentiment at a time when Spain was still ruled by the nationalist dictator Francisco Franco, and to legitimate Spanish settler claims to the Canary Islands. It covers the Canarian past from the geological formation of the islands through to the end of the Spanish conquest and provides a highly romanticized version of this past. Professor Salvador Lopez Herrera, a native of Tenerife, worked as a journalist on the island until 1939. In that year he relocated to Madrid where he completed a PhD thesis and subsequently became a historian of Spanish and Portuguese colonialism in the Americas, specializing in Brazilian history. This book, written toward the end of his career, was a tribute to the land of his birth and emphasized its integral relationship with his adopted homeland.

Questions for Consideration

All settler societies construct mythologized and idealized histories that deny or justify the violence perpetrated in their displacement of Indigenous peoples. Analyze the ways in which Herrera does this, noting in particular the ways in which he presents the conquest of the Canaries. If you live in a settler society, consider how the histories taught to you in school, at university, and through public memorials reflect settler interests and marginalize Indigenous roles, rights, and viewpoints. Reflect on why settler mythologies tend to be extremely resilient and romantically imagined, even in the face of a great deal of evidence to the contrary.

Salvador Lopez Herrera, *The Canary Islands through History*[14]

Chapter XI

A.—The Colonization of the Canary Islands under the Patronage of the Spanish Monarchs

At the time of the conquest, various pressures led to the subjection of the native tribes, but the law established by the conquerors was far from cruel. It is true that many outrageous violations of human rights took place during the war that culminated in the conquest of the islands, but the Catholic Monarchs promptly gave orders to curtail such abuses.

As soon as the conquest was accomplished, the natives actually enjoyed the same rights as other Spanish subjects, as stipulated in the chart drawn at San Cristóbal de La Laguna in 1514.

That the native race was not considered an inferior one is clearly shown by the high number of mixed marriages that took place. The romance between Dácil and Captain Gonzalo Castillo, which was to inspire Lope de Vega's famous play <<the Guanches of Tenerife and the Conquest of the Canaries>> may be considered the poetic symbol of an important social phenomenon: the brotherhood of the two races.[15] It also accepted how the Spaniard accepted the Guanches as their equals, even before this primitive race had forgotten its habits and customs and learned those of a new civilization.

The Spanish kings were particularly eager to allot the lands equitably. The royal warrant given on 20 January, 1487, by which the Catholic Monarchs accepted the distribution of land and water made by General Pedro de Vera, included the following clause: "If any member or members of the community living in the aforesaid island of Gran Canaria, were wronged because of this partition, they should be heard and then their wrongs amended according to what the law provides in these cases."

In those islands where the crown had direct intervention, the actions taken were animated by the highest aims. The Spanish kings never allowed the natives to become slaves, and it was always attempted to deal justly with them. If under the rule of the monarchs the natives were sometimes transported as slaves, Espinosa

---

14. Salvador Lopez Herrera, *The Canary Islands through History* (Madrid: Editorial Dosbe, 1978), 171–77.

15. Dácil, a Guanche princess and Ben Como's daughter, married a conquistador, Captain Fernando García del Castillo. The two apparently fell in love after Castillo was taken captive and Dácil was deputed to take care of his wounds. A handful of marriages between the Canarian elite and Spaniards have become a symbol of a presumed cultural blending between conqueror and vanquished in settler stories presented by Herrera and others.

categorically asserted that: "The Kings immediately ordered their release and granted them the right to live as free men."

Likewise, the Spanish church was always strongly opposed to slavery. The churchmen protected the natives against the Portuguese, who often captured the Canarians, either through false promises or by violence, and took them to the island of Madeira where they were to till the soil. When Fray Fernando Calvetos was appointed bishop of Rubicón in Lanzarote in 1431, he ardently strove to abolish this inhuman trade and strictly forbade the sale of any islanders, whether baptised or not. But on realising that his spiritual threats were to no avail, he brought the case before the Holy See and Pope Eugene IV issued a bull dated 25 October 1434, which read "On behalf of the new converts in the Canaries, we forbid, under the gravest bans, the ill treatment and the subjection to slavery of any of these islanders, for these horrible cruelties only serve to make them abhor Christianity."

. . . Indeed a rapid and thorough amalgamation of the two races took place, through the friendship sprung between the conquered and their conquerors, through mixed marriages, and also, through the genuine admiration the Spaniards felt for the splendid virtues of the Canarians. This may be said to be a unique example in the history of colonization and conquest. . . .

The Canarians not only fought in the islands for their own protection, but they also played a key role in all Spanish military enterprises. They heroically participated in the African Wars; they generously sent their own people to colonise America. Canarians were also found in Flemish battlefields and in Extremadura, Portugal, and Cataluna, whenever the Spanish kings needed their faithful sons. And finally, they were to shed their blood in the war of Succession and in the War of Independence. . . .

The spiritual bonds between the Archipelago and the Peninsula are today as firm as ever. These ties of patriotism and affection may be called indissoluble.

Chapter 2

"Improved from the Face of the Earth": The Destruction of Queensland's Aboriginal Peoples

In the first half of the 1860s, a young Oxford graduate, George Carrington, regarding his prospects for advancement in England to be limited, decided to seek his fortune in the newly established and booming colony of Queensland, where the outlook seemed so much brighter. Finding it not to be quite the land of opportunity he had hoped, he spent four years during the mid-1860s traveling through the expanding territory doing whatever work he could find. After returning to England, Carrington in 1871 published a book recounting his experiences in which he summarized settler attitudes and behavior toward Aborigines thus:

> It is the fashion usually, to speak of these poor people as "aborigines": the idea meant to be conveyed that they are a relic, so to speak, of the past, intruders in the path of the white man, and to be improved from the face of the earth accordingly. The argument seems to be, that God never intended them to live long in the land in which He placed them. Therefore, says the white man, in his superiority of strength and knowledge, away with them, disperse[1] them, shoot and poison them, until there is none remaining; we will utterly destroy them, their wives and their little ones, and all that they have, and we will go in and possess the land.
>
> This is no rhapsody or overstatement, but represents, in words, the actual policy which has been pursued toward the natives of the Australian colonies, and which is being acted upon vigorously in Queensland today.[2]

This is a perceptive and surprisingly accurate summary, even though it was written roughly halfway through the dispossession and genocidal destruction of Queensland's Aboriginal peoples. Carrington, however, happened to be in Queensland when colonial expansion was at its most frenzied and conflict with its Aboriginal peoples at an apex. Queensland experienced a frenetic land rush during the first half of the 1860s, followed by a severe recession in the latter half of the decade that contributed to Carrington becoming a sojourner rather than a settler.

---

1. A common Australian euphemism for massacre.
2. George Carrington, *Colonial Adventures and Experiences by a University Man* (London: Bell & Daldy, 1871), 143–44.

Queensland covers a huge area, taking up almost the entire northeastern quarter of the Australian continent. Encompassing nearly 670,000 square miles, it is two and a half times the size of Texas. With the Tropic of Capricorn running through central Queensland, its climate is subtropical in the southern coastal areas, temperate to semiarid in the interior, and tropical in the north. While it includes an impressively diverse range of topographical, climatic, floral, and faunal types, a very large part of it is suitable for pastoral farming, with sheep predominating in the southern and central areas and cattle farther north. Queensland came into being in 1859, when it was separated from New South Wales, which initially covered the eastern half of the continent. As such, Queensland was a political creation of British imperialism.

Of all the Australian colonies, Queensland had the largest area suitable for farming and the largest Indigenous population. Not surprisingly, the colony experienced the most intense and prolonged conflict in the dispossession of Australia's Aboriginal peoples. Its size, large areas of rugged and isolated terrain, and the fact that the administrative center, Brisbane, lay in the far southeastern corner all contributed to settler impunity in their dealings with Indigenous peoples. Initially, most settlers came from Victoria and New South Wales—and later, from within Queensland itself—and were thus experienced in the use of force to clear land of Aboriginal inhabitants and counter their resistance. Queenslanders developed a reputation, not only in Australia, but also within the British Empire, for being particularly brutal colonizers. This was especially the case after 1859, when the territory fell under the governance of a settler elite rather than officials appointed by the Colonial Office. Queensland therefore represents the prime case study for genocide on the Australian continent, even though the destruction of the Tasmanian Aborigines is more widely known in this respect. Tasmania, from the 1870s, already had gained global notoriety as a colony where the entire Indigenous population had been exterminated.

Aboriginal Peoples and Early European Contact

Archaeological evidence indicates that the Aboriginal peoples of Australia, who were hunter-gatherers, have occupied the continent for between 50,000 and 60,000 years. The mainstay of their diet consisted of a wide variety of plant foods that they gathered seasonally, and game they hunted using spears, clubs, snares, and bows and arrows. Where the opportunity presented itself, they gathered shellfish and fished using traps and harpoons. Aboriginal peoples exploited other resources such as gathering honey, birds' eggs, and insects. Their economy was cooperative, with clear protocols for sharing food within, and often among,

Torres Strait

PAPUA NEW GUINEA

Coral Sea

Cape York Peninsula

Gulf of Carpentaria

PACIFIC OCEAN

Cooktown
Palmer River
Hodgkinson River
Etheridge
Gilbert
Cairns
Mulgrave River

Townsville
Star River
Charters Towers
Ravenswood
Bowen
Mount Wyatt
Mackay
Cape River

Canoona

QUEENSLAND
Cullin-la-Ringo
Rockhampton

Hornet Bank Station
Maryborough
Gympie

AUSTRALIA
Condamine River
Darling Downs
Brisbane

NORTHERN TERRITORY
BOUNDARY AFTER 1862
BOUNDARY UP TO 1862

Great Barrier Reef

Great Dividing Range

SOUTH AUSTRALIA

NEW SOUTH WALES

N

Key

Land occupied by 1852

Land occupied by 1853–62

Occupied in the land rush of 1862–66

Main settlement streams in the 1860s

Main settlement streams in the 1870s and 1880s

Merri Merriwa ▲

0   200 miles

0   200 km

Queensland.

hunting bands. Like all hunter-gatherers, Aborigines had an intimate knowledge of their natural environment to which they had intense spiritual connections. Hunter-gathering made for relatively sparse population densities. The current scholarly consensus is that Australia had a population ranging between 750,000 and 1,000,000—and Queensland between 250,000 and 300,000—at the start of colonization in 1788.

Aboriginal society was organized into small loosely knit bands, typically of between fifteen and fifty people, consisting of three to six family units, usually covering three generations. There was a gender-based division of labor in that men hunted while women were mainly gatherers. Bands lived in makeshift shelters or caves and moved seasonally within defined areas following game or the availability of plant foods and water. Hunting bands affiliated through kinship formed extended social networks that might encompass several hundred people linked through reciprocal arrangements including intermarriage, the sharing of resources, gift giving, and various forms of exchange. Although they shared a similar mode of subsistence, Aboriginal economies differed from one area to the next depending on the natural environment. Nor were Aboriginal peoples culturally homogeneous. Apart from regional variations in social customs and material culture, they spoke a diversity of languages, most of which were mutually unintelligible beyond a particular sociolinguistic group. Bands coalesced into larger kin-based units referred to in the literature as clans, which in turn formed larger political units, referred to as tribes or nations. Australia had perhaps as many as 600 sociolinguistic groupings, and Queensland, being the most populous part of precolonial Australia, had about 250.

As far as we know, first contact between Aboriginal and European seafaring explorers occurred in 1606, when the Dutch explorer Willem Janszoon landed along the northern Queensland shore. Over the better part of the next two centuries there were several other explorers and navigators from England, France, Holland, and Spain who landed along its coastline, and their interactions with Aborigines were not without conflict. In 1770, the English navigator Lieutenant James Cook, on behalf of King George III, claimed the entire eastern half of Australia for Britain, naming it New South Wales. Britain set down its first colony in Australia in 1788 at Port Jackson, where Sydney stands today. The earliest British settlements in Australia—first New South Wales and then Tasmania in 1803—were established primarily as penal colonies. Britain founded these settlements because it had lost its other penal colonies along the east coast of North America as a result of the American Revolution, which ended in 1783.

The first stage in the colonization of Queensland came in 1824 with the establishment of a penal colony at Moreton Bay, near the present site of Brisbane, then still part of New South Wales. Moreton Bay, the most remote of the penal settlements, was set up as special punishment for "recalcitrants" and "incorrigibles." In all, the colony housed somewhere between 2,000 and 3,000 convicts before being closed down in 1839. Although there was some cooperation with Aboriginal peoples in the vicinity of the Moreton Bay settlement, especially during the earlier period, the relationship with colonists was overwhelmingly marked by strife. Colonists generally disrespected Aborigines, desecrated sacred sites, shot game, and exploited other resources without requisite permission, raped Aboriginal women, and were abusive almost as a matter of course. This is not surprising given that the colony consisted almost entirely of convicts and soldiers. Aborigines, in retaliation, killed stock and attacked colonists who, in turn, resorted to shooting Indigenes. Throughout its fifteen-year existence, the Moreton Bay colony was a conflict zone, with violence reaching a peak in 1831–1832, which included a massacre of about twenty Aborigines by British soldiers on Moreton Island. While the penal colony was disastrous for Aborigines in its immediate vicinity, its overall impact was small because it lasted for a limited time, involved small numbers of interlopers, and Indigenes had some scope for taking evasive action. This colonial beachhead, however, provided a foretaste of what was to follow.

Through the latter half of the nineteenth century Queensland had two major frontiers, each driven by the colony's two main economic activities, stock farming and mining. Each had a distinct dynamic that drew large numbers of settlers into the territory, and each acted as largely independent vectors for the dispossession and destruction of Aboriginal societies. Other economic activities, such as crop farming, timber harvesting, fishing, and pearling, were of relatively minor importance in this regard.

The Pastoral Frontier

The pastoral frontier was by far the most important in spurring settler penetration of the interior and conflict with Indigenous peoples. It was not only the most enduring and extensive of the frontiers, but also the most damaging to Aboriginal society. The pastoral enterprise in nineteenth-century Queensland consisted initially of sheep, millions of them, but later also of large herds of cattle, and to a lesser extent pigs, goats, and horses. The pastoral invasion started in southeastern Queensland in the early 1840s, when it was still part of New South Wales. The initial move by sheep farmers into the Darling Downs district was the extension northward of pastoral farming that had started three decades earlier in the hinterland of Sydney and helped fuel the industrialization of Britain, which was largely predicated on the cotton and wool industries. A boom in wool production in New South Wales from the mid-1810s onward radiated into surrounding areas. This pastoral advance reached southern Queensland by about 1840; by 1890, virtually all land in Queensland suitable for pastoral farming had been seized by settlers.

This extensive land grab did not happen at a steady pace, but spasmodically, and was marked by several phases of expansion. The first occurred from the 1840s till about 1852, when the southeastern corner of Queensland was occupied. The second lasted about a decade from 1853 till about 1862 and was in essence an extension of the first. By the time of Queensland's separation from New South Wales in 1859, there were already over 1,300 stations harboring over 3,000,000 sheep in southern Queensland. This was followed by a frenzied land rush that lasted till 1866 and in which virtually all land suitable for pastoralism was grabbed by settlers. During this time, the pastoral frontier of Queensland raced ahead at an annual rate of as much as 200 miles. This feverish expansion, as so often happens, was followed by a retreat during the severe economic recession of 1866–1872. Falling wool prices and higher haulage costs from outlying areas resulted in a reversal of the tide of settlement as over 400 pastoral stations were abandoned. And then from the mid-1870s to the late-1880s, another wave of pastoral expansion saw the re-occupation of sheep runs abandoned the decade before. By the early 1890s, there were about 21,000,000 sheep and 7,000,000 cattle on Queensland farms.

Stock farming entailed dispersed settlement and by its very nature was expansive, taking up large areas rapidly. The occupation of land was often temporary, especially in drier areas, as farmers moved on with their stock in search of better grazing and water. Because stock farming was damaging to the ecosystem, the grazing capacity of the land diminished over time, and many farmers needed to move on after a few years. Graziers generally did not take up permanent farms but leased tracts of land from the state, which meant that they were not tied to a particular holding nor did they need to sink large amounts of capital into land ownership. In the Australian context, most stock farmers, even the more affluent ones with large-scale operations, were referred to as squatters because they preferred leasing land. The mobility of squatters meant that the frontier was all-the-more fluid, and they could move that much faster as they sought greener pastures. Many took up as much land as they could in boom times, hoping to sell at a huge profit to newcomers. This largely explains the speculative frenzy driving land rushes.

By and large, the displacement and exclusion of Aborigines from land claimed by settlers was enforced through naked violence. Invading stock farmers used their access to superior force—guns, horses, and the backing of the colonial state—to chase Indigenes off land to which they had leases or that they claimed. Bands were driven off their land at gunpoint and often massacred. Sometimes the more cunning tactic of presenting resident Aborigines with poison-laced food was used. The pastoral frontier thus generated a great deal of conflict as Aborigines resisted their dispossession, defended their sources of food and water, and sought to retain access to sacred locales.

Sheep and cattle had severely detrimental effects on the ecosystem, and their presence greatly diminished the ability of Aborigines to live off the land. Plant foods were trampled and supplanted by the impact of grazing by domesticates. Predators, such as dingoes and hawks that were a threat to farm animals, and herbivores, such as kangaroos, wallabies, and later rabbits that competed with livestock for grazing, were shot and poisoned in great numbers. This acutely diminished the hunting prospects for Aborigines. Competition over access to water was another major area of contention because farmers tended to occupy and appropriate water sources and exclude Aborigines. What is more, stock consumed large amounts of water, depleting and polluting supplies. Settler disruption of natural cycles and their degradation of the environment had catastrophic consequences for Aborigines. The influx of settlers with their herds and flocks into a particular area almost inevitably meant that it was not long before Aboriginal communities faced malnutrition, even starvation.

This in turn resulted in stock raids and mounting Aboriginal resistance to colonial invasion. Aborigines struck back by spearing stock and killing pastoral workers and settlers. There were times when Aboriginal opposition forced farmers to abandon their leases, resulting in financial ruin. Aboriginal resistance predictably led to settler reprisal, often with the intention of exterminating Aborigines within the vicinity. It was not unusual for settlers and their dependents from surrounding stock stations to band together in armed, mounted posses that went on the rampage in response to Aboriginal aggression. And it was not unusual for such sorties to result in dozens of, and sometimes over a hundred, Aboriginal deaths with many innocent people, including women and children, being killed. In a few extreme cases several hundred Aborigines were killed in reprisal attacks. Entire bands would be wiped out, and in larger massacres, entire clans were depleted. The Queensland government throughout the period of frontier expansion maintained an extremely lethal paramilitary force, the Queensland Native Police Corps. It consisted of Aboriginal troopers under the command of white officers, and its main duties were to quell Aboriginal resistance and clear the land for settlement.

A pattern of settler invasion, Aboriginal retaliation, followed by organized mass violence on the part of the settler establishment was observable as the frontier advanced in largely northerly and westerly directions. Because the pastoral invasion of Queensland was both rapid and extensive, avoidance was not much of an option for Aborigines as there was very little open, habitable land. For Aborigines to relocate almost inevitably meant moving to marginal land or encroaching on other peoples' territory. Settler invasion thus resulted in a notable increase in inter-Aboriginal conflict as bands were displaced and competed with others for a share of diminishing resources.

There was no concession to Aboriginal ownership of the land in law nor any attempt to coexist peacefully with them on the part of settlers, despite the Colonial Office in 1848 stipulating that where crown land was leased, Aboriginal inhabitants be allowed to continue practicing their traditional lifestyles.[3] Most pastoralists openly flouted this condition of their leases. After taking possession of land, farmers usually sought to exclude Aborigines in what they saw as defense of their property. Thus, if inhabitants stood their ground or displaced people tried to return to their land, they were likely to be shot; indeed, Aborigines who were deemed to be trespassing were usually fired upon, often on sight. Queensland stock farmers in general also sought to exclude Aborigines as workers from their stock farming operations despite a perennial shortage of labor in frontier areas. The major reason for this was settlers' sense of vulnerability. Their small numbers and scattered settlements gave rise to anxiety about Aboriginal retribution—of stolen livestock, sabotage, and attack. A few high-profile massacres of settlers served as constant reminders of this danger. Perceptions of Aborigines as ill-suited to pastoral work and the availability of alternative sources of labor in the form of European, Melanesian, and Chinese workers also played a part. It was only once Aboriginal resistance was broken and there was little fear of retaliation that Aborigines were taken up as farmworkers in any number.

The Gold Mining Frontier

The gold mining frontier was mainly an alluvial one, in which prospectors panned for nuggets along stream beds. Here settler penetration also took the form of a series of rushes. Wherever gold was discovered there was a rush of thousands, sometimes tens of thousands, of prospectors, diggers, laborers, and other fortune seekers into the area. The first Queensland gold rush came in 1858 at Canoona along the central coastline of Queensland. This rush was abortive because the

---

3. Under British law, Australian Aborigines had no sovereignty over, or property rights in, land they occupied. Colonization thus vested ownership of the entire continent in the crown. This legal doctrine, later referred to as *terra nullius* (nobody's land), remained the law throughout the colonial period.

deposit was small and quickly worked out. It nevertheless drew nearly 20,000 people hopeful of making a quick fortune. There was a great deal of disorder and lawlessness in and around the mining camps giving a foretaste of what was to come with future scrambles. A substantive mining frontier was opened nine years later when gold was discovered along the Gympie River in southern Queensland. There was another major gold rush of over 50,000 people at the Palmer River diggings in the far north of the colony in 1873, as well as a series of smaller rushes at Etheridge (1863), Star River (1866), Cape River (1866), Mount Wyatt (1867), Gilbert River (1869), Merri Merriwah (1869), Ravenswood (1870), Charters Towers (1871), Hodgkinson (1876), and Mulgrave River (1879).

An important feature of the Queensland mining frontier is that it resulted in large, sudden influxes of people into what usually had been seen as wilderness, mostly in the north, away from stock farming areas. The hordes who flocked there tended to be lawless, violent, and rapacious. Gold prospectors were highly mobile and tended to spread out across the landscape in the vicinity of gold finds in the hope of striking it rich. They built shanties and set up tent towns; dug up the land, cleared surrounding vegetation, and chopped down trees; took over rivers and streams, polluting and diverting the water; drove away and hunted out the fauna; abused and killed Indigenes in the area; and generally did not want to employ Aborigines, preferring to bring in cheap Chinese and Melanesian labor. A gold rush spelled disaster for Aboriginal groups in the wider vicinity of the find and resulted in intense Aboriginal resistance. During the 1870s alone, as many as one hundred incomers were killed on the Palmer River diggings and another fifty or so at the other smaller rushes.

Gold rushes, as well as smaller copper, silver, and tin mining operations, propelled settler penetration of the interior by drawing colonists not only from the other Australian colonies, but also from the rest of the world, especially from Britain and China. It stimulated the colonial economy by creating a demand for a wide range of goods and services. Foodstuffs, especially meat, were in high demand, benefiting the pastoral industry. In those areas where alluvial fields gave way to reef mining, which entails digging for gold in quartz veins, the result was permanent settlement and the building of infrastructure—roads, railway lines, and port facilities—that helped open up the hinterland. For Aborigines the inevitable outcome was dispossession, displacement, and famine as tens of thousands of people invaded their territories. The isolated and rugged terrain of alluvial gold fields, however, meant that miners, who often operated alone or in small groups, were vulnerable to attack. The Gilberton and Mount Wyatt goldfields were, for example, abandoned for a while because of Aboriginal attacks and fear of further hostilities. Aboriginal aggression resulted in vicious mass reprisals from prospectors. The impact of mining was not as extensive as pastoralism but was every bit as severe in its impact on Aboriginal communities.

Civilian-Driven Violence and Demographic Collapse of Aboriginal Societies

By 1911, when Australia's first national census was conducted, the Aboriginal population of the entire continent had collapsed to little more than 30,000, while the immigrant population had grown to 4,500,000. This represents a disastrous shrinkage of between 96 and 97 percent in 123 years. Queensland's Aboriginal population by 1911 was no more than about 20,000, which represents a decline of over 90 percent from precolonial levels. The settler population of Queensland meanwhile had grown from a small number of convicts and soldiers in the latter half of the 1820s to over 600,000. It is estimated that in Queensland perhaps 1,500 settlers and their dependents were killed in frontier conflict. The slightly higher survival rate of Aborigines in Queensland, despite its more intense conflict, can be attributed to parts of the tropical north and coastal islands not being suitable for settler economic activity. There were few Aborigines left in the settled areas.

There are a number of mutually reinforcing factors that explain this demographic collapse. The more important are colonial violence, starvation, child confiscation, a declining birthrate, sexual violence, and disease. The focus of necessity needs to be on colonial violence, as this was the fundamental cause of the demographic collapse and created the conditions in which the other factors had their impact. Colonial violence consisted of two interrelated parts, namely, civilian-driven violence and that perpetrated by the state and its military forces. In colonial Queensland there was an unusual synergy between the two. With the colony granted self-governing status in 1859, settler interests found direct and growing expression in government policy, and the restraining influences of the Colonial Office diminished over time.

It is not possible to establish precise statistics of numbers killed either by settlers or the colonial state. What is patently clear from the historical record, however, is that the mass killing of Aborigines was both commonplace and systematic on the Queensland frontier. The most recent estimate by Raymond Evans, the doyen of Queensland frontier studies, puts the figure at over 65,000— and this does not include deaths by starvation, sexual violence, or disease. While much of the bloodshed was hidden and evidence deliberately destroyed for fear of prosecution and moral censure, a good number of colonists nonetheless confessed to murder and massacre in diaries, memoirs, and in the press. Some openly boasted, especially among themselves and people they felt they could trust, of killing Aborigines and participating in massacres. English adventurer William Stamer, in a memoir recalling his travels through southern Queensland in the late 1850s, confirmed the circulation of many "stories that were told of the diabolical manner in which whole tribes were rubbed out" by unscrupulous squatters. These accounts reported how Aborigines "had been hunted and shot down like wild beasts . . . and poisoned wholesale by having arsenic or some other substance given to them as food."[4]

A few perpetrators had the impunity to brag of their dark deeds publicly. In a notorious example, a settler who identified himself as an "old pioneer," in an article titled "Taming the Niggers" in the *Townsville Herald* of February 2, 1907, described in detail his participation in two genocidal massacres that destroyed the Kuungkari people of central Queensland thirty years earlier. These massacres were in revenge for the killing of John Fanning, manager and part owner of the Isis Downs pastoral station. The author, signing himself H7H, the Isis Downs cattle brand, claimed that in the first massacre: "It was estimated that over 150 myalls[5] 'bit the dust' that morning, and unfortunately many women and children shared the same fate." The second was a dawn attack on a camp that " . . . would make Hell's Furies blush. . . . How those gins[6] and kiddies shrieked when we got among them." He relates that when they later on "in daylight came to view the white man's work of vengeance bucks, gins, and piccaninnies[7] were laying dead in all directions, and not a thing in camp moved or breathed." Justifying such wholesale slaughter of innocent people H7H explained that: "The writer never held a man guilty of murder who wiped out a nigger. They should be classed with the black snake and death adder, and treated accordingly."[8]

Many colonists, some of them prominent citizens, openly advocated the extermination of Aborigines. Calls for the extermination of Aborigines were commonly made in the wake of attacks on settlers. Carl Lumholtz, Norwegian explorer and ethnographer who traveled to Australia in 1880 and spent much of his four-year sojourn in northern Queensland, published an influential account of his experiences there. He reported that: "In Northern Queensland I often heard the remark: 'The only treatment proper for the blacks is to shoot them all . . . they are not fit to live.'"[9]

4. William Stamer, *Recollections of a Life of Adventure*, vol. 2 (Bedford: Applewood Books, 1866), 98.

5. A pejorative term for Aborigines unassimilated to Western culture.

6. Aboriginal women.

7. Respectively, men, women, and children.

8. See also Henry Reynolds, *Why Weren't We Told: A Personal Search for the Truth about Our History* (Camberwell: Penguin Books, 1999), 107–8.

9. Carl Lumholtz, *Among Cannibals: Account of Four Years' Travels in Australia and Camp Life with the Aborigines of Australia* (Firle, Sussex: Caliban Books, 1979; first published London, 1889), 373.

Skull Hole massacre. This engraving, said to depict the Skull Hole massacre, appeared in Carl Lumholtz's *Among Cannibals*. A squad of a dozen Native policemen attacked a group of perhaps twenty Aborigines at the Skull Hole lagoon near the Palmer goldfields in the first half of the 1880s. While some were brought down trying to scramble up the cliff-face, most were shot trying to hide among lily pads in the adjoining lagoon. Skulls would wash out during floods, which gave the lagoon its name.

Several observers noted a precipitous decline in Aboriginal populations soon after settler penetration of particular regions. A correspondent to the *Port Denison Times* of April 17, 1869, for example, decried the "mournful sight" of no more than "about 30 male survivors out of all that tribe, which not long ago could be numbered in the hundreds." He blamed the Native Police who, after committing massacres in the surrounding countryside: ". . . visited the public house . . . the heels of their boots covered with brains, and blood and hair." Pastoralist William Chatfield, owner of the Natal Downs cattle station, who was sympathetic to Aborigines and sought to employ them, criticized the Native Police for provoking conflict and of committing atrocities. He noted that the Indigenous population in that region of north-central Queensland had been reduced to a quarter of its original size. Similarly, in 1896, Archibald Meston, appointed special commissioner to investigate the condition of Queensland Aborigines, reported that twelve tribes in the far north of the Cape York Peninsula that had numbered about 3,000 had been reduced to no more than 100 within a few years.

While most of the slaughter of Aborigines happened by means of shooting, the other favored method of mass murder was that of poisoning, especially through the distribution of arsenic or strychnine-laced food. Settlers sometimes poisoned water holes as well. Not only were there many reports of settlers in frontier areas resorting to poisoning but the way in which it was often mentioned indicates that it was fairly common practice. A commemorative history of Queensland published at the turn of the twentieth century confirmed that: "Wholesale poisoning was not an uncommon method of freeing a run of Aborigines," noting that such acts were "still fresh in the memory of Queenslanders."[10] Poisoning readily suggested itself as a means of mass murdering Aborigines as virtually all farmers on the frontier used toxins to kill livestock predators and herbivores that competed with their animals for grazing. Industrial processing had made these toxins cheaply available by the mid-nineteenth century. Poisoning had the advantages that, unlike massacring, it could be effected with relatively little effort or organization, and by a single perpetrator. Indeed, William Stamer identified "One 'lady' on the Upper Condamine [who] had particularly distinguished herself in the poisoning line, having . . . disposed of more natives than any squatter by means of arsenic."[11] The usual practice was to leave adulterated flour where Aborigines would be sure to find it, or more treacherously, to give them poisoned flour or food as a present, or even as payment for work. Poisonings were particularly pernicious as they generally targeted Aborigines

---

10. Anonymous (compiled by Alcazar Press), *Queensland, 1900: A Narrative of Her Past Together With Biographies of Her Leading Men* (Melbourne: W. H. Wendt & Co., nd.), 90.
11. Stamer, *Recollections*, 98.

indiscriminately, resulted in extremely painful deaths, and involved diabolical levels of deceit.

Among the more notorious incidents were the poisoning of about sixty Giggabarah people near Kilcoy Station in 1842, and at least fifty Kabi-Kabi near Whiteside Station in 1847. Both opportunistic mass murders occurred at clan gatherings when the fruiting of bunya nut trees, native to southeastern Queensland, prompted festive congregations of people from far and wide. Bags of toxic flour were presented to both groups by local squatters. Another well-known mass poisoning is described in some detail by Harold Finch-Hatton, in recollections of his experiences on the Queensland frontier. This incident occurred at Long Lagoon in central Queensland when a "gentleman who shall remain nameless"—in all probability Finch-Hatton's elder brother Henry—resorted to elaborate trickery to poison Aborigines in revenge for four of his shepherds being killed. He loaded a large cart with supplies as if to deliver rations to shepherds in the field, and along the way, engineered for a wheel to come off in full view of "a large mob of Blacks." Seemingly annoyed, he left the cart and went back to the station. The Aborigines took the food, heavily laced with strychnine, down to the edge of the lagoon, where they consumed it. Finch-Hatton reports that: ". . . not one of the mob escaped. . . . More than a hundred Blacks were stretched out by this ruse. . . . In a dry season, when the water sinks low, their skulls are occasionally to be found half buried in the mud."[12]

Once farmers leased land from the state, they had legal title to it in terms of colonial law and felt they had the right to move Aborigines off their runs. If Aborigines resisted removal from ancestral land, the result was bound to be murder and massacre. There was a major economic incentive with an immediate payoff for squatters to free their holdings of Aboriginal threat. Not only did the value of the land increase, often substantially, but wages also declined as there was no longer a need to offer danger pay to attract workers. Although an exaggeration, there was substance to Commandant Frederick Walker's boast that the activity of his Native Police contingent along the Macintyre River in 1849–1850 increased the value of runs fivefold in a matter of six months.

A recurring reason for killing Aborigines and massacring groups of them was revenge. Not only were large numbers of livestock driven off and speared, but a fair number of settlers and their dependents were killed on the frontier by Aborigines. It is estimated that on average between fifteen and twenty incomers, mostly adult males, were killed annually during the decades of frontier expansion.

---

12. Harold Finch-Hatton, *Advance Australia: An Account of Eight Years' Work, Wandering, and Amusement, in Queensland, New South Wales, and Victoria* (London: W. H. Allen & Co., 1886), 133–34.

There were numerous frenzied responses to Aboriginal attacks, with vigilante gangs being formed to hunt down and kill any Indigenes they could find. It was particularly when settler families, especially women and children, were killed by Aborigines that reprisals by vigilante gangs of colonists were savage. A correspondent to the *Port Denison Times* expressed settler sentiment on the matter by claiming that for every white killed by an Aborigine "we take say fifty, exacting not an eye for an eye, and a tooth for a tooth, but as many eyes and teeth as we can get."[13] In the case of some of the larger retributory onslaughts, the fifty for one estimate was no exaggeration. In general, settler retribution was out of all proportion to Aboriginal offenses.

Revenge killings reached a peak during the second land rush. Aboriginal bands across a wide frontier, put under severe pressure by this frenzied pastoral expansion, reacted fiercely, on occasion attacking and massacring groups of settlers. Graziers moving into new territory far from settled areas felt very vulnerable and thus tended to overreact to threats. In this period, there was a series of Aboriginal attacks on settlers that were met with hysteria and mass reprisal. Notable incidents include the killing of five station workers at Mount Larcom the day after Christmas in 1855; the Hornet Bank massacre of October 1857, in which eleven colonists, including seven members of the Fraser family and one Aboriginal employee, were slaughtered; the killing of two parties of Europeans at Castle Creek and Clematis Creek in early 1860; and the massacre of nineteen colonists, the largest by Aborigines in Australian history, at Cullin-la-Ringo in October 1861. The rape and murder of barmaid Fanny Briggs in Rockhampton in November 1859—initially blamed on local Aboriginal men but later found to have been committed by Native policemen—also provoked an enraged response.

The settler backlash in each of these cases was frenzied as contingents of Native Police accompanied by parties of white vigilantes went on killing sprees. Not only were there massacres of Aborigines within a wide area, but killings were also random. Vigilante gangs killed every Aborigine they came across including a number of "station blacks." Women and children, and others who obviously had not participated in violence against settlers, were slaughtered. In reprisal for the Hornet Bank killings, vigilantes and Native Police went on a killing spree taking somewhere between 300 and 400 Aboriginal lives over the next few weeks. An even greater number, perhaps as many as 500 Aborigines, were also killed in response to the Cullin-la-Ringo massacre.

The principle of collective punishment was commonly applied in frontier reprisals. The logic behind such unbridled retribution was to make Aborigines

---

13. *Port Denison Times*, March 2, 1867.

in general pay for the crimes of perpetrators so that the reprisals served as deterrents for any Aborigines contemplating resistance to white intrusion. There was usually little or no attempt to find the perpetrators of violence against settlers but to attack the nearest Aborigines or to scour the countryside and kill any they encountered. Perpetrators at times annihilated entire communities living in the vicinity. Collective punishment was also a result of the dehumanization of Aborigines in that their individuality was denied and corporate blame was assigned under a blanket racial othering of all Aborigines as inherently malevolent and therefore guilty by association.

As these manifestations of dehumanizing behavior indicate, frontier violence was deeply modulated by racism. Not only did Queensland settler society regard itself, by virtue of its Western European heritage, to be at the apex of human development, but regarded Australian Aborigines as among the lowest specimens of humankind, to the point of many questioning and denying their humanity. This extreme othering of Aborigines was colored by the circulation of polygenist as well as Social Darwinist ideas in Queensland society. The former, current in Western society for over two centuries by that time, asserted that the various races were the product of separate creations, whether by God or nature, contradicting the more conventional monogenetic views of humanity having a common origin. This denial of a shared ancestry served as a means of animalizing Aborigines further and removing moral constraints against violence toward them. Aborigines were popularly seen as a "doomed race," for long protected by the isolation of Australia, but rapidly dying out in the face of the advance of "civilization." To many perpetrators this mode of thinking was further incitement to violence as Aborigines were regarded as an encumbrance to humanity, and hastening their demise, a service to it.

Besides utmost brutality toward Aborigines and a complete lack of empathy for their suffering among so many frontier settlers, there were other noteworthy indicators of their extreme dehumanization. One was the collection by colonists of Aboriginal body parts as trophies and mementos of their nefarious exploits. Jonathan Watson, manager of the Lawn Hill station in the Gulf Country, provides an excellent example. He gained notoriety in the region for his collection of about forty pairs of severed Aboriginal ears collected during raids and nailed to the walls of his homestead. He also kept an Aboriginal skull as a spittoon, presumably as a show of utmost contempt for Indigenes. Others collected teeth, skulls, or finger bones among other skeletal parts as grim keepsakes or as specimens for racial science, museums, and personal collections. Two further indicators of extreme dehumanization were that Aborigines were killed for the most trivial of reasons and were sometimes hunted as game. An editorial article in the

Port Denison Times of August 8, 1868 referenced both in a single sentence: "It is not at all uncommon to try the range of a Terry's breechloader on a mob of blacks, or to hunt them like kangaroos for sport." George Carrington confirmed that the Aborigine ". . . has come to be considered in the light of a troublesome wild animal to be shot and hunted down, whenever seen in the open country."[14] Such attitudes were not confined to settlers. English adventurer Arthur C. Bicknell, who traveled through northern Queensland in the early 1890s, partly to record the "manners and customs" of Aborigines before "they will have disappeared from the face of the earth," one night found himself stranded in the wilderness after his cart had overturned. Contemplating the probability of an Aborigine attack, he consoled himself with the thought that: "I had with me a five-shooter and twenty rounds of ammunition . . . quite expecting that I might get a brace or two of black game before the morning."[15]

Not all Australian male settlers were cold-blooded killers. The slaughter generally happened on the frontier and moved with it from the southeast in northerly and westerly directions over a period of a little more than half a century. Among frontier farmers there was a handful of compassionate souls who protested against the violence of their peers and the Native Police, and who sought to employ Aborigines. Even some of these, however, confessed to having killed Aborigines—as did George Carrington. In the more settled areas there was calm, largely because Aborigines there had already been driven out or killed. What could be said of those behind the frontier is that the majority of settlers openly or silently condoned such killings, and many simply could not care less. There was a handful of people, the most vocal being clergymen and progressive journalists, who protested vigorously. But they were a tiny minority and ostracized in settler circles. Some were intimidated to the point of leaving the colony. Even the most ardent humanitarians were not opposed to the settler project per se, but wanted it implemented in a more humane fashion.

Government Culpability and the Native Police Force

The Queensland state was directly involved in the violent destruction of Aboriginal society and was culpable in three main ways. Firstly, it vigorously promoted squatter interests, thereby facilitating the dispossession of Aborigines and the perpetration of violence against them. Secondly, it failed to do anything to stop the violence or to prosecute settlers who committed atrocities against Aborigines,

---

14. Carrington, *Colonial Adventures*, 153–54.
15. Quoted in Alison Palmer, *Colonial Genocide* (Adelaide: Crawford House Publishing, 2000), 45.

even in the face of blatant criminality. In that way it encouraged a culture of impunity among settlers. Thirdly, the Queensland government administered the Native Police Corps that killed large numbers of Aborigines across the length and breadth of the colony throughout the era of frontier expansion. Not only was the Native Police an extremely deadly force, it was one of the Queensland government's key instruments of policy toward Aboriginal society until the closing years of the nineteenth century.

Most Queensland government representatives and officials in the upper echelons of the administration during the nineteenth century, in one way or another, had a stake in the pastoral industry. The government thus overwhelmingly represented the interests of the squatter elite. Also, the state, to a very large extent, was dependent on the revenues generated by pastoral farming, as it was by far the colony's largest economic sector. It was thus in the interests of the Queensland elite, the state as a whole, individual officials, and its law enforcement agencies, to turn a blind eye to settler violence against Aborigines, support Indigenous removal, and suppress Aboriginal resistance. One fact says it all: despite decades of pervasive violence and utter brutality toward Aborigines on the frontier, not a single settler was successfully prosecuted in Queensland courts until 1883, when a Townsville man, Edward Camm, was sentenced to life imprisonment for raping an Aboriginal child.

The Native Police came into being in the northern pastoral areas of New South Wales in 1848 as an initiative of farmers for protection against Aboriginal attack. After serving under the New South Wales government for a decade, the force was subsequently taken over, administered, financed, and expanded by the Queensland government from 1859 onward. The Native Police was a paramilitary force, consisting of contingents of usually between six and ten Aboriginal troopers under the command of one or two white officers, and lived in camps that moved along with the frontier. The government resorted to the use of Aboriginal policemen because few colonists were prepared to do this dirty and dangerous work for such low pay, and because they were regarded as more effective fighters under bush combat conditions. Troopers were recruited from Aboriginal tribes far away, usually from New South Wales and Victoria, so that they had no affinities with local Aborigines. Some were the brutalized child survivors of massacres and orphans who had grown up on the fringes of colonial society and for whom this work was a form of preferment. Native Police were chosen for their tracking skills and bush craft essential for effective operation in the rough terrain of the Queensland frontier. Furthermore, Indigenes were less susceptible to endemic diseases, learned local languages more easily, and understood Indigenous culture. That Aboriginal evidence was inadmissible in court quelled fears that officers

Queensland Native Police. Queensland Native Police detachment at Rockhampton, December 1864, under the command of Lieutenant George "Black Jack" Murray, second from left. Two years later, Murray was appointed chief inspector of the force and had a long career as a magistrate after he left the Native Police in 1877. Note the racial hierarchy and emphasis on deadly force reflected in the photograph.

might be compromised by the testimony of native troopers. A divide-and-rule tactic was to assign recruits from different language groups to detachments to minimize their chances of banding together against officers.

Native Police squads were extremely lethal, being armed with efficient, modern firearms. From the mid-nineteenth century onward, there was a big leap in firearm technology giving guns longer ranges, greater accuracy, and increasingly rapid firing capability. From the early 1860s, the Native Police's earlier muzzle-loading rifles were replaced with far superior breech-loading Terry rifles. From the mid-1870s, they were issued the more effective Snider rifles, and from the mid-1880s, switched to the even deadlier Martini-Henry firearms. Native Police also carried revolvers and cutlasses that were used in close combat. These huge military advantages were amplified by Native Police being mounted. The speed and power of horses gave them great ascendancy in mobility, allowing them to cover long distances rapidly, as well as advantages of height and greater maneuverability in closer skirmishing. Horses were also invaluable in instances of hot pursuit. They were particularly potent in flat, open country but less effective in rocky or wooded terrain. The effectiveness of the Native Police was also enhanced by their access to modern, industrial technology such as steamboats, railways, and telegraph.

The stated purpose of the Native Police was to patrol the frontier and to protect livestock stations vulnerable to attack. From no more than five or six contingents in the 1850s, by 1863 fourteen detachments, and in 1869 twenty-four squads were deployed on the frontier. A great deal of the Native Police's time was spent patrolling the borderlands as a form of visible policing and intimidation to deter Aboriginal attack. But its brief was also to be proactive in preventing attacks on colonists. Native Police contingents thus often went on the offensive against Aboriginal communities for no substantive reason, especially when they felt that congregations of Aboriginal people were dangerously large or their behavior was in any way perceived to be threatening. In 1866, officers were given express instructions "at all times and opportunities, to disperse any large assembly of blacks without unnecessary violence."[16] This gave the more murderous officers an excuse to attack gatherings of Aborigines without cause.

Unprovoked attacks from time to time occurred when Aborigines congregated to perform cultural and spiritual ceremonies. In one such incident in 1862, eight Aborigines were shot and killed without any provocation by Native Police at a gathering at Caboolture, thirty miles north of Brisbane. A similar assembly near Rockhampton in 1865 aroused completely unsubstantiated fears of attack in Samuel Birkbeck of the nearby Glenmore station. He summoned the Native Police who killed eighteen Aborigines in the ensuing "dispersal," subsequently burning and burying the bodies. Another three large-scale massacres of Aborigines gathering for ceremonial purposes in the Birdsville area during the 1880s resulted in several hundred casualties. These wanton onslaughts arose from a combination of ignorance of Aboriginal cultural practices, settlers on isolated frontiers being easily panicked because of acute fears of Aboriginal aggression, and large gatherings of Aboriginal peoples presenting Native Police contingents or white vigilantes with opportune targets.

The purpose of the Native Police was also punitive—to exact revenge for Aboriginal aggression. Under some of the more bloodthirsty white officers, and in the aftermath of Aboriginal retaliations, especially when settler women or children were killed, Native Police units operated very much as mobile death squads, roaming the countryside in and beyond the frontier, killing any Aborigines they encountered. Their favored method of attacking an Aborigine camp was to surround it at night and attack at dawn. A description of one such encounter is provided in the recollections of settler William Telfer. In mid-1849, commandant Frederick Walker and a contingent of ten native policemen arrived in Bigambul territory on the Condamine River in the future southern Queensland, where several sheep stations had been abandoned in the wake of twelve white men having been killed and a large number of stock being lost. In one of several sorties

---

16. *Queensland Government Gazette*, March 10, 1866.

in which the Bigambul were effectively destroyed, Walker traveled through the night to surprise one of their camps. Telfer reported that: ". . . at daybreak they made an attack on the sleeping camp. Some of them [Aborigines] fled . . . making for the scrub but were met by the native police who drew their swords cutting and slashing the fugitives a great number were slain also a lot shot dead."[17] Some thirty-five years later another settler, Jack Kane, provided a vivid eyewitness account of another such massacre southwest of Cairns on the Cape York Peninsula

> At Skull Pocket police officers and native trackers surrounded a camp of Indindji blacks before dawn, each man armed with a rifle and revolver. At dawn one man fired into their camp and the natives rushed away in three other directions. They were easy running shots, close up. The native police rushed in with their scrub knives and killed off the children. . . . I didn't mind the killing of the "bucks" but I didn't quite like the braining of the kids.[18]

It would appear from these and other descriptions of massacres that for some, both black and white, service in the Native Police and joining vigilante gangs served as an outlet for psychopathic impulses. The sadistic pleasure that some perpetrators took in bloodletting shines through in the eyewitness account of vigilante Hazelton Brock of a massacre in about 1875 of a large number of Guwa people pursued by a Native Police contingent accompanied by fourteen settler cutthroats in retaliation for the murder of a single settler a week earlier. After attacking a sizable Guwa encampment from three sides, forcing about 200 of them to jump a thirty-foot precipice into a creek, and pinning them in the water against the riverbank, "lead poured thick and heavy on them . . . [until] the blacks were thinned out to about half, nearly all the men being killed." Brock recalled that

> The troopers had been getting more and more excited, until at last they threw down their guns and drew their sheath-knives, which they all carried, jumped into the water, and engaged in hand-to-hand struggle. But it did not last long; the blacks had only a nulla-nulla[19] or two, and the troopers fought with the ferocity of tigers.[20]

---

17. Roger Millis, *The Wallabadah Manuscript: The Early History of the Northern Districts of New South Wales; Recollections of the Early Days by William Telfer Jr.* (Sydney: New South Wales University Press, 1980), 41.

18. Quoted in Timothy Bottoms, *Conspiracy of Silence: Queensland's Frontier Killing Times* (Sydney: Allen & Unwin, 2013), 147.

19. A nulla-nulla, also known as a waddy, is a pointed Aboriginal weapon resembling a club.

20. Quoted in Bottoms, *Conspiracy of Silence*, 172–73.

Although dispossession and major bloodletting were essentially over by about 1890, frontier-type violence continued on a smaller scale into the 1910s, after which Queensland could, in colonial terminology, be regarded as having been "pacified." Native Police patrols were scaled back from the 1890s, but the force was only fully demobilized in 1914.

After exhaustive research into the history of the Queensland Native Police, Jonathan Richards comes to the conclusion that: "The evidence clearly shows that the Native Police in Queensland operated under the direct control of the colony's most senior administrators—the Executive Council. The governor, in concert with the colonial secretary and other ministers, decided where to deploy the Native Police, who to appoint and which officers to dismiss."[21] It is no exaggeration to say that the Queensland government used the Native Police to wage undeclared war on Aboriginal society—in its entirety.

Ancillary Forms of Social Destruction

In addition to murder, massacre, and poisoning, there were a number of collateral contributors to the demographic collapse of Queensland's Aboriginal population. The most important were starvation, sexual exploitation, child confiscation, a low birthrate, and disease. The point to bear in mind is that barring the partial exception of communicable disease, these ancillary forms of social destruction were all intentionally inflicted—intentional in its juridical sense, that is.

Many Aboriginal people died of dehydration and starvation as a result of their being displaced from their traditional lands and their concomitant loss of access to food and water. There was no possibility of Aborigines and settlers living amicably together as their land usage and social values were utterly incompatible. Settler economic activities destroyed Aboriginal food sources and disrupted the natural cycles on which they depended. Many people who were uprooted had little option but to move to marginal land where they might be able to subsist for a while through a combination of foraging and stock rustling. This was a dangerous existence, as farmers were wont to hunt down and kill rustlers. Also, drought regularly spelled death for displaced communities in the outback who found themselves stranded without food or water. There were many reports by colonists of emaciated Aboriginal communities and of groups dying of starvation.

---

21. Jonathan Richards, *The Secret War: A True History of Queensland's Native Police* (St. Lucia: University of Queensland Press, 2008), 216.

Sexual abuse of Aboriginal women by settlers was a major cause of conflict on the frontier and contributed significantly to Aboriginal population decline. With gender ratios in the settler population as high as 1-to-10, and seldom below 1-to-6, on the frontier; with a relatively young, heavily armed, predominantly male, invader population given to drinking and sexually predatory behavior; with racist and macho attitudes prevalent; and culprits able to act with impunity; the assault, abduction, and rape of Aboriginal women and children on the frontier was common. Retaliatory attacks by Aborigines were often in response to the abuse of women and children.

Many Aboriginal women were seized by settlers to serve as both sexual captives and domestic servants. It was not unusual for some younger women and children to be spared during massacres expressly to be exploited in these ways. Some pastoral stations detained Aboriginal women as "stud gins" to attract labor and to do menial work. Many Aboriginal women taken captive or separated from traditional society had little option but to endure such abuse, as they became dependent on their persecutors for survival and usually faced severe punishment, or even death, if they tried to escape. The labor, reproductive capacity, and other contributions of these women were lost to Aboriginal society, while their so-called half-caste children would in time augment the captive labor supply of the settler economy.

A high proportion of sexual abusers were infected with venereal diseases, especially syphilis and gonorrhea, which had a double impact on Indigenes who had little immunity to these pathogens. Firstly, these diseases were extremely virulent in people with low immunity and thus killed significant numbers of Aborigines. Secondly, most who survived the infection were rendered infertile due to the damage done to their reproductive organs.

The abduction, confiscation, and forced assimilation of Aboriginal children severely undercut the reproductive capacity of Aboriginal society—both biologically and culturally. The loss of these children meant that the emergent cohort within Indigenous societies was seriously diminished and that of settler society complemented, at the very least with cheap, servile laborers. The abduction, and subsequent gifting and sale, of Aboriginal children by settlers in the Queensland outback was common during the era of frontier expansion and for several decades thereafter.

Native Police, both officers and troopers, were frequently involved in the abduction of children. The Northern Protector of Aboriginals Report for 1902 confirmed that: "It is known that in past years a most obnoxious practice grew up of the police supplying their friends *etc* with aboriginal children. . . . This 'trucking' in children is still going on." The report for the following year elaborated that: "A large number of individuals have an idea that they can trade an aboriginal as they would a horse or a bullock." An article in the Brisbane newspaper, the *Bulletin* of June 19, 1880 disclosed that:

> In several far northern districts it is by no means uncommon for residents to ask the native troopers to procure young blacks for them; and the writer has frequently seen a long string of native police filing into a township—some of them carrying in front of their saddles black children from two to ten years of age.

Even more damaging in the longer run was that the reproduction of Aboriginal society was subverted through a severe decline in its birthrate. Social dislocation brought about by settler invasion disrupted the biological reproduction of Aboriginal society in myriad ways. Very importantly, the fertility of Aboriginal women was acutely affected by malnutrition, sexual abuse, venereal disease, and the psychological trauma of living through the murder of family members, the massacre of their communities, and the utter mayhem that came with their lifeways being destroyed. Besides such severe and chronic stress subverting conception, it is probable that people actively refused to rear children under such chaotic and dangerous circumstances, resorting to abortion and infanticide.

Infectious diseases, such as smallpox, tuberculosis, influenza, measles, and whooping cough introduced by Europeans and to which Aborigines had little immunity, were the biggest killers. At the time, colonists often interpreted this as a manifestation of racial weakness, God's punishment of savage depravity, or God's way of clearing the land for white settlement. Contagious disease is often seized upon by present-day apologists and denialists to argue that Aboriginal societies were destroyed unintentionally by a neutral agent and through "natural causes." This is, however, far too simplistic and self-serving an interpretation of the role of disease in the destruction of Aboriginal society. In the first place, the spread of disease occurred in the context of Indigenous communities being traumatized by displacement and massacre, and whose immune systems were severely compromised by malnutrition and psychological stress. Social dislocation also undermined these communities' ability to care for the sick. Casualty rates were thus much higher than they would otherwise have been. What is more, Queensland authorities did nothing to stem the spread of these diseases or to alleviate suffering. While there is no evidence of the intentional spread of infectious diseases such as smallpox as occurred in North America, this does not hold true for venereal diseases. Most colonial carriers knew they had a venereal disease and were aware that it would be spread through sexual intercourse. Indeed, there is evidence that some abusers deliberately sought to spread their venereal infections. Others believed that they could cure their illness by passing it on to a partner.

After the Closing of the Frontier

The Queensland frontier started winding down from the end of the 1880s onward, as the last of the land of economic value to the settler economy was taken in the far northern and western areas of the colony. Mass violence against Aborigines subsided over the next decade, and the activities of the Native Police were progressively phased out. Occasional massacres nonetheless occurred well into the twentieth century. Among the better known was that on Bentinck Island in 1918, when a large proportion of the Kaiadilt people, who numbered just over one hundred, were hunted and killed by a party of settlers wanting to occupy the island. As the frontier closed and Aboriginal resistance was no longer much of a threat, a change in both settler attitudes and government policy toward them became evident. Settlers were now more willing to employ Aborigines, who in time became a significant element of the workforce in stock farming as well as other parts of the colonial economy. Government attention started turning to how survivors were to be accommodated within the post-frontier order.

By the turn of the century, there were no more than about 20,000 Aborigines left in Queensland, largely concentrated in the recently conquered north and northwest. The general view was that Aborigines were a "dying race," and that their dying out needed to be managed effectively by the government so as to minimize conflict with whites and to maximize their utility as cheap labor. The most effective response to this situation was seen to be segregation and tight management of Aboriginal lives. In contrast, those supposedly of "mixed race" were regarded as a group that would survive, but because of their defective genetic makeup would be given to criminality, prostitution, and social disorder in general. Their existence was an embarrassment to colonial society and there were fears that they would in the future create problems for white Australia unless their development was socially engineered in a productive direction. The solution to the "half-caste problem" was seen to be assimilation, especially of children, and the "breeding out of color" over several generations, until they disappeared altogether as an identifiable element in Australian society. For much of the twentieth century government policy thus envisaged the complete disappearance of Aborigines, and was geared toward this objective.

The first sign of a change in the government's approach as the frontier started closing, was the support given to missionary enterprises from the late 1880s onward. Moving Aborigines onto mission stations was a convenient means of implementing racial segregation and channeling labor into farmwork. In the following decade, thousands of Aborigines were forcibly moved to mission stations, usually located on unproductive land. Missionaries were also seen as useful

Djabugay. Part of a group of sixty-four Djabugay people living in Kuranda near Cairns in northern Queensland, who were about to be moved to the Monamona mission station in February 1916.

agents in helping to "civilize" Aborigines, especially children, through schools that were meant to teach them skills and habits that would assist in integrating them into colonial society as menial laborers.

It was not until 1897 that new government policy toward Aborigines was concretized in the form of the ironically named Aboriginals Protection and Restriction of the Sale of Opium Act. The act did very little to protect Aborigines, who were now wards of the state, but a great deal to sanction and institutionalize further harm to them. Although the Queensland state did not have the resources to impose these measures fully, and implementation was at first haphazard, its eliminationist intentions toward Aborigines are clear; its capacity to reinforce control over Aboriginal lives increased over time; and those Aborigines who fell under its influence suffered enormous personal and social harm. Subsequent amendments such as those of 1901, 1928, 1934, and successor legislation in 1939 and 1965, became progressively comprehensive and discriminatory.

The Aboriginals Protection Act gave the state and designated functionaries the power of near-total control over Aboriginal lives. It appointed an Aboriginal Protector in each administrative district, usually the local police chief, who was responsible for implementing its provisions. The act set up a system of closed and strictly segregated reservations, from which Aborigines were not allowed to move without permission from the protector. They were effective prisoners there, and commonly referred to as "inmates" or "interns." They could be forcibly relocated to any reserve or between reserves, and such forced removals became ever more frequent across Queensland through the first half of the twentieth century. Protectors could, among other things, determine where people were allowed to live, what work they could do, what they were paid, withhold their wages, deny couples the right to marry, remove their children by force, and send them to another location. People were subjected to forced labor, families were broken up, and many children sent to mission schools far away. So-called full-blooded children were trained for manual labor, usually on nearby farms, while many "half-castes" were removed from their families and made available for adoption or fostering by white families or raised in state or missionary institutions as part of the state's assimilationist policy. On reserves, Aborigines were forbidden to speak their native languages, practice traditional customs, or perform cultural and spiritual rituals that were crucial for reproducing social and cultural ties.

The government set up a special reservation on Palm Island, forty-five miles north of Townsville, as a punishment center for recalcitrant Aborigines. Here conditions were harsh, and punishments included imprisonment, flogging, and exile on a diet of bread and water on nearby, even more isolated, Eclipse Island. Reservations had high mortality rates as a result of disease, poor living conditions, malnutrition, and general neglect. It was only from the 1970s onward that conditions were ameliorated in the face of intensifying Aboriginal protest and resistance, and the changing human rights environment after World War II. The failure and dismantling of the White Australia Policy, as well as the global impact of the American Civil Rights and South African Anti-Apartheid Movements, were significant influences.

The Case for Genocide

The annihilation of Queensland's Aboriginal societies is plainly a case of genocide. Intent to destroy the victim group—the key criterion for determining genocide—is easily inferred from the consistently lethal and socially pernicious actions of civilian perpetrators as well as the unrelenting and organized violence of the state toward Aboriginal peoples. Civilian-driven and state-led violence were tightly interlaced through common economic, social, political, and ideological interests. Many perpetrators openly supported the extermination of Aborigines; and both armed, mounted settler posses, as well as Native Police contingents, time after time acted in local exterminatory fashion. The killing of Aborigines was systematic, occurred throughout the colony over an extended period, and targeted the Aboriginal people as a whole. Neither women, children, nor the elderly were spared. Both murder and massacre were often gratuitous and unprovoked, and perpetrators knowingly killed many innocent people. Aborigines were often shot on sight, hunted as prey, or killed for trivial reasons. Moreover, an extreme dehumanization of Aborigines facilitated mass violence against them. In other words, Aboriginal people were generally killed for no other reason than that they were Aborigines. That so many people died in stealth attacks, such as dawn-light ambushes of camps and mass poisonings, and that there were so many killings but so few prisoners taken, strengthen the case for genocide. There can be little doubt that nearly all Aboriginal communities in colonial Queensland suffered genocidal destruction in the process of dispossession in that they were no longer able to reproduce themselves biologically or culturally as functional social entities. Indeed, the frontier policy of successive governments until the 1890s was in effect one of undeclared genocidal war against Aborigines. The resultant reduction of their population by 90 percent over half a century of carnage is by any standard an excessively high death toll.

With the closing of the frontier and passage of the Aboriginal Protection Act in 1897, government policy shifted from overtly extirpatory methods of murder and massacre to more covert strategies of social destruction. Given the comprehensive abuse of Aboriginal human rights, neglect of their basic needs for health and well-being, cultural suppression, child confiscation, assimilation of "half-castes," and other inimical actions by the state and civilian population, there cannot be the slightest doubt that accusations of "ongoing genocide" after the closing of the homicidal frontier phase are fully justified.

Timothy Bottoms summed up the essence behind the destruction of Queensland's Aboriginal societies succinctly: "Aboriginals were killed for being there and being in the way of the great land theft."[22] It was the settler establishment's vision of ridding their society of an Aboriginal presence altogether that establishes intent and makes the violence unequivocally genocidal.

At about the same time, on what might be envisaged as the other side of the world, Euro-American settlers pouring into California precipitated an even more acute genocide of Indigenous peoples. In both instances, the rapidity of genocidal destruction came from the ineluctable consequences of the industrial revolution. And in both cases ancient cultures made way for highly productive economies that consolidated the spread of Western dominance.

---

22. Bottoms, *Conspiracy of Silence*, 45.

SOURCES

"The Way We Civilise": Contending Views on Frontier Violence in Colonial Queensland

Our first two documents are extracts from the sixty-page pamphlet, *The Way We Civilise*, which consists of a collection of fourteen newspaper editorials condemning violence by settlers and Native Police against Aborigines, as well as of twenty-seven letters in response from readers, published between May 1 and July 17, 1880 in the *Queenslander* newspaper. The editorials were written anonymously by Carl Feilberg, a Danish-born Australian journalist and newspaper editor, and were commissioned by Gresley Lukin, owner of this leading weekly paper. Feilberg was editor of the *Queenslander* at the time, and frontier conflict in the northern and western parts of the colony was at its height. The pamphlet was widely distributed as part of an unsuccessful campaign led by Lukin and Feilberg to try to force the Queensland government into setting up a Royal Commission of Enquiry into the conduct of the Native Police.

As political commentator, Feilberg supported a wide range of progressive causes of which defending the interests of Aboriginal peoples was his most passionate and abiding. His advocacy of Indigenous rights, as well as those of other downtrodden groups, such as indentured laborers from China and the Pacific Islands, took a great deal of courage because it evoked outright hostility from Queenslanders. Experiencing intensified ostracism and victimization as a result of these articles, Feilberg decided to move to Melbourne in 1882. He had also suffered demotion at the hands of the new owners after the Brisbane Newspaper Company, of which the *Queenslander* was part, was sold in December 1880.

Although *The Way We Civilise* stirred up a great deal of controversy, prompted extensive parliamentary debate on the possibility of holding a Royal Commission of Enquiry, and subsequently provided other humanitarians with ammunition, it had no discernible impact on prevailing sentiment within the settler establishment nor on the treatment of Aboriginal peoples in Queensland. Largely forgotten after the closing of the frontier, *The Way We Civilise* has in the last two decades been resurrected to become one of the most widely referenced primary sources on Queensland's frontier history. Today it stands as a searing indictment of Queensland's settler establishment.

The very first editorial and the very first letter in response, are presented here. These two documents set out the basic positions of the opposing sides of the controversy. Subsequent contributions were in essence elaborations on, and responses to, these opening salvos.

Questions for Consideration

What motives for the columnist's condemnation of frontier violence are you able to discern from the article? How fair a reflection of frontier violence does he provide, and what evidence is there in this article that settler violence was genocidal in nature? Assess the effectiveness of Feilberg's arguments in terms of their logic and morality rather than their impact on government policy or settler attitudes. Are you able to detect a patronizing attitude toward Aborigines in Feilberg's writing?

The Way We Civilise[23]

It is necessary, in order to make the majority of the community understand the urgent necessity for reform, to dispense with apologetic paraphrases. This in plain language is how we deal with aborigines: On occupying new territory the aboriginal inhabitants are treated in exactly the same way as the wild beasts or the birds the settlers may find there. Their lives and their property, the nets, canoes, and weapons which represent as much labor to them as the stock and buildings of the white settler, are held by the Europeans as being at their absolute disposal. Their goods are taken, their children forcibly stolen, their women carried away, entirely at the caprice of the white men. The least show of resistance is answered by a rifle bullet; in fact, the first introduction between blacks and whites is often marked by the unprovoked murder of some of the former—in order to make a commencement of the work of "civilising" them. Little difference is made between the treatment of blacks at first disposed to be friendly and those who from the very outset assume a hostile attitude. As a rule the blacks have been friendly at first, and the longer they have endured provocation without retaliating the worse they have fared, for the most ferocious savages have inspired some fear, and have therefore been comparatively unmolested. In regard to these cowardly outrages, the majority of settlers have been influenced by the same sort of feeling as that which guides men in their treatment of the brute creation. Many, perhaps the majority, have stood aside in silent disgust whilst these things were being done, actuated by the same motives that keep humane men from shooting or molesting animals which neither annoy nor are of service to them; and a few have always protested in the name of humanity against such treatment of human beings, however degraded. But the protests of the minority have been disregarded by the people of the settled districts; the majority of the outsiders who take no part in the outrages have been either apathetic or inclined to shield their companions and the white brutes who fancied the amusement, have murdered, ravished, and

---

23. Anonymous [Carl Feilberg], *The Way We Civilise; Black and White; The Native Police: A Series of Articles and Letters Reprinted from the "Queenslander"* (Brisbane, 1880), 3–5.

robbed the blacks without let or hindrance. Not only have they been unchecked, but the Government of the colony has always been at hand to save them from the consequences of their crime. When the blacks, stung into retaliation by outrages committed on their tribe, or hearing the fate of their neighbours, have taken the initiative and taken white blood, or speared white men's stock, the native police have been sent to "disperse" them. What disperse means is well enough known. The word has been adopted into bush slang as a convenient euphemism for wholesale massacre. Of this force we have already said that it is impossible to write about it with patience. It is enough to say of it that this body, organised and paid by us, is sent to do work which its officers are forbidden to report in detail, and that a true record of its proceedings would shame us before our fellow-countrymen in every part of the British Empire. When the police have entered on the scene, the race conflict goes on apace. It is a fitful war of extermination waged upon the blacks, something after the fashion in which other settlers wage war upon the noxious wild beasts, the process differing only in so far as the victims, being human, are capable of a wider variety of suffering than brutes. The savages, hunted from the places where they had been accustomed to find food, driven into barren ranges, shot like wild dogs at sight, retaliate when and how they can. They spear the white man's cattle and horses, and if by chance they succeed in over-powering an unhappy European they exhaust their savage ingenuity in wreaking their vengeance upon him, even mutilating the senseless body out of which they have pounded the last breath of life. Murder and counter murder, outrage paid by violence, theft and robbery, so the dreary tale continues, till at last the blacks, starved, cowed, and broken hearted, their numbers thin, their courage overcome, submit to their fate, and disease and liquor finish the work which we pay our native police to begin.

This is the ordinary course of events, but occasionally a variation occurs, and the process of quieting the blacks is unusually prolonged. This is particularly the case in the North, where the blacks are more determined, better armed and have more mountain and scrub retreats than in other parts of the colony. . . . Conse-quently there is no part of Queensland in which more lives have been lost, or where the bush is so thoroughly unsafe for the single traveller. It is difficult to estimate the extent of the loss that has been directly incurred, and still more difficult to calculate the indirect injury suffered by the district. Prospecting for minerals could only be carried out by well armed and equipped parties—and this itself has been a serious drawback to the European miners. But the heavi-est loss is being experienced now that the mining excitement has subsided. For, as the writer of the Cooktown paper says, there is plenty of good soil inviting settlement; but how many men dare fix their home in the bush when they know that neither their property nor their lives will be safe from attacks of desperate

savages, whose natural cunning would have been intensified by their long struggle for life with the whites. Evidently settlement must be delayed until the work
of extermination is complete—a consummation of which there is no present
prospect—or until some rational and humane method of dealing with the blacks
is adopted. It is surely, advisable, and even at this eleventh hour, to try the more
creditable alternative, and to see whether we cannot efface some portion at least
of the stain which attaches to us. . . .

—*Queenslander*, May 1, 1880.

✦✦✦✦✦

The Way We Civilise: Justifying Frontier Violence

This candid rejoinder to the preceding newspaper editorial typifies the attitude of
most perpetrators of mass violence against Aborigines on the Queensland frontier and of their supporters in settled areas.

Questions for Consideration

How does Never Never justify his advocacy of the complete annihilation of
Aboriginal society? What uncomfortable truths nonetheless come through
in this riposte? How does racial stereotyping inform his worldview? What
does the writer mean by "restlessness of culture" and how is this supposed to
advantage the "invading race" in the struggle for dominance? What common
ground is shared by Never Never and Feilberg, and what does this indicate about
the nature of colonialism, and of settler colonialism in particular?

LETTERS TO THE EDITOR

WHITE VERSUS BLACK

Sir,— . . . I am not writing this in defence of our Black Police system, but I am
writing against a sweeping vilification of all white pioneers who find it necessary
to preserve their property by the strong hand. Nothing is easier than to sit down
at a desk or table, and—on paper—work out a civilising code that shall make the
savage a docile tractable being, anxious to work and eager to please; and nothing
harder than to take one's flocks and herds and go out into the desert and carry
theory into practice. As I intend to speak decidedly and openly on the subject, I
may say that I have lived for sixteen years in this colony, and as a rule in outside

country always; that I have been to the settlement of North and West, and have had to hold responsible situations where blacks had to be utilised for want of other labor. I think I may say that I have been as successful in getting as much work as possible out of them as other men; and that my experience pretty well comprises the boundaries of Queensland. I say this merely to show that I am not writing on a strange or unknown subject but one that has been continually under my notice. Furthermore, I am what would be called a "white murderer," for I have had to "disperse" and assist to disperse blacks on several occasions. The blackfellow of Queensland is an embodiment of contradictions: he is a brave man and an abject coward; an angel for good nature, and demon for cruelty; the personification of laziness, and yet capable of untiring perseverance; a riddle, and a hopeless one, so far as guessing him is concerned. A blackfellow learns our vices, and unlearns what savage virtues he possesses, and with fatal facility. . . . The question then arises, What lives are we to sacrifice—black or white? Shirk it as we will, this is the question. So long as we have country to settle, so long as men have to trust their lives to their own right hands, so long shall we come into contact with the natives and aggressions and reprisals shall take place. The article I refer to as yet commits itself to nothing, and, beyond a gird at the policy so long pursued, says nothing tangible to reply to. The great feature of the case it leaves untouched— namely, that if, as the *Queenslander* says, the Native Police are an exterminating force, it is a pity that the work is not more thoroughly and effectually done. Is there room for both of us here? No. Then the sooner the weaker is wiped out the better, as we may save some valuable lives by the process. If the blackfellow is right in murdering white men for invading and taking possession of his country then every white man, woman, and child who sits at home at ease in our towns and townships is a murderer, for if they had the courage of their opinions they would not stop on in a colony built up on bloodshed and rapine. Do they do this? do our black protectors—our philanthropists of today—go out and enquire into the truth of the many stories that are in from the back country, or do they rather sit in the high places and partake in the corn and oil, leaving it to the sinful to go out and bear the heat and burden of the day? I rather think they do the last. Hide it as you will, our policy towards the black is bad, but it is only the game we played all over the world; and it starts with the original occupation of the country and any other policy would be equally outrageous that entailed the taking of the land from the blacks. Say that we make reserves, and put the natives on them— have them guarded and watched, and cared for—is not that just as arbitrary and high handed as shooting them? Would *we* recognise the justice of a superior race coming here, curtailing our boundaries, picking out our best country for their use, and instituting a fresh code of religion, law, morality for our benefit? Would we submit tamely, or prefer a quick and easy death to it? By its very presence and publication here the *Queenslander* recognises the utility, to put it mildly, of dispossessing the blacks, and until it takes its departure to another country, and there preaches its sermon, its voice has a very hypocritical ring about it. We all want to get on here, and we all want to get somebody else to do the work needful; and if there is any dirty work necessary we are the first to cry out against it— when we are in a position to do so. This is the black question, as put forward by the protectors of the poor savage. I know full well that I shall hear of atrocities, of barbarities, and other disgraceful proceedings committed by whites; but that does not touch the point at issue. The unanswerable fact remains that by overrunning this or any other country we expose the natives to the chances of suffering the rigors of guerrilla warfare—always the cruellest and the worst—and, knowing that, we come here and take up our quarters with our eyes open; by our very presence in the land justifying the act of every white ruffian in the outside country. We are all savages; look beneath the thin veneer of our civilisation and we are very identical with the blacks; but we have this one thing not in common—we, the invading race, have a principle hard to define, and harder to name; it is innate in us, and it is the restlessness of culture, if I dare call it so. The higher we get in the educated scale, the more we find this faculty; and if we do not show it in one shape we do in another. We work for posterity, we have a history, and we have been surrounded by its tales and legends since infancy. We look upon the heroes of this history as familiar friends, and in all our breasts there is a whisper that we too by some strange chance may be known to posterity. This brings us here to wrest the lands of a weaker race from their feeble grasp, and build up a country that our children shall inherit; and this feeling is unknown to the native of Australia. He has a short history but it is more a matter of gossip than anything else, and only goes back one generation. He has no thought of the future, because he never knew of anyone being remembered more than a lifetime, therefore he has no interest but to pass through life as easily as possible, and he never seeks to improve land for those who will come after him. This justifies our presence here; this is the only plea we have in justification of it, and once having admitted it we must go the whole length, and say that the sooner we clear the weak useless race away the better. And being a useless race, what does it matter what they suffer any more than the distinguished philanthropist, who writes in his behalf, cares for the wounded half-dead pigeon he tortures at his shooting matches. . . . We are pursuing the same policy in Zululand and Afghanistan, and, I suppose, on a more barbarous scale; the recital of all the atrocities going, of all the shooting and slaying by the Native Police, never alters the fact that, once we are here, we are committed as accessories, and that to prove the fidelity of our opinions we should leave the country. I cannot touch upon anything definitely this time, as the *Queenslander* is not committed as yet to advocating any particular line of policy. I only want to show how we cannot—if we take the position of conquerors—expect anything else but harsh treatment towards the conquered in outlying places where men are not under so much constraint. . . .

Yours &c.,

Brisbane, 4 May.
Never Never.
—*Queenslander*, May 8, 1880.

◆◆◆◆◆

Social Darwinism

Through the latter half of the nineteenth century and up until the end of World War II, racial discourse in Australia, especially in relation to Aborigines, was dominated by Social Darwinist thinking. The term started gaining general currency, especially in the English-speaking world, in the1870s, thanks to the writings of Herbert Spencer, who coined the phrase "survival of the fittest" in his *Principles of Biology* (1864). Deeply influenced by Charles Darwin's *Origins of the Species* (1859), Spencer extended its theories into the areas of anthropology, sociology, and moral philosophy. Nevertheless, similar ideas and treatises about the inevitable extinction of "dark races" and "savages" when brought into contact with "civilization," had already been circulating for decades—and in Australia from the early nineteenth century onward.

Australian colonial society generally saw Aborigines, particularly because they were hunter-gatherers, as "unfit" and in the process of rapidly dying out in the face of competition with the superior Caucasian race. In colonial terms they were a lower form of humanity, a relic of an earlier stage of human evolution, that had been shielded by Australia's isolation; and a "doomed race" because they were unable to adapt to the demands of modernity. On their part, Social Darwinists regarded humanitarian concerns as misplaced because the unbending laws of nature, and hence evolution, could not be transcended. At best humanitarians could "smooth their dying pillow" as a popular catchphrase put it. The doomed-race theory generally operated as a self-fulfilling prophecy as proponents acted in favor of their assumptions and predictions. The accompanying article is typical of Social Darwinist discourse around Aboriginal extinction in Australia during the latter decades of the nineteenth century.

Questions for Consideration

Explain the premises and assumptions on which the Social Darwinist thinking in this article is based. In what ways would Social Darwinist ideas have encouraged violence against Indigenes by settlers in their personal capacities and by the state? How would they have assuaged perpetrator guilt? Do you agree with the judgment that Social Darwinism and settler colonialism were strongly congruent? Explain your answer.

D. MacAllister, "The Australian Aborigines," *Melbourne Review*, 1878[24]

The Australians surely demonstrate, by their evident doom, that races below the level where self-prompted progress exists are unable to adapt themselves to the conditions forced upon them by civilization, and that, therefore, they must perish when brought into contact with it. The same great fact is being exemplified in every land where savagery has been brought into sudden conflict with a high civilization. Even among the less rude of savage peoples, as the Maoris, the Fijians, or some of the American Indians, although they may hold their own, and bravely too, for some time, yet all sink in the struggle, because of their inability to keep step with the forward movement, or to adapt themselves to the new conditions constantly brought to bear upon them by the civilization by which they are surrounded.

As to the future of these people, there is scarcely room for two opinions: the fiat of Fate has gone forth, and nothing seems capable of staying the progress of their extinction. The introduction of civilization and the civilized European has done its work, by introducing to the natives numbers of diseases before unknown to them; these, including alcohol, tobacco, and syphilis, combined with the physical changes effected by the axe, the plough, and the cattle of the white man, in their country and on their climate, tell a sad tale of havoc and death among their continually lessening numbers.

The total extinction, however, of these people, which seems, and is so certain, is not without an important significance to those who are conversant with the theory of "Evolution," or who have kept abreast of "The Drift of Modern Thought," for being admittedly on the very lowest link of the long chain embraced by mankind, we cannot fail to recognize in their extinction a decided widening of the chasm by which mankind is now cut off from its animal progenitors. Not only is the chasm thus widened, but the difficulty of its ever being bridged over becomes greater, and the chances less—and how know we but that the fate which

---

24. D. MacAllister, "The Australian Aborigines," *Melbourne Review* 3 (1878), 153–58.

is now so rapidly overtaking this race, in its competition with the higher white races, may not have removed races of beings still lower in the scale of civilization and humanity than the Australian Aborigines? For rude and unprogressive even as they were, it is possible they may have trampled out of existence races of creatures far their inferiors in the characteristics of humanity, although, perchance, as high proportionally to the civilization before which succumbed, as the Australians now are to that of Europe.

Thus, then, we see a double process at work, by which is being effected the extinction of all traces of the unity of the organic chain. One, the dying out of the lowest races of men; the other, the steady forward movement of those races which are able to hold their own in their internal struggles and against natural changes.

◆◆◆◆◆

Aboriginals Protection and Restriction of the Sale of Opium Act, 1897

This act embodied the Queensland government's policy toward Aborigines after the closure of the frontier. It sought to segregate Aborigines on state-proclaimed reservations and regulate every aspect of their lives in the expectation that those of "full-blood" would die out but that a remnant "mixed blood" group would survive. The latter, if left to their own devices, would be rejected by colonial society and form an underclass prone to vagrancy, criminality, and social disorder because of their racially inferior constitution. The Aboriginal Protection Act was intended to manage the dying out of "full-bloods" and eliminate the "half-caste" problem through a multigenerational program of the separation, and assimilation of "mixed race" children into colonial society. The act was thus predicated on the complete disappearance of the Aboriginal population and later in accord with the White Australia Policy pursued after federation in 1901 through to the end of World War II. In this policy, the Australian government gave British immigrants preference over all others and excluded people of non-European origin, especially Chinese and Pacific Islanders. Section 31 of the Aboriginal Protection Act reprises all of its major provisions, making for a useful summary of the act as a whole.

Questions for Consideration

To what extent does the act support accusations of "ongoing genocide" after the closing of the frontier? Which provisions may be seen as genocidal in intent? Explain why some clauses of the act, which may sound harmless or even beneficial when taken in their plain prose sense, were in reality extremely detrimental to

Aboriginal society when read in context. How are "half-castes" treated differently from "full-bloods" by the act and to what desired effect?

Queensland

ANNO SEXAGESIMO PRIMO VICTORIAE REGIAE[25]

No. [17]
A Bill to make Provision for the better Protection and Care of the Aboriginal and Half-caste Inhabitants of the Colony, and to make more effectual Provision for Restricting the Sale and Distribution of Opium[26]

31. The Governor in Council may from time to time, by Proclamation, make Regulations for all or any of the matters following, that is to say,—

(1) Prescribing the mode of removing—aboriginals to a reserve, and from one reserve to another;

(2) Defining the duties of Protectors and Superintendents, and any other persons employed to carry the provisions of this Act into effect;

(3) Authorising entry upon a reserve by specified persons or classes of persons for specified objects, and defining those objects, and the conditions under which such, persons may visit or remain upon a reserve, and fixing the duration of their stay thereupon, and providing for the revocation of such authority in any case;

(4) Prescribing the mode of distribution and expenditure of moneys granted by Parliament for the benefit of aboriginals;

(5) Apportioning amongst, or for the benefit of, aboriginals or half-castes, living on a reserve, the net produce of the labour of such aboriginals or half-castes;

(6) Providing for the care, custody, and education of the children of aboriginals;

(7) Providing for the transfer of any half-caste child, being an orphan, or deserted by its parents, to an orphanage;

(8) Prescribing the conditions on which any aboriginal or half-caste children may be apprenticed to, or placed in service with, suitable persons;

---

25. In the sixty-first year of [the reign of] Queen Victoria.
26. See https://www.foundingdocs.gov.au/resources/transcripts/qld5_doc_1897.pdf for a copy of the bill.

(9) Providing for the mode of supplying to any half-castes, who may be declared to be entitled thereto, any rations, blankets, or other necessaries, or any medical or other relief or assistance;

(10) Prescribing the conditions on which the Minister may authorise any half-caste to reside upon any reserve, and limiting the period of such residence, and the mode of dismissing or removing any such half-caste from such reserve;

(11) Providing for the control of all aboriginals and half-castes residing upon a reserve, and for the inspection of all aboriginals and half-castes, employed under the provisions of this Act or the Regulations;

(12) Maintaining discipline and good order, upon a reserve;

(13) Imposing the punishment of imprisonment, for any term not exceeding three months, upon any aboriginal or half-caste who is guilty of a breach of the Regulations relating to the maintenance of discipline and good order upon a reserve;

(14) Imposing, and authorising a Protector to inflict summary punishment by way of imprisonment, not exceeding fourteen days, upon aboriginals or half-castes, living upon a reserve or within the District under his charge, who, in the judgment of the Protector, are guilty of any crime, serious misconduct, neglect of duty, gross insubordination, or wilful breach of the Regulations;

(15) Prohibiting any aboriginal rites or customs that, in the opinion of the Minister, are injurious to the welfare of aboriginals living upon a reserve;

(16) Providing for the due carrying out of the provisions of this Act;

(17) Providing for all other matters and things that may be necessary to give effect to this Act.

Chapter 3

"Not a Bad Indian to Be Found": The Annihilation of Native American Societies in California

In the late afternoon of August 28, 1911, at a slaughterhouse about a mile east of the small town of Oroville in north-central California, an emaciated and half-naked Native American man, perhaps fifty years old and five feet, six inches tall, was found cowering under an oak tree within the compound by a worker who knocked him to the ground thinking he was a thief. The starving man had emerged from nearby forested hills recently ravaged by fire that had destroyed his main sources of food. The intruder did not resist when detained by the workers or when taken into custody by the local sheriff. Thanks to translator Sam Batwi, an octogenarian and one of the last surviving Yana speakers brought in a few days later from Redding, about one hundred miles north, it was established that the captive was apparently the last surviving member of the Yahi tribe, the southernmost of the four subsections of the Yana peoples, whose territory had lain on the east bank along the upper reaches of the Sacramento River.

The detention of this supposedly "last wild Indian in North America," as he came to be commonly described, caused an immediate sensation throughout the nation, and caught the attention of prominent anthropologist Alfred Kroeber at the University of California, Berkeley. With the permission of the Bureau of Indian Affairs, Kroeber took the detainee to San Francisco, where he housed him in his museum and employed him as a janitor to make it more convenient to study his language and culture. Here the man known as Ishi—an anglicized version of the Yahi word for "man"[1]—became the subject of intensive anthropological study by Kroeber and other anthropologists, and an object of curiosity to the general public, who visited the museum mainly on Sundays. Thousands came to watch this genial and obliging live museum exhibit enact elements of his aboriginal culture, such as crafting arrowheads and spearpoints, making fire using sticks, building brush shelters, posing in Native American dress, and performing traditional chants. Often ill because of his lack of immunity to communicable diseases common in the settler community, and to which he was irresponsibly exposed by his handlers, Ishi died of tuberculosis on March 25, 1916.

---

1. His real name never became known as his cultural beliefs forbade him from uttering it unless formally introduced by another Yahi. Nor was he allowed to speak of the dead.

Ishi was a survivor of the genocide of the Yana peoples, who are estimated to have numbered about 3,000, and of which the Yahi constituted little more than 400 prior to the American conquest of California. With their territory located largely in the gap between the northern and central goldfields, and with the main wagon trail through which gold-seekers poured into California bisecting their homeland, the Yana were among the first to experience the vortex of violence and epidemic disease unleashed by the California gold rush from the late 1840s onward. For about two decades, the Yana resisted homesteader invasion of their land and, when starving, raided settler stock

Ishi on his first day in captivity.

to replace depleted game and destroyed food sources. Vigilante groups of settlers struck back with murder and massacre, frequently of innocent people. From 1856, the dynamic behind settler brutality started shifting from summary shootings and episodic punitive assaults to larger, more systematic search-and-destroy sorties. By 1858, settler violence had escalated into a concerted campaign of extermination as continued raids by the desperate Yana excited settler fears for their safety and property. Outnumbered, outgunned, displaced from traditional food sources, and vulnerable to infectious disease, Yana numbers rapidly thinned through the 1850s and 1860s. With food scarce and being restricted to inhospitable mountainous areas, many died of starvation, especially in winter. Others were rounded up and banished to faraway reservations, where they were still not safe from settler predation. Rampant disease, malnutrition, and institutionalized neglect of their most basic needs ensured a high mortality rate on reservations.

Ishi was born around 1862, a terrifying time for the Yana, who faced further intensification of this cataclysmic violence after a wagon driver and three children were killed by Indians near Antelope Creek. In September and October 1864, the exterminatory campaign against the Yana heightened into a frenzy when two large vigilante gangs went on a rampage in response to the killing of two white women and the serious injury of four children left for dead. The vigilante bands roamed the countryside killing all Native Americans they encountered, including "friendly Indians" and even those in the employ of fellow settlers. This paroxysm of violence reached its climax in September 1864 with the massacre by a large posse of vigilantes of an estimated 300 Yana who had gathered near Oak Run for a ceremonial dance. After this, sporadic killing of Yana, most of whom took to hiding in secluded uplands, continued for some years. The last significant massacre of Yana occurred in April 1871 when as many as thirty were killed by a vigilante band when trapped in Kingsley Cave along the mid-waters of the Mill Creek. An incident during this massacre revealed the genocidal intent of vigilante gangs hunting Yana. Norman Kingsley, a rancher who was part of that vigilante squad and after whom the cave would subsequently be named, could not bear to shoot the Yana children with his high-powered Spencer rifle because: "It tore them up so bad." He shot them with his Smith & Wesson revolver instead.[2]

It is thought that Ishi, then a toddler of about three, and a few family members were among the survivors of the Three Knolls Massacre of August 1865, in which the greater part of their band known to settlers as the Mill Creeks, were killed. Survivors went to ground in remote, rugged terrain and lived off a combination of hunter-gathering and pilfering from nearby homesteads over the next four and a half decades. Theirs was a wretched existence of trauma, constant danger, and hunger. There were about half a dozen fleeting sightings of this dwindling group of "wild Indians" reported over the years. In 1908, surveyors from the Oro Power and Light Company chanced upon their hideout shielded by cliffs and dense undergrowth in an isolated part of Deer Creek Canyon known as Grizzly Bear's Hiding Place. There were only four members of the fugitive party left—Ishi, his mother, an uncle, and a middle-aged woman who could have been his sister, wife, or cousin. Three fled leaving the decrepit mother behind. She was largely ignored by the surveyors, who ransacked the camp. By the time Ishi was detained three years later, he was the sole surviving member of this group. His mother and uncle had died, and the younger woman had very recently drowned in the nearby Feather River. Ishi's hair was still cropped short in mourning when he was taken captive.

Ishi's story and the genocidal destruction of the Yana are emblematic of the experience of the Indigenous peoples of California under United States rule. That Ishi was unquestioningly accepted as the last of his tribe and the last surviving

---

2. Thomas Waterman, "The Yana Indians," *University of California Publications in American Archaeology and Ethnology* 13, no. 2 (1918): 59.

California.

"wild Indian" of North America is testimony to the degree of social destruction suffered by the Native American societies of the continent. Post-1848 California presents us with one of the more dramatic demographic collapses of an aboriginal population in colonial history. The rapid demographic swamping of Native Americans with the onset of the gold rush and an unusual degree of lawlessness, coupled with intense Indian hating, a feverish desire to strike it rich quickly, and the pandering of both state and federal governments to settler interests facilitated genocidal violence against Indigenes.

Surveying their handiwork after the dawn massacre of a Native American camp by a vigilante death squad out on a two-month-long hunt for Yana in 1859, one of the perpetrators, a young and enthusiastic Indian killer, Robert Allen Anderson, in his memoirs half a century later commented: "There was not a bad Indian to be found, but forty good ones lay scattered about."[3] This attempt at wit and the impunity with which it was made underscores the exterminatory framing that the settler establishment had adopted toward Indigenous society in general.

The Indigenous Peoples of California

California, which is the third largest state in the United States and covers nearly 164,000 square miles, has a wide variety of ecological zones, much of which was well-watered and rich in plant and animal life in precolonial times, providing Indigenes with a relatively secure existence. Nearly all aboriginal Californians were hunter-gatherers who had inhabited the region for at least 12,000 years. Only along the fertile flood plain of the Colorado River in the far south did some peoples raise a few crops to supplement their hunter-gathering economies. Foraging communities in California lived relatively prosperous lives and tended to be more sedentary than most hunter-gatherers, given the natural bounty of much of the land. This was particularly true of the well-watered, winter-rainfall areas of central California with its Mediterranean-type climate, while the extensive forested regions in the north and along the coast were also conducive to human habitation. It was only the desert landscapes of the southeast and the mountainous areas that were barely habitable. Well over half the population was thus concentrated in the fecund heartland of California with its mild climate and natural abundance.

Prior to the gold rush, enormous herds of antelope, deer, and elk grazed California's extensive grasslands, notably in the Central Valley, providing hunters

---

3. Robert Allen Anderson, *Fighting the Mill Creeks: Being a Personal Account of Campaigns against Indians of the Northern Sierras* (Chico: The Chico Record Press, 1909), 24.

with abundant prey, as did a variety of smaller game animals, including birds and rabbits. Rivers seasonally teemed with fish, especially salmon and steelhead trout, while coastal areas and estuaries were rich sources of fish, shellfish, and sea mammals. Extensive groves of oak trees supplied communities with abundant acorns, a staple of the Californian Indian diet. Grass seeds, fruit, berries, nuts, insects, and tubers were also gathered. Additionally, Indigenous communities managed the ecology in a variety of ways to improve yields, and like their Australian counterparts, practiced fire-stick farming. Controlled, low-intensity burning of undergrowth promoted the spread of grassland, which attracted and supported herbivore populations. It also prevented large, potentially catastrophic fires. Precolonial California was thus among the most densely settled regions of the continent north of Mexico, with an estimated population of about 320,000.

Indigenous Californians were culturally diverse, speaking an exceptional variety of languages. As many as one hundred languages, grouped by linguists into five families, were spoken in the territory. Anthropologists have identified over sixty sociolinguistic groups, usually referred to as tribes, each of which can be subdivided into smaller cultural segments as with the Yana, which have been classified into Northern, Central, Southern, and Yahi subsections. Each of these subtribes consisted of several bands, or village-based communities. Clusters of villages covering perhaps 200 to 300 square miles of territory usually operated as politically independent entities. Chiefs, dependent on the trust of the communities they led, had little personal power or wealth. The extended family functioned as an economic unit, with men doing the hunting and women most of the foraging. These were thus highly egalitarian societies, whose communal lives revolved around hunting, feasting, ceremonial dance, and spiritual rituals. They were loosely bound into larger social units connected through these cultural ties, as well as systems of exchange and reciprocity, diplomacy, competition, and sometimes, conflict.

Before the Gold Rush

California was in an isolated part of the world and not a very attractive prospect from a Western colonial perspective until the mid-nineteenth century when substantial deposits of gold were discovered along the western slopes of the Sierra Nevada foothills. Permanent European occupation came only in 1769, when Spain started settling the area, known as Alta (Upper) California, to strengthen its ill-defined claim to what is today the southwestern United States. Spanish rule in California came to an end when Mexico won independence in 1821 after a decade-long armed struggle. California nonetheless remained a neglected economic backwater on Mexico's northwestern fringes. The next major development in California's political evolution came when Mexico was forced to cede a large tract of over 500,000 square miles of territory that included California to the United States with the signing of the Treaty of Guadalupe Hidalgo on February 2, 1848. This treaty officially ended the Mexican–American War (1846–1848) precipitated by disputed Texan territory. The United States had, however, already conquered California by mid-January 1847.

Spanish colonization of California was the culmination of three and a half centuries of colonial expansion that started with the fifteenth-century Canarian enterprise. It then swept through the Caribbean, and into Central and South America, unleashing genocidal havoc on many Indigenous societies. California, however, did not experience the intense violence and exploitation that characterized Spanish colonization of much of the rest of Spanish America. The isolation of California meant that by the start of the gold rush, there were no more than 10,000 to 12,000 non-Indians, mainly Spanish speakers, in the entire region. Spanish colonization nonetheless brought catastrophic change for Native American communities along the southern two-thirds of its coastal area where the mission presence was concentrated.

Starting in the far south with the establishment of a fort and a mission station at San Diego in mid-1769, the Franciscan Order, with the blessing and some financial aid from the Spanish crown, set up twenty-one mission stations along the coast as far north as San Francisco Bay over the next half century. These missions formed the foundation of the Spanish presence in California, as there were few settlers and only a small number of soldiers to support their evangelical enterprise. In addition to cementing Spanish claims to the territory, the main objective of the missionaries was to convert the Indians to Christianity and assimilate them to Hispanic culture. This required Native American communities to be concentrated in and around mission stations so that they could be instructed, disciplined, and their lives regulated. Since few Indians were open to missionary blandishments, this civilizing mission was implemented largely through force and aided by the desperation of communities wracked by communicable diseases introduced by Europeans. Each mission station had soldiers garrisoned within, or close by, to help with forced recruitment, discipline, and punishment of recalcitrants, as well as the capture of runaways. Priests generally claimed absolute authority over their charges whom most infantilized as racial inferiors incapable of reason. These proselytizers were for the most part exacting in their demands and cruel in the administration of corporal and other punishments.

In the half century of the missionary period, tens of thousands of people and entire coastal communities were uprooted and relocated to mission stations, where they were forcibly inducted into new lifeways, taught new skills, subjected to forced labor, and housed in crowded, unsanitary conditions. Sexual violence, mainly by soldiers against Indigenous women, was rife resulting in widespread venereal diseases that often proved fatal, as Native Americans lacked immunity to them. Exposed also to a range of other deadly pathogens and forced to subsist on meager diets, Indians at mission stations died in large numbers. Depression, cultural suppression, and constraints on biological reproduction, mainly through separation of the sexes and harsh living conditions, all contributed to the destruction of communities that fell under the jurisdiction of the missions.

Mexican independence in 1821 and the subsequent secularization of the missions did not benefit their inhabitants much. Having been taught economically useful skills and inculcated with new work habits, mission Indians were of considerable value to the several hundred Mexican ranch owners who populated the area by this time. Although nominally free, thousands of Native Americans, through a combination of economic pressure, debt bondage, and violence, were coerced to labor on ranches where they worked for little more than food, clothing, and shelter—a system of peonage operative in the rest of Mexico. It was especially in the 1830s and 1840s that waves of epidemic disease, most notably smallpox and malaria, swept through Californian Indian society killing tens of thousands of people.

The upshot of eight decades of Hispanic colonial rule was that the Native American population of California was more than halved to about 150,000 on the eve of American conquest. Many coastal peoples suffered far greater losses than this average, and a strong argument for genocide of such communities under Hispanic rule can be made. As ruinous as Hispanic colonialism was to Indigenous California, American conquest was to accelerate its decline much more precipitously. The basic reason for this difference lies in Albert Hurtado's succinct contrast between the Hispanic custom in which "the native people were assimilated and exploited" and the Euro-American tradition in which "the only good Indians were dead Indians."[4]

Although the gold rush, which started gaining momentum in the latter half of 1848, was the main catalyst for the genocide of California Indians, indiscriminate violence by Euro-Americans against Indigenous people preceded it by two and a half years. Euro-Americans had started coming to California from as early as 1818 and formed a significant minority by the mid-nineteenth century. Once American military operations in California got underway in the second quarter of 1846, the Euro-American community began asserting itself in anticipation

---

4. Albert Hurtado, *Indian Survival on the California Frontier* (New Haven: Yale University Press, 1988), 12.

of annexation by the United States, and Native Americans became subject to more intense forms of violence by them. The invading US Army itself perpetrated several massacres and smaller-scale killings of Indians, even though some were recruited as foot soldiers against their Mexican overlords. There was also a notable increase in sexual abuse, slave raiding, dehumanizing treatment, demonization, collective punishment, and other depredations by Euro-American civilians toward Indians during this period. Already on the eve of the gold rush, a few Euro-American settler voices started calling for the extermination of Indigenous peoples.

The decade prior to the gold rush was a momentous one in the life of the United States. New ideas of racial science gained popularity through the 1840s, as did the associated doctrine of Manifest Destiny, the belief that the United States as a matter of divine providence was destined to expand across the North American continent "from sea to shining sea." Between 1845 and 1848, the United States exploded in size by more than half with the annexation of Texas, the acquisition of the Oregon Territory from Britain, and the Mexican cession, extending now all the way to the Pacific coast. This rapid ascendancy helped fuel American racial arrogance, above all toward Native Americans.

The Gold Rush and the Onset of Genocidal Collisions, 1848–1850

California's isolation changed dramatically after 1848 when gold was discovered in northern California and the greatest gold rush in history ensued. While the immigrant population doubled in 1848 with the arrival of 10,000 to 12,000 gold-seekers, in 1849 alone another 70,000 immigrants—the famed '49ers—streamed into California, further tripling the non-Indian population. By late 1852, Governor John McDougal estimated the newcomer population to have more than tripled again to over 300,000. Newcomers consisted mainly of Euro-Americans, but also of people from around the world, especially from Latin America, Europe, and China. The gold rush changed California rapidly and had far-reaching consequences for its Indigenous peoples. The environmental and social impacts characteristic of gold rushes observable elsewhere, notably Queensland—of Indigenous food sources being destroyed, water polluted, native peoples displaced, murdered, and massacred—all occurred in California, except on a much larger scale and with greater ferocity.

Although sawmill operator James Marshall struck gold at Sutter's Mill at Coloma on January 24, 1848, it was only by July that a large part of the internal settler population had been drawn to the central goldfields. Several thousand

Indians participated in the early stampede, mainly as forced laborers or slaves, some as employees, and a few as independent miners. The first Indigenous peoples to be affected by the rush were those on whose land gold was found, such as the Miwok, Nisenan, Wintu, Konkow, and Maidu.

An early impact of the gold rush was a large increase in slave raiding in many parts of California to obtain mine workers and also to fill labor gaps caused by the exodus to the goldfields that had left other parts of the economy severely hobbled. Despite this, much of 1848 was relatively peaceful as Indigenous communities were as yet more inclined to accommodate early gold-seekers than resist their encroachment violently. The initial crop of prospectors was also less inclined to resort to excessive force as they were dependent on Indian labor and were substantially outnumbered by them on the goldfields, most of which were still located beyond the settled areas. Besides, many early gold-seekers had pre-existing relationships with Indigenes and the negative effects of mining on native peoples were as yet limited.

This changed as throngs of outsiders started arriving, profoundly transforming interactions with Indigenous people in the mining areas. Most came in tented wagons via the northern Oregon-California Trail or the less popular southern Santa Fe Trail, while some braved an arduous three- to six-month sea journey around stormy Cape Horn. Most overlanders, who traveled in dire, though exaggerated, fear of Indian attack along the way, came heavily armed, brimming with Indian-hatred, and primed to respond with violence to threats, real or imaginary. Frontier mining camps, by their very nature, were lawless environments, given the lack of institutional regulation, and populated as they were by single, heavily armed, younger men given to excessive alcohol consumption. Newcomers, moreover, tended to see Native Americans as dispensable racial inferiors and obstacles in their path to wealth. Few settlers paid any attention to Indian ownership or occupation of land, believing that they had a just claim to it by right of conquest.

It was in particular Oregonians, the first outsiders to arrive in large numbers from September 1848 onward, who changed the dynamic of interaction between settler and Indigene in the goldfields. They were given to intense hatred of Native Americans because of ongoing fierce conflict in Oregon. With their arrival, attacks on Indians in the mining areas increased in frequency, scale, and intensity, which encouraged other colonists to violence. Besides wanting to displace Indigenes, settler bloodletting during the early part of the gold rush was increasingly motivated by revenge, as Native Americans responded to gold-seeker incursions with force. Not only were the fires of vengeance and hatred stoked, but more importantly, dislocated Indigenous societies were left even more dependent on raiding for survival. Thus, what might have started out as small skirmishes tended to escalate, with settlers increasingly resorting to vigilante action by armed, mounted posses prone to indiscriminate killing, collective punishment, and locally exterminatory sorties. Though this earlier conflict in the gold mining districts was unorganized beyond the level of the vigilante gang and episodic in nature, localized eradication of Native American society was the inevitable result, given the huge asymmetry in firepower, and the demographic balance swiftly swinging in favor of settlers. In a matter of a few years, immigrant intolerance and the wholesale killing of Indians resulted in the destruction of Indigenous societies in the goldfields themselves.

Foundations of the Genocidal Settler State, 1846–1853

The institutional structure and legal framework that California developed under US jurisdiction from as early as 1846 onward disadvantaged Native Americans severely, accelerated their dispossession, and facilitated violence against them by settlers, the military, and the territorial, and later state, government itself. Starting with the proclamation of martial law on September 15, 1846, the US military administration entrenched the Mexican system of Indian servitude that served as the springboard for tyranny and mass violence. In November 1847, the military administration instituted a pass system to tighten control of Native Americans, especially the movement of laborers and to criminalize as vagrants those not already trapped in the colonial economy. The pass system, imposed only on Indians, marked them as the lowest category of racial inferiors.

Two years later, in November 1849, California voters ratified the state's new constitution and elected representatives as part of its move to civilian government. By mid-December, California's legislature held its inaugural session under its first civilian governor, Peter H. Burnett. In September 1850, California was admitted to the Union as its thirty-first state. The settler establishment was in full control of the state of California, which proved to be an unmitigated disaster for Indigenes, as federal officials tended to abdicate responsibility for the administration of Native Americans to state officials who supported settler interests. The state in turn both failed to protect Indigenes from settler abuse and became a major perpetrator of mass violence against them.

Already in April 1850, the new legislature passed the ironically named Act for the Government and Protection of Indians. This act was the main instrument that defined the legal status of Native Americans in California and made them vulnerable to violence and extreme forms of exploitation. Importantly, it prohibited the conviction of any "white man" on the testimony of Indians, and together with later legislation, severely restricted their participation in legal and political processes, essentially placing them on the same level as mental incompetents and felons. And by legalizing the corporal punishment of Indians, the act helped dehumanize them. This extremely pernicious piece of legislation encouraged the murder, abduction, enslavement, sexual exploitation, and perpetration of other social harms against Native Americans.

Passed in the context of an extreme shortage of labor, the act sought to hone the existing system of Indian servitude to take full advantage of this pool of ultra-exploitable workers. To this end, it instituted a form of debt peonage through two convict leasing clauses. The first allowed employers to pay the fines of Indian convicts and then have them work for up to four months to pay off the debt. The second specified that convicts could be put up for auction to the highest bidder for whom they would work for a stated period without pay. The act ensured a constant supply of convict laborers by empowering settlers to have Indians arrested for trivial and easily trumped-up charges such as loitering, begging, vagrancy, drunkenness, and disorderly behavior. Needless to say, many employers plied workers with cheap alcohol to keep them in a state of dependence. A combination of force and alcoholic addiction recycled workers, once snared, through the system repeatedly. Prisons thus operated as clearing houses for forced Indian labor as thousands were processed through the revolving door machinery created by the Protection Act. Backbreaking labor, execrable living conditions, physical abuse, alcohol dependence, malnutrition, and disease ensured rapid attrition of this workforce.

An extremely deleterious effect of the act was that it allowed the adoption of Indian children by settlers with the consent of parents or "friends," and for them to be held as apprentices without pay until the ages of fifteen for females and eighteen for males. This not only encouraged the abduction of Indian children, but also an effective slave trade in them. An 1860 amendment extended these ages to twenty-five and thirty respectively, initiating a slave-raiding boom directed preeminently at Native American children and younger women. It was not uncommon for Indian parents to be murdered by traffickers so that their children could be sold into slavery with the killers posing as "friends" taking care of "orphans." The children were generally held in bondage well beyond the stipulated ages, as their precise birthdates were not known. Many remained in servitude for life, as they became dependent on masters and were essentially helpless against their threats and use of force. The conditions of the act were ameliorated in 1863, partly as its worst excesses were untenable in the wake of the Emancipation Proclamation that came into force on January 1 of that year. By this time, the declining Indian population and a growing reserve of cheap immigrant laborers, largely from China and Latin America, made them more dispensable. Clandestine kidnapping, trafficking, and forced labor of Indians, especially younger women and children, nonetheless continued after this.

In addition to denying Indians basic human or citizenship rights, refusing them the vote, or participation in political processes, the California Legislature also set up machinery for the physical annihilation of Native Americans by passing laws enabling citizens to form volunteer militia companies. The state government signaled its sanctioning of Indian killing by both funding volunteer companies and not putting in place strict controls over their activities. This institution was to prove an extremely lethal weapon in the settler drive to dispossess and annihilate Indigenous societies.

The way in which California's Indians lost title to their land played an important role in their exposure to settler violence. In an attempt to legitimate the expropriation of Native American land in terms of existing US policy, Congress set up a three-man Special Commission in March 1851 to negotiate treaties with tribal leaders for their cession of Indian land to the federal government in return for establishing Indian reservations together with promises of food, clothing, tools, and protection from settlers. Congress saw this as necessary to legalize the expropriation of Indigenous land and to protect Indians from extermination. Between March 1851 and January 1852, the commission signed eighteen treaties with representatives from 139 Indian groups to create eighteen reservations totaling an area of 11,700 square miles covering about 7.5 percent of California. When the terms of the treaties became known in February 1852, there was a huge outcry of opposition from the settler establishment, not least from within the California Assembly. Many immigrants had already settled within the proposed reservations, others coveted parts of this land, and most felt that the treaties were far too generous. Concerted political lobbying by California politicians, notably its senators, and the fact that the commissioners had exceeded their budget fourteen-fold, resulted in all eighteen treaties being repudiated by the US Senate in July 1852. Instead, Congress established five small military reservations on federally owned land totaling no more than 195 square miles, a mere 1.6 percent of what had been proposed by the Special Commission.

The Senate's failure to ratify these treaties, which were bungled by the commissioners but signed in good faith by Native American leaders, left these native communities more vulnerable to exploitation, persecution, and settler aggression than ever before. This was especially the case with those Indians who had moved out of ancestral lands onto provisional reservations in the hope of state protection and the chance of starting a new and more secure life. They were unable to return to their traditional lands, which had in the meantime been appropriated by settlers, and once again found themselves violently displaced by newcomers. After the treaties were revoked, many Native Americans were forced onto marginal land, others into servitude with immigrants, and yet others into the temporary and very dangerous strategy of living off a combination of foraging on vacant land and stock theft. Because titles to military reservation land were not explicitly awarded to Indians, jurisdiction over the land remained uncertain. California Indians were thus not regarded as wards of the US government as in other states. That the army on these grounds refused reservation residents full protection left them utterly exposed to settler violence and exploitation.

Given the expeditiousness with which the California Legislature implemented a regimen that enabled the extreme exploitation and wanton killing of Native Americans, it is not surprising that Governor Burnett, could in his second annual message to the legislature on January 6, 1851 maintain: "That a war of extermination will continue to be waged between the races until the Indian race becomes extinct must be expected." While Burnett put the blame for this violence on Native Americans' inability to adapt to modernity, and their extinction to be "beyond the power or wisdom of man to avert," it was under his governorship and with his full support that much of the machinery for genocide was put in place.[5] By this time, it was clear that the destruction of Indigenous societies throughout California was becoming a state-sanctioned project. California was a democracy for settlers but a vicious tyranny of the majority for Native Americans.

Demographic Collapse

At the start of the gold rush, Indigenes outnumbered settlers by more than 10-to-1; within a generation settlers outnumbered Indians by a ratio approaching 40-to-1. That the mining areas were also the areas of highest concentration of Native Americans ensured that the gold rush had an immediate and acute demographic impact as Indians started dying in growing numbers and newcomers flooded the territory. Squeezed between exceptionally high mortality and plummeting fertility rates, California's Indian population suffered a catastrophic demographic collapse of about 80 percent in the quarter century following the discovery of gold, while the immigrant community catapulted to about 600,000. Even more dramatic was the estimated 65 percent plunge in the Native American population that occurred by the mid-1860s.

Central to this crash was the direct killing of Native Americans by settlers and colonial forces and the confiscation of their land. Much of it was also due to other lethal effects of conflict and conquest, such as starvation, exposure, exhaustion from overwork, and greater vulnerability to disease. Social destruction of

---

5. Peter H. Burnett, "State of the State Address, January 6, 1851," The Governors' Gallery, California State Library, accessed February 17, 2020, https://governors.library.ca.gov/addresses/s_01-Burnett2.html.

Indigenous societies also came from nonlethal practices, such as people being taken captive, child removal, psychological trauma, cultural suppression, sexual exploitation, outrageously unjust levels of incarceration, and a variety of hindrances to biological reproduction, including separation of the sexes, venereal disease, unrelenting stress, and harsh living conditions.

While concerted mass violence against Native Americans was initiated early on during the gold rush, it did not take long for the carnage to radiate outward from the mining areas, become overtly genocidal, and engulf nearly all of the state. Already by November 1852, the contours of the California catastrophe were apparent to the state's Indian Affairs superintendent, Edward Beale. In a heartfelt but futile appeal for federal funding to alleviate the plight of Native Americans, he observed that Indians were being:

> Driven from their fishing and hunting grounds, hunted themselves like wild beasts, lassoed, and torn from homes made miserable by want, and forced into slavery, the wretched remnant which escapes starvation on the one hand, and the relentless Americans on the other, only do so to rot and die of a loathsome disease. . . . I know that they starve; I know that they perish by the hundreds; I know that they are fading away with a startling and shocking rapidity, but I cannot help them. It is a crying sin that our government, so wealthy and so powerful, should shut its eyes to the miserable fate of these rightful owners of the soil.[6]

Pivotal to the swift spread of violence was that as the immigrant population grew, so demand not just for land but also for forced Indian labor increased. The rapidly growing immigrant community encouraged local food production and the provision of a range of goods and services that helped disperse the population, settler landholding, and conflict beyond the prospecting areas. Importantly, the inevitable failure of the mining bonanza to provide the burgeoning gold-seeking population with easy riches—or for most, even an acceptable living—pushed disappointed immigrants into other forms of economic activity, which almost inescapably resulted in the dispossession of Native Americans. There was from the early 1850s already an accelerated move of prospectors into pastoralism and crop growing, as well as into logging, fishing, and hunting. And during the 1850s and 1860s, desperados known as "Indian hunters" made a living from violence toward Native Americans, such as trafficking Indian captives, bounty hunting, or joining militia expeditions.

---

6. Cited in Brendan Lindsay, *Murder State: California's Native American Genocide, 1846–1873* (Lincoln: University of Nebraska Press, 2012), 279.

Ways of Killing

The precipitous decline in California's Indigenous population was in substantial part due to the direct killing of Native Americans on the California frontier and came from ongoing homicides, a multitude of massacres, and only a handful of small encounters that could be described as battles. Homicides were common on the California frontier, ranging from settlers shooting Indigenes on sight through to fatal beatings of workers; from colonists wanting to rob Indians, especially of gold, or to clear them from ancestral land through to summary justice for minor, sometimes imagined, offenses; or for reasons of revenge and collective punishment through to bounty hunting and wanton cruelty. As damaging as these homicides were, and as much as they reflected the genocidal ethos within the California settler establishment, it was the organized mass killing of Native Americans that was responsible for most of the casualties.

On the California frontier, organized killing of Native Americans was perpetrated through three institutions whose principal function was the infliction of mass violence—first, the US Army; second, volunteer militia companies that were constituted and funded by the California Legislature to suppress resistance by Indigenes; and third, vigilante gangs that were settler frontier associations for committing violence against enemies, mainly aboriginal peoples. The three complemented one another and routinely collaborated in a variety of ways to achieve their common goals of securing settler control of the land, suppressing Indigenous resistance, and ultimately destroying Indigenous society.

Vigilante Gangs

The vigilante band was a common feature of frontier settler communities globally, as it was their most obvious means for collective offense and defense given the absence or weakness of the colonial state. Such bands were organized to clear land of Indigenes, quell native resistance, launch preemptive strikes, engage in hot pursuit of raiders and attackers, exact revenge, organize forays to acquire forced labor, and support formal military forces on the frontier. Frontier vigilante gangs, though temporary and varied in their individual manifestations, and despite being extralegal associations, were nonetheless institutions, albeit informal ones. They were communal organizations formed with clear social purposes and recognized norms that regulated the behavior of members. As such, they constituted an integral part of their respective frontier cultures. In California their activities were aided and abetted by the state in many ways, ranging from arming and provisioning them to providing institutional support, such as implementing a legal regime and criminal justice system that gave perpetrators effective immunity from prosecution.

Vigilante action was evident on the California frontier from the very early days of American rule, but became particularly salient once the gold rush got underway, as demonstrated by the attacks carried out by newly arrived immigrants from 1849 onward. A posse could be called together for a single act of mass violence or could operate sporadically or concertedly for weeks, or even months, on end. They were mounted, well-armed, and although prone to disorderly behavior, were generally disciplined and ruthless in their dealings with Native Americans. The asymmetry of force, bolstered by the 1854 Act to Prevent the Sale of Firearms and Ammunition to Indians, allowed small groups of settlers to massacre much larger numbers of Indians, a frequent occurrence on the frontier. Though vigilante parties tended to be smaller, more localized in their focus, and more sporadic in their operation than formally constituted militia companies, some were sizeable, well-equipped, and every bit as lethal. Vigilantes might call on formal forces for help, operate in tandem with militia or the army, or sometimes merge with one or the other to create a single attacking force.

Vigilante assaults were more marked in newly settled areas, where the state presence was minimal, Indian resistance considerable, and settlers motivated by the primal emotions of fear and greed. Settler avengers, especially from the early 1850s onward, went on killing sprees, often at the slightest provocation—sometimes nothing more than a missing or stolen head of stock. Such easy resort to bloodshed by civilians was symptomatic of the genocidal outlook of settlers on the California frontier. Systematic violence of this sort very quickly depleted hunter-gatherer populations in newly penetrated areas and happened with regularity as American settlement spread across California. Repeatedly in the latter phases of campaigns against targeted groups or the clearance of particular areas, vigilante bands acted as mobile death squads seeking out and exterminating remaining bands of Indigenous survivors. Their preferred method, as in Queensland, was to encircle sleeping encampments through the night and launch surprise attacks by dawn light. In both cases, this tactic was an obvious response to the targeted communities being scattered in small groups across extensive landscapes.

In 1862, in the wake of extensive army and vigilante bloodletting in Mattole Valley, Lieutenant Charles Hubbard noted, regarding the region's colonists: "Cold-blooded Indian killing [is] considered honorable, [even the] murdering [of] squaws and children,"[7] His observation applied to frontier communities in general. There were, in effect, no restraints on vigilante rampages against Native Americans, and perpetrators could be fairly certain they would face no consequences for their actions. Vigilante activity was commonly incentivized by some

---

7. Quoted in Benjamin Madley, *An American Genocide: The United States and the California Indian Catastrophe* (New Haven: Yale University Press, 2016), 302.

PROTECTING THE SETTLERS.

"Protecting the settlers." This drawing of a dawn-light settler ambush of a Native American village in California with the caption, "Protecting the settlers," appeared in *Harper's New Monthly Magazine* of August 1861. It served as an illustration to an article by John Ross Browne, an Irish-born American traveler, writer, and government agent. Browne was critical of settler vigilante action.

communities offering scalp bounties. Another inducement was that vigilante groups could be formalized into, or be amalgamated with, militia companies and be paid for their "work." The Eel River Rangers, a formally constituted militia unit led by notorious Indian-killer Walter Jarboe, started out as a vigilante gang sponsored by judge, and later California attorney general, Serranus Hastings, the largest landholder in the Round Valley region of Mendocino County. The ubiquity of vigilante action through to the mid-1860s made it a major contributor to the genocide.

State Militias

Given that militias were an integral part of American colonial society dating back to the early seventeenth century and were regularly deployed against Native Americans, it is no surprise that the California Legislature set up a militia system that played an extensive role in frontier conflict. In April 1850, the California Assembly passed legislation sanctioning the formation of volunteer militia companies by citizens generally referred to as "rangers." After following prescribed procedures relating to the naming, enlistment, election of officers, adoption of a uniform, and other stipulations, they could petition the governor for arms and provisions. The opportunities offered by the militia laws were warmly welcomed by the settler establishment. The first militia company was set up a month after the passage of the act with operations starting in May 1850 and directed at the Nisenan people. There was no shortage of recruits, as the provision of food and equipment, the promise of payment, and opportunities for looting were attractive to many younger men who were disappointed by their dwindling prospects in the goldfields. Federal land bounty laws of 1850, 1852, and 1856, which promised parcels of land of up to 160 acres to militiamen or volunteers who served in a state militia for at least fourteen days, were another important inducement. In little more than a decade, to the end of 1861, twenty-one major volunteer militia expeditions were organized involving over 3,400 militiamen. They resulted in the death of over 1,500 Indians and cost the state of California in excess of $1.3 million.

There were few restraints on militia companies when it came to killing Native Americans, and members had effective immunity, as they were protected by law. Even if they ran afoul of the law, the unwillingness of the state to prosecute provided them with peace of mind. Militias, especially the earlier expeditions, were prone to inefficiency and corruption, particularly as a result of collusion between commanders and suppliers. From the latter half of 1852 onward, however, militia companies were generally smaller, more efficient, and focused on Indian killing. Several ranger units acted in local exterminatory fashion, combing the countryside for Indians to kill. Some started out as vigilante outfits, or absorbed such parties into their ranks. They often cooperated with vigilantes, and greatly encouraged their unlawful activities. Militias received extensive support from the army in the form of arms and other supplies, both directly and through donations to the state arsenal. There were several joint operations with the army, but from early 1862, the militia system was superseded by the army.

US Army

The US Army played a pivotal role in the genocide of California's Native Americans. Firstly, during martial rule between 1846 and the end of 1849, it was the military administration that laid the groundwork upon which the civilian government built the genocidal settler state by reinforcing Indigenous peoples' condition of rightlessness, their segregation, and vulnerability to extreme exploitation and violence. Secondly, the army participated directly in the slaughter of Indians, committing numerous massacres, including most of the larger ones. It regularly collaborated with militias and vigilante groups, helped arm and provision them, and at crucial points escalated the tempo of killing. Important also was what it failed to do, namely, use the considerable force at its disposal to protect Indians or deter perpetrators.

The army got in on the action early on. Indeed, a full five weeks before the United States declared war on Mexico on May 13, 1846, John C. Frémont, a major in the US Army who spearheaded its campaign in California and had already traversed the northern parts of the state with a formidable force from September 1845, perpetrated a massacre of several hundred Wintu people gathered along the Sacramento River to harvest salmon during their biannual run. The attack on this peaceful gathering, which included many women and children, was triggered by the unfounded fears of nearby American settlers that these Wintu were congregating to attack them. This gratuitous act of bloodletting and other killings of Indians by American forces during the Mexican–American War foreshadowed the catastrophe that was to engulf Native American society soon after California was ceded to the United States.

The army played a critical part in the escalation of mass violence against Indians in the early stages of the gold rush with the perpetration of a series of retaliatory massacres of Pomo and Wappo peoples in the Clear Lake region between December 1849 and May 1850. The involvement of the army in this round of bloodletting was precipitated by the murder, a few days before Christmas 1849, of Charles Stone and Andrew Kelsey, sadistic co-owners of the Big Valley Ranch near Clear Lake about one hundred miles north of San Francisco. Stone and Kelsey were killed by a group of their Pomo and Wappo workers, whom they had repeatedly and severely brutalized over several years. The Pacific Division of the US Army under the command of General Persifor Smith was determined to punish the Pomo people as a whole so severely that it would serve as a deterrent to further violence against settlers. The US 1st Dragoons, an elite, mounted unit stationed at Sonoma sent out detachments to the area on Christmas Day. They committed several indiscriminate massacres of Indian communities in the locality with the help of vigilantes as acts of collective punishment. This unleashed vigilante action against Native Americans in an expanded area, including the Napa and Sonoma districts, which continued into March.

The dragoons meanwhile geared up for a massive assault on the Pomo of the Clear Lake region. When the army was ready in mid-May 1850, its operations culminated in two horrific massacres, in which as many as 150 Native Americans, mostly women and children, were killed in an orgy of bloodletting by US soldiers. The first and larger occurred on what subsequently became known as "Bloody Island" on May 15, along the northern reaches of Clear Lake. The second took place about twenty miles west at Cokadjal, on an island created by a slough along the Russian River described by expedition commander Brevet Captain Nathanial Lyon as the "perfect slaughter pen."[8]

This set of massacres by the US Army is notable on several counts. Firstly, it reinforced the principle of collective punishment on the California frontier because it, quite absurdly, held an entire tribe and all other Indians who happened to be in the vicinity responsible for the actions of a few and arbitrarily exacted the ultimate penalty on hundreds of innocents irrespective of age, gender, or communal affiliation. The key point about these bouts of collective punishment is that victims were killed for who they were rather than for what they had done. Secondly, the entire operation was driven by the commanding officer's conviction of the power of pedagogic violence in that it was meant to instill such fear in the Indigenous population as a whole that it would be taught an enduring lesson. As such, the retaliation was deliberately and massively disproportional to the offense. Both principles from early on came to characterize settler aggression on the Californian frontier. Collective punishment and pedagogic violence were integrally connected and highly prone to genocidal outcomes as they entailed indiscriminate attacks on entire communities and Indigenes generally. Part of their attraction to perpetrators was that they provided a ready-made excuse for exterminatory onslaughts. Thirdly, it exposed the genocidal outlook of influential decision-makers within a key organ of state and communicated to settlers generally that it was acceptable to kill Native Americans.

---

8. Cited in Madley, *American Genocide*, 134.

That no attempt was made to rein in accompanying vigilante murderousness sent a clear message of impunity to civilians contemplating violence. Indeed, when several offenders were arrested in the Sonoma and Napa regions by farmers incensed that their Indian workers and other innocent people were being killed, those charged were allowed to skip bail and were never pursued by the criminal justice system despite living openly in defiance of the law. Most importantly, these massacres by the army were the crucial trigger for ramping up vigilante violence against Indian communities throughout the frontier from the early 1850s onward. The army set a terrifying precedent not lost upon others considering mass atrocities against Native Americans. While direct violence by the army abated by mid-1850, the killing of Indigenes by vigilantes and militia escalated through the decade, initially mainly in gold mining districts, but soon throughout the state. Periodic killing of Native Americans by the army continued through the 1850s until it erupted with renewed intensity after the outbreak of the American Civil War.

Although the Civil War, which broke out in April 1861 and lasted four years, was largely fought in the eastern and southeastern regions of the country, it had a profound impact on the genocide unfolding in the far west and on the role of the army in this violence. Rather than distract the settler establishment from hostilities with Indians, the Civil War served to intensify conflict with them. Violence on the California frontier during the latter part of the 1850s and the first half of the 1860s was exacerbated by the federal government's attention being focused on the impending secession of the Southern states and the Civil War, which stretched its administrative, financial, and military resources to the limit. The federal government, at the best of times, had little regard for the wellbeing and lives of Indians on the frontier, much less so for those of its most distant state in a time of existential crisis. With a distance of 2,400 miles as the crow flies between the two capitals, Washington's influence on what happened on the ground in California was tenuous. Both federal officials and the state government had a great degree of freedom to act in their own interest, which was usually to the detriment of Native Americans.

Soon after the outbreak of the Civil War most regular soldiers in California were redeployed to theaters of combat. To shore up the state's security, the secretary of war asked the California governor John Downey to establish volunteer infantry and cavalry regiments of the US Army. There was an enthusiastic response to the call for men to enlist for three years, as the pay was attractive and alternative economic opportunities in short supply with thousands of immigrants continuing to flood into the state. All in all, thirteen regiments were formed, and over 15,700 men were enlisted, a good proportion of whom served in a variety of capacities outside of the state—some as far afield as Pennsylvania and Massachusetts.

The California Volunteers, as these combat units were collectively known, constituted a powerful military force that could now also be deployed against Native Americans. The California Volunteers, which replaced state militia companies, changed the dynamic of state-sponsored violence against Indigenous peoples dramatically. Smaller, temporary, volunteer militia expeditions sponsored by the California state were replaced by a larger, more lethal standing force led by professional officers. Importantly, military action against Indians was now directly funded and provisioned by the federal government. The *Humboldt Times* of March 7, 1863 rejoiced that: ". . . an opportunity is now offered to rid our county forever from the curse of Indians at the expense of the Federal Government."[9]

By the end of 1861, there were nearly 6,000 California Volunteers, some of whom from mid-1862 onward were systematically deployed against Native Americans. The Volunteers started campaigning against Indians in northwestern California, a long-standing epicenter of resistance, with a series of massacres that killed over a hundred people. Additionally they captured and deported many more to reservations. Over the next two years, the Volunteers launched numerous campaigns against Native American communities across the length and breadth of the state, killing several hundred and dispatching large numbers to reservations. The methodical use of the Volunteers in this way broke the back of remaining Indigenous resistance by the time the Civil War ended. As was the case in 1850 with the army's Clear Lake campaign, increased violence against Native Americans by the US Army encouraged more intense vigilante action. This resulted in an escalation of conflict on the frontier to new levels. Massacres by vigilantes continued for some months after the Volunteer campaigns ceased by mid-1864.

Despite its principal role in the genocide, there is one sense in which the army was less exterminatory in its dealings with Indians compared to vigilante gangs and militias. The army took more prisoners and was more concerned with deporting them to reservations with the help of Department of Indian Affairs officials. Life on the reservations, however, proved to be so lethal that it can justifiably be regarded as part of a broader pattern of genocidal destruction of Native American society. Militias and vigilantes were more murderous and thorough in their work of physical destruction, usually preferring not to be hampered by prisoners, even though they may have had some value as forced laborers.

---

9. Quoted in Madley, *American Genocide*, 317.

Indirect Killing and Nonlethal Ways of Social Destruction

Because of the intensity of violence on the California frontier and most of the bloodletting being concentrated in little more than one and a half decades—from the time the gold rush started in earnest in early 1849 and sustained killing died down by early 1865—the focus thus far has largely been on direct killing. It goes without saying that large numbers of Native American people also died in a variety of other ways immediately related to settler conquest. Neither can it be denied that nonlethal means of social destruction contributed greatly to the genocide.

Thousands of Native Americans perished of starvation and exposure that came with being displaced from their land. Groves of oak trees were leveled or put out of bounds; game animals were hunted to near extinction; edible plants and grass seeds were destroyed by stock; Indigenous peoples were denied access to fishing grounds; and sources of water were often polluted or placed off-limits. Not only did settler economic activity destroy food sources, consume environmental resources, and disrupt the natural rhythms on which Native Americans depended, but settler insurgents were generally diligent when it came to wrecking their food stores, shelters, and vital equipment, such as canoes, nets, and hunting gear. Displaced people were left with little option but to enter the employ of colonists, frequently as virtual serfs or slaves, or move to secluded highland areas where food was scarce, the climate inhospitable; and yet they were not safe from attack by settler posses intent on hunting them down.

From the early 1850s onward, removal of displaced Native Americans to one of five tiny military reservations became an option for the California and federal governments. Reservations played a significant role in the demographic collapse of Indigenous populations housed there. While removal to a reservation was in itself not necessarily genocidal, it was extremely damaging to the social fabric of aboriginal societies. In California, however, every aspect of reservation policy was implemented in extremely brutal fashion. To begin with, the process of capture for removal to reservations—usually conducted by army or militia units in the wake of military action that commonly included massacre—was on the whole excessively violent. Then the transfer, usually to distant locations over rough terrain on foot, was an exhausting and traumatic experience that exacted many lives. And once on reservations, most Native Americans were detained under psychologically debilitating and exceedingly lethal conditions.

Removal to a reservation not infrequently provoked conflict among inhabitants, as traditional enemies were regularly crowded together, exacerbating resentments and promoting competition for resources among groups. Reservations were in effect open-air prisons, as internees were not allowed to leave, and those who did try to escape were usually hunted down and regularly killed by soldiers, militiamen, and vigilantes. Indeed, Indians outside of reservations and not in the employ of settlers were generally regarded as fair game by vigilantes and the military. Food was so scarce on reservations that malnourishment was the norm for internees, and malnutrition left people vulnerable to disease. Consequently, the mortality rate due to both chronic and infectious diseases was exceptionally high. In some instances, internees starved to death, and many of those who tried to escape did so to avoid starvation. The scarcity of food was exacerbated by pervasive corruption among reserve officials who colluded with suppliers to divert provisions and defraud the government.

Reservations, which were not fenced or patrolled, hardly provided residents with any protection against settler depredations. Marauders freely entered reservations to perpetrate violence, steal stock, exploit resources, such as grazing and timber or the internees themselves as forced labor—often with the collusion of reservation officials. Vigilantes were generally able to come onto reservations with impunity to harass, rape, and kill occupants. There were, indeed, several massacres of Indians on reservations by settlers. Thus, instead of serving as havens of safety as the federal government claimed, reservations in reality functioned as detention centers, where the Indian population could be segregated, concentrated, and controlled at minimal cost. Viewed as one element within the full array of harms perpetrated against Native American society, the role of reservations as instruments of genocide is undeniable.

The subjection of tens of thousands of Indians to bondage, whether through legal means or effective slavery, also played an important part in the destruction of Indigenous societies. Forced labor, whether effective slavery, indenture, or apprenticeship, redeployed the most productive human resources of Indigenous societies for the benefit of the settler establishment and critically disrupted processes of biological and cultural reproduction. Widespread child confiscation undercut the regenerative powers of these societies severely and the removal of able-bodied males, either as captives or for seasonal agricultural labor, hampered reproduction. Most damaging, however, was the loss of its most fecund females, whether as forced laborers, concubines, or through other forms of sexual violence, as it meant that in addition to the critical functions they performed, their childbearing capacities were lost to Native American societies.

Also, many Indian workers were severely maltreated, not infrequently with fatal consequences. The gold rush and subsequent rapid economic development of California created a severe shortage of labor to the extent that some settlers embarked on raids to acquire or sell Indigenes as forced laborers and sex slaves. While adult males were in strong demand, especially during the earlier part of the gold rush, a robust trade in children and younger women developed through the 1850s and 1860s. The state and the army did very little to stop these nefarious activities. Indeed, the California government sanctioned the maltreatment of Indian laborers through its labor code that legalized the extreme exploitation of Indigenes. Workers were frequently beaten, faced death for trying to escape from masters, and some died of exhaustion through overwork. Many masters and employers, partly through greed and partly through racial antipathy, regarded Native American labor not as a sustainable resource worth nurturing, but as one to be consumed for immediate profit, a practice condoned by the state's labor code. The intensive exploitation and abusive treatment of the Indian workforce is indicative of the genocidal outlook of many colonists on the frontier.

Disease, the single biggest cause of death, was not a neutral vector that exacted its toll independently of settler agency, as apologists and deniers are wont to assert. While pathogens were for the most part spread unintentionally, the impact of epidemic diseases—such as smallpox, cholera, tuberculosis, typhoid, malaria, and measles—was all the more catastrophic on a population suffering dispossession, malnutrition, exposure, exhaustion from overwork, and deep psychological trauma. Though generally not as dramatic in impact as mass violence, the damage inflicted by contagious diseases was relentless and unceasing in the havoc it wrought.

Venereal disease, a major vector of social destruction, needs to be evaluated differently from other infectious diseases, as it was usually transmitted knowingly and through acts of violence. Sexual exploitation of Indian women and a great deal of sexual violence perpetrated by settlers infected with venereal diseases ensured that these spread quickly among Indigenes, killing many, debilitating others, and sending the birthrate into a downward spiral. Not only did Native Americans die in disproportionate numbers from venereal diseases because they lacked immunity to them, but these illnesses also resulted in infertility and large numbers of miscarriages, still births, and neonatal fatalities. Venereal diseases were particularly injurious to the prospects of Indigenous societies' demographic recovery, as it tended to kill and sterilize many more women than men. Chronic venereal disease also lowered peoples' resistance to other diseases.

As in many other Western settler colonies across the globe, Californians promoted theories of the inevitable extinction of the "savage" to explain and justify the destruction of Native American society. The *Daily Alta California* of December 15, 1850, for example, portrayed Indians across the American continent as having "faded . . . away like a dissipating mist before the morning sun from the presence of the Saxon."[10] The metaphor of the rising sun dispelling mist or snow was commonly applied by settlers to the dying out of Indigenes because to them it neatly captured the supposed inevitability and impersonal nature of this process.

---

10. Cited in James Rawls, *Indians of California: The Changing Image* (Norman: University of Oklahoma Press, 1984), 173.

And, by ascribing the outcome to a providential agent, whether God or nature, it conveniently absolved settlers of blame. California senator John B. Weller, in an 1852 speech before the Senate, epitomized the common settler attitude of Euro-American entitlement at the expense of the very right to existence of Native Americans:

> The Indian is placed between the upper and nether millstones and he must be crushed! The fate of the Indian is irrevocably sealed. . . . In the providence of God they must soon disappear before the onward march of our countrymen. Humanity may forbid but the *interest* of the white man demands their extinction.[11]

Weller, who went on to serve as governor of Californian between 1858 and 1860, clearly felt morally justified in the use of violence against Native Americans, as did many of his fellow Californians. Not only did they feel little remorse for their actions, but actually regarded them as honorable. Doomed race theories, especially in settler colonial contexts, operated as self-fulfilling prophecies as they encouraged settlers to behave in ways that helped Indigenous societies on to their assumed destinies of extinction.

After the Season of Slaughter

Systematic deployment of the army on the California frontier tapered off by mid-1864 as the Civil War wound down, and a few months later vigilante attacks started diminishing as army support, both material and moral, for their depredations was withdrawn. Not only had the military climate changed, but by this time there were not that many Indians within easy reach left to kill or who threatened settler aspirations. Surviving Native Americans were either in the employ of colonists or were living out of sight in remote, inhospitable areas that settlers did not regard as having economic value. Others languished on desolate reservations. Regardless, periodic killings by the army and scattered vigilante attacks against Indians continued for the better part of a decade. The last of the sizeable massacres came in mid-February 1866, when a squad of nearly eighty cavalrymen accompanied by vigilantes pursued a band of Northern Paiute raiders across the border into Oregon and massacred perhaps as many as 120 people, about a third of whom were women. The last significant armed conflict occurred in the first half of 1873 with a series of skirmishes in far north-central California known as the Modoc War. As many as 400 soldiers in all were mobilized to forcibly move

---

11. The Congressional Globe: The Debates, Proceedings and Laws of the First Session of the Thirty-Second Congress, Volume XXIV, Part III, August 12, 1852, 2175. Emphasis in the original.

about 150 Modoc people to the Klamath reservation in southern Oregon. In several clashes in the lava fields south of Tule Lake, where this group of Modocs made its last stand, perhaps as many as forty Modocs were killed, and survivors were taken prisoner. After the main leaders were hanged and others imprisoned, the rest were dispatched into exile in Indian Territory in what is today Oklahoma.

While the Modoc War provides a convenient marker for the closing of the California frontier as well as of the murderous phase of the genocide, James Rawls, in his landmark study of changing perceptions of Californian Indians from the earliest days of European contact, identifies the early 1870s also as the time when Euro-American attitudes toward Native Americans moderated significantly.[12] A distinct softening in demeanor toward Indigenes emerged in the dominant society as they were no longer seen as a threat. Native Americans started attracting the attention of anthropologists, who were eager to study their cultures, and of humanitarians, who recognized some of the injustices they had suffered. From the late nineteenth century, several religious and secular organizations were formed by philanthropists to help relieve Native American social distress and to advocate for some form of redress. A campaign started in 1922 to compensate Californian Indians for the land they had lost, eventually after many twists and turns, in 1972 resulted in a payment of little more than $600 each to about 65,000 people deemed to have been descendants of the aboriginal inhabitants of the state. Some Native Americans saw this derisory offer of less than fifty cents per acre as outrageous and refused to accept payment.

Despite violence toward them having subsided markedly from the early 1870s, the demographic decline of Native American society nonetheless continued apace till the late 1890s—from about 30,000 in 1870 to little more than 15,000 in 1900. Deleterious living conditions, a high infant mortality rate, and disease continued to take a toll, as did cultural suppression and various efforts at forced assimilation, most notably through government boarding and day schools, reduced federal funding for reservations, attempts at loosening communal ties to land, and reducing the powers of tribal authorities. Population numbers only started stabilizing by the turn of the twentieth century as, among other things, communities developed improved resistance to introduced diseases and the infant mortality rate started dropping. After that, the population started growing very slowly to about 20,000 in 1950.[13] There has subsequently been an explosion

---

12. Rawls, *Indians of California*, 205.

13. These population statistics are based on a combination of census figures and estimates by demographers. Whatever their shortcomings, they do provide a good sense of demographic trends through the last century and a half. See Rawls, *Indians of California*, 214; Madley, *American Genocide*, 347; Lindsay, *Murder State*, 128.

in the number of Native Americans living in California with some estimates placing it as high as 700,000 today as a result of improvements in health and nutrition, and more importantly, through immigration and changing patterns of ethnic self-identification.[14]

The "Brilliant" and the "Sordid": A Clear Case of Genocide

The destruction of California's Native American societies under US rule is an obvious case of genocide. The process was so swift and decisive, and the exterminatory intent of perpetrators so conspicuous and well documented that it, in my opinion, qualifies as the preeminent example of genocide in the conquest of the United States. Virtually all sectors of the settler establishment either participated or acquiesced in the genocide: civilian society through pervasive vigilantism, land confiscation, and wanton violence, as well as extreme sexual and economic exploitation of Indigenes; the state of Californian through its deployment of militia units, legislation enabling severe maltreatment of Native Americans, and refusal to prosecute offenders; and the federal government through the havoc inflicted by the US Army, retrospective funding of militia activity, and a general failure of oversight. The heaviest blame needs to be placed at the door of the state of California as it demonstrated a consistent and extraordinary political will to destroy Native American society. Indeed, it is difficult to escape the conclusion that the California government institutionalized Indian killing. The ready recourse by both civilian and military perpetrators to exterminatory rhetoric and violence, often for the smallest of infractions, for preemptive reasons, or without provocation is a clear indication of a pervasive genocidal mindset within the settler establishment, particularly since it is inconceivable that they would have reacted in this way toward white transgressors. Many victims were killed for no other reason than that they were Native American.

A day after California instituted its civilian government on December 21, 1849, Peter H. Burnett in his "Governor's Message" made the prediction that "Either a brilliant destiny awaits California or one of the most sordid and degraded."[15] While Burnett was confident that it was the former that would be achieved, from an early twenty-first-century perspective, it is clear that both have

---

14. See, for example, "Native American Statistical Abstract: Population Characteristics," California Tribal Court-State Court Forum, accessed May 18, 2020, https://www.courts.ca.gov/documents/Tribal-ResearchUpdate-NAStats.pdf.

15. Peter H. Burnett "State of the State Address, December 21, 1849," The Governors' Gallery, California State Library, accessed May 8, 2020, https://governors.library.ca.gov/addresses/s_01-Burnett1.html.

been accomplished—splendid achievements have been attained on a foundation of genocide. Ishi, as were other survivors of the genocide, was a victim of both the sordid and the brilliant.

SOURCES

Prelude to the Clear Lake Massacre, May 15, 1850

Our first source is an extract from a document produced by William Ralganal Benson (1862–1937), a hereditary chief of the Pomo people who lived in the Clear Lake region of coastal northern California. Benson produced this report to explain events surrounding the Clear Lake Massacre of May 15, 1850 from the perspective of survivors. Perhaps as many as 150 Eastern Pomo and Clear Lake Wapo people were killed by US soldiers under the command of Brevet Captain Nathaniel Lyon. Born about twelve years after the massacre, Benson knew several people who had lived through this event. Serving as elder and historian of the Pomo, he collected the testimonies of survivors to produce his account, which was published in an article coauthored with Max Radin, professor of law at the University of California, Berkeley. According to Radin, who contributed nothing more than a short introduction to the article, this text was produced entirely at Benson's initiative and was reproduced in unadulterated form.

Benson's father, Addison, one of the earliest settlers in the region, lived permanently among the Pomo after marrying Benson's mother, Gepigul, who belonged to one of its leading families. Because his father died while he was still a child, Benson was raised within Pomo culture, speaking only his native language. In adulthood he taught himself to read and write English, and to use a typewriter. Having received no formal schooling, Benson's spelling tends toward the phonetic, and aspects of his English usage are unconventional. He served extensively as interpreter and informant for anthropologists studying Native American cultures in the region, because of his deep knowledge of local indigenous practices and his reputation for authenticity.

Our excerpt comes from the opening section of Benson's account and outlines the treatment Native American workers and other indigenous peoples received at the hands of ranch owners Charles Stone and Andrew Kelsey. They were among the first settlers in the area and were co-owners of the Big Valley Ranch located near the southwestern shore of Clear Lake in 1847. Because they were starving, a group of Stone and Kelsey's workers paid two of their number, Shuk and Xasis, to kill an ox for them. In the sections following the extract, Benson reveals that the hirelings used two of the ranch's best horses to lasso an ox, but because it was raining and the ground was slippery, Shuk's horse fell and bolted. The conspirators were left with a major dilemma because Stone and Kelsey were sure to wreak fearsome revenge on their Indian workers and possibly on neighboring communities as well. After debating possible responses through the night, the party decided to kill Stone and Kelsey. That Stone and Kelsey were at that point holding Shuk's wife as a sex slave, probably contributed to the decision to kill them.

Benson, who had interviewed all five men who had participated in Stone and Kelsey's murders, goes on to describe the preparations of surrounding Indian communities for the inevitable reprisals by settlers. Most retreated into hideouts, stockpiling whatever food they could. Perhaps as many as two hundred people, mainly women and children, took refuge on what subsequently came to be known as Bloody Island, situated along the northern shore of the lake. Finally, Benson recounts episodes in the violence unleashed by the US Army on those who had taken shelter on the island.

Questions for Consideration

How would you describe Stone and Kelsey's treatment of their Native American laborers? What factors contributed to their behavior toward indigenous workers? Consider the institutional, situational, racial, emotional, and economic catalysts for their labor practices—as well as any others you can think of. What evidence for the salience of these aspects do you see in this document? Would you agree that Native American workers were generally treated worse than slaves in other parts of the United States? Why might this have been the case? How would you describe the tone of Benson's writing and the quality of his account? What makes Benson's text especially valuable to historians? What cautions do we need to exercise in using it?

William Ralganal Benson, "The Stone and Kelsey 'Massacre'"[16]

. . . there were two indian villages. one on west side and one on the east side [of Stone and Kelsey's ranch]. the indians in both of these camps were starveing. stone or kelsey would not let them go out hunting or fishing. Shuk and Xasis was stone and kelsey headriders looking out for stock. cattle horses and hogs. the horses and cattle were all along the lake on the west side and some in bachelors

---

16. Max Radin and William Ralganal Benson, "The Stone and Kelsey 'Massacre' on the Shores of Clear Lake in 1849: The Indian Viewpoint," *California Historical Society Quarterly* 11, no. 3 (September 1932): 266–73.

valley. also in upper lake. so it took 18 indian herdsman to look after the stock in these places. Shuk and Xasis was foremans for the herds. and only those herds got anything to eat. each one of these herders got 4 cups of wheat for a days work. this cup would hold about one and ahalf pint of water. the wheat was boiled before it was given to the herders. and the herders shire with thir famlys. the herders who had large famlys were also starveing. about 20 old people died during the winter from starvetion. from severe whipping 4 died. a nephew of an indian lady who were liveing with stone was shoot to deth by stone. the mother of this yong man was sick and starveing. this sick woman told her son to go over to stones wife or the sick womans sister. tell your aunt that iam starveing and sick tell her that i would like to have a handfull of wheat. the yong man lost no time going to stones house. the young man told the aunt what his mother said. the lady then gave the young man 5 cups of wheat and tied it up in her apron and the young man started for the camp. stone came about that time and called the young man back. the young man stoped stone who was horse back. rode up to the young man took the wheat from him and then shoot him. the young man died two days after. such as whipping and tieing thier hands togather with rope. the rope then thrown over a limb of a tree and then drawn up untell the indians toes barly touchs the ground and let them hang there for hours. this was common punishment. when a father or mother of young girl. was asked to bring the girl to his house. by stone or kelsey. if this order was not obeyed. he or her would be whipped or hung by the hands. Such punishment occurred two or three times a week. and many of the old men and woman died from fear and starvetion. these two white men had the indians to build a high fence around thir villages. and the head riders were to see that no indian went out side of this fence after dark. if any one was caught out side of this fence after dark was taken to stones and kelseys house and there was tied both hands and feet and placed in a room and kept there all night. the next day was taken to a tree and was tied down. then the strongs man was chosen to whippe the prisoner.

the starvetion of the indians was the cause of the massacre of stone and kelsey. the indians who were starving hired a man by the name of Shuk and a nother man by the name of Xasis. to kill a beef for them.

✦✦✦✦✦

The Condition of Native Americans in the Goldfields, 1853

In this letter, Edward A. Stevenson, who had recently been appointed special Indian agent for El Dorado, Placer, Amador, and Calaveras Counties, reports to his superior Thomas J. Henley, superintendent of Indian affairs of California, on the condition of Native Americans within his agency, which straddled the eastern border between the central and southern goldfields. His brief included instructing Indians under his jurisdiction on government policy, and persuading them to relocate onto one of the military reservations to avoid conflict with settlers. Although Stevenson evinces a degree of sympathy for Indians, unusual for the time, he was not above exploiting Indian labor for personal profit or diverting federal funding intended for their subsistence into his own pocket. Stevenson's report came but five years into the gold rush and was focused on an area that had been remote from settled areas before 1848. This is a measure of the rapid impact that the stampede of immigrants into prospecting areas had on Native American communities.

Questions for Consideration

It may be argued that Stevenson emphasized certain aspects of the social condition of Native Americans but played down or failed to comment on others. Do you find this to be true? If so, what did he overlook or downplay, and how do you explain these lapses? Stevenson's letter reflects his values and perspectives. Elaborate on what these were and how they are manifested in the text. Consider the moral judgments implied in his comments and how they would affect this letter's value as historical evidence. To what extent does he admit that Native Americans were unfairly treated? What were his proposed remedies for their predicament and how effective do you think they would have been? Do you think that Stevenson was disingenuous and condescending in his behavior toward Native Americans? Cite evidence from the text to support your response. The letter also provides evidence of the institutional barriers and ecological challenges that Indians encountered. What were they?

Indian Agent, Stevenson, to Superintendent
of Indian Affairs, Henley[17]

Diamond Springs
Eldorado County
December 31st 1853

Sir:

. . . These Indians, some eight thousand in number, are divided into about one hundred and twenty-five separate bands or communities and some of them very

---

17. Robert Heizer, ed., *The Destruction of California Indians* (Lincoln: University of Nebraska Press, 1993), 13–16.

difficult of access, and are to be found straggling about every mining camp in the mining regions. Many of them being without any settled place of habitation; and many of them have already imbibed the very worst vices of civilization, and are becoming vitiated and degraded, a pest and nuisance to the localities where they resort. It is a frequent occurrence to find white men living with Indian women and because the Indians dare remonstrate against this course of conduct they are frequently subject to the worst and most brutal treatment. . . . The poverty and misery that now exists among these Indians is beyond description and is driving the squaws to the most open and disgusting acts of prostitution, thereby engendering diseases of the most frightful and fatal character. I had occasion a few days since to visit an Indian Camp, and on my arrival found one of their head men or chiefs. I conversed with him on the subject of removing the Indians to a Reservation. He answered me in quite good English saying that he was in favor of that course because he was satisfied that if they remained where they were they must all starve or fall a victim to that fatal disease that the white men had brought among them, but says he "I shall die before their removal can be accomplished, therefore, it matters but little to me." I asked him his reasons for thinking so, when to my surprise he showed me his legs which were covered with ulcers peculiar to the disease I have referred to. He asked me if the Big Chief of the White men would cure them of this dreadful disease if they went to a reservation. I told him yes . . . In one camp in the Eastern portion of this County I found nine squaws so far advanced with this disease that most of them were unable to walk. I turned in disgust and sorrow from a sight more revolting than I had ever before witnessed. In this diseased, unsettled, dispersed and otherwise unfavorable condition, nothing can be done to reclaim or improve them until they shall be removed to a place where those evil influences are less likely to surround them.

In all my travels through the country I have invariably found that the better class of Indians are in favor of removing and willing to go to any place where they can have a permanent home, while the more worthless and drunken are opposed to any policy that would in the least interfere with their debased passions and appetites. I believe it is an admitted fact by every person at all conversant with Indian character that the use of ardent spirits stands more in the way of their civilization than anything that can be mentioned. When they are sober they are as easily managed and influenced to do what is right as most other people; but they all seem to have a strong appetite for whiskey, and will use every means in their power to obtain it and once under its influence their reason is gone. They are then ready for any acts of violence, brutality and crime that a savage nature can invent, and although the law in this State is very severe against those who sell them liquor, it is almost impossible to prevent them from obtaining it. I have endeavored to find out by Indians where they get liquor, but they will not inform. I have, however, succeeded in convicting and fining those persons in this county for selling or giving away liquor to Indians, which will have a tendency to lessen the traffic in that article among them. The Indians in this portion of the State are wretchedly poor, having no horses, cattle or other property. They formerly subsisted on game, fish, acorns, etc., but it is now impossible for them to make a living by hunting or fishing, for nearly all the game has been driven from the mining region or has been killed by the thousands of our people who now occupy the once quiet home of these children of the forest. The rivers or tributaries of the Sacramento formerly were clear as crystal and abounded with the finest salmon and other fish. I saw them at Salmon Falls on the American river in the year 1851, and also the Indians taking barrels of these beautiful fish and drying them for winter. But the miners have turned the streams from their beds and conveyed the water to the dry diggings and after being used until it is so thick with mud that it will scarcely run it returns to its natural channel and with it the soil from a thousand hills, which has driven almost every kind of fish to seek new places of resort where they can enjoy a purer and more natural element. And to prove the old adage that misfortunes never come singly the oaks have for the last three years refused to furnish the acorn, which formed one of the chief articles of Indian food. In concluding this brief report I deem it my duty to recommend to your favorable consideration the early establishment of a suitable reservation and the removal of these Indians thereto, where they can receive medical aid and assistance which at the present time they so much require.

E. A. Stevenson
Spec. Indian Agent

Hon. Thos. J. Henley
Supt. of Indian Affairs
San Francisco Cal.

❖❖❖❖❖

A Native American Woman Narrates Her Experience of the California Frontier

While firsthand testimony of indigenous survivors relating their experience of genocidal violence on settler frontiers is scarce, the voices of women are rare indeed. And what makes the document from which these excerpts are taken even more extraordinary is that it is the product of collaboration between two remarkable women, Edith Van Allen Murphey (1879–1968), a self-taught range botanist who had arrived in California from New York in 1903, and Lucy Young, a Wailaki woman in her early nineties and a highly respected elder in her community living on the Mendocino reservation.[18] The two struck up a lifelong friendship in 1927, when Murphey starting drawing on Young's knowledge of local plants and ethnographic knowledge. Like Benson, Young was extensively used as an informant by anthropologists.

Lucy Young dictated her story to Murphey in 1939. Murphey makes it clear that her transcription of the interview does not embellish the testimony in any way and that the words are Lucy's own. While by far the greater part of the narrative is taken up with Young's account of her childhood experiences, mostly during 1862–1863, she does provide a summary of her life toward the end of the article. The themes that dominate Young's childhood memories are the massacring of family and community members, the child trafficking she witnessed and experienced, and the implied sexual servitude of Native American women.

Although her narrative does not elaborate specifically on the sexual exploitation of Native American women, nor of her own experiences in this regard, it is apparent from other sources that Young's childbearing years were spent as a concubine and sex slave.[19] As a teenager on the run from traffickers she ended up under the protection of a settler named Abraham Rogers who looked after her and soon took her as a concubine. They lived together for perhaps thirty years and had four children. Although the union was forced on her, Young appears to have had a stable life with Rogers. It is not clear how the relationship ended, but she then for five years landed in the clutches of Arthur Rutledge, who kept her chained to prevent her from escaping. Rutledge repeatedly raped and beat her resulting in several miscarriages, until he let her go when he found a white woman to marry. Because of a reluctance to discuss her sexual abuse, Lucy Young

18. Her original name was T'tcetsa meaning "little one." She was given the name Lucy by Abraham Rogers, the first settler to force her into concubinage at the age of about fifteen. She retained the name and adopted the surname Young when she married Sam Young, a Wintun man, in 1914. They remained together till Lucy died in 1944, aged about ninety-eight. The eighty-seven-year-old Sam died five weeks later.

19. See, for example, Ida Rae Egli, *No Rooms of Their Own: Women Writers of Early California* (Berkeley: Heyday Books, 1992), 47–50; Anon. [Thomas Keter?], "Lucy and Sam Young and Soldier Basin" (unpublished paper, no date), accessed June 2, 2020 available at http://wordpress. solararch.org/wp-content/uploads/2021/02/b03_lucy_and_sam_young_overview.pdf.

admitted to a significant degree of self-censorship in the account she provided Murphey. She doubted that an unvarnished version would be published.[20]

Questions for Consideration

How well does Lucy Young's chronicle fit with what you already know about conflict and human trafficking on the Californian frontier during this time? In what ways could Lucy's behavior be interpreted as resistance to her oppression? Indian experience of frontier violence was highly gendered. What evidence in the extract is there for this? Reflect in particular on the relationship between settler men and indigenous women and girls, and how deeply their interactions were gendered and racialized. How did the institutional structures and ideological underpinnings of California settler society enable the dual exploitation of Indigenous women in domestic and sexual servitude?

Edith Murphey and Lucy Young: "Out of the Past . . ."[21]

[Up to this point, Lucy described her life on the run, together with her mother and younger sister, over a period of more than six months, after the greater part of their community had been massacred by soldiers. The three were captured and taken to Fort Seward. Lucy, about ten years old, was about to be separated from her family.] One white man come there [Fort Seward], want take me South Fork Mountain. His woman got li'l baby. He want me stay his woman. . . . This Inyan woman whip me all time. Didden' talk my language. 'Bout week all I stay. Commence rain pretty hard. He tell me go get water. I go down, water muddy. I get it anyway. He ask me, make sign, "Where you get this water?" I showum down to river. He think I get water in hole near house. He throw out water, commence whip me, tell me go get water.

I go down river, pretty steep go down. I throw bucket in river. I run off. Never see bucket no more. I had soldier shoes, take off, tie around neck. Water knee deep. I just had thin dress, can run good. Come up big high bank. Keep look back see if that woman follow me. . . . Water up to my waist. I run through. Get to Fort Seward before I look back.

---

20. Kayla Rae Begay, "Wailaki Grammar" (D. Phil. diss., University of California, Berkeley, 2017), 10.
21. Edith Van Allen Murphey and Lucy Young, "Out of the Past: A True Story Told by Lucy Young of Round Valley Indian Reservation," *California Historical Society Quarterly* 20, no. 4 (December 1941): 349–64.

At last I come home.[22] Before I get there, I see big fire in lotsa down timber and tree-top. Same time awfully funny smell. I think: Somebody get lotsa wood.

I go on to house. Everybody crying. Mother tell me: "All our men killed now." She say white men there, others come from Round Valley, Humboldt County too, kill our old uncle, chief Lassik, and all our men.

Stood up about forty Inyan in a row with rope around neck. "What this for?" Chief Lassik askum. "To hang you, dirty dogs," white men tell it. "Hanging, that's dog's death," Chief Lassik say. "We done nothing, be hung for. Must we die, shoot us."

So they shoot. All our men. Then build fire with wood and brush Inyan men been cut for days, never know their own funeral fire they fix. Build big fire, burn all them bodies. That's funny smell I smell before I get to house. Make hair raise on back of my neck. Make sick stomach, too. . . .

That white man, same evening got me, took to his house. Then took me down South Fork again. I ride behind. He talk his women. He had cowhide rope. Short one. He upped that. Give woman good whipping with that. He stay all night, next morning go back Fort Seward. 'N other Inyan boy where I was. I didden' know he spoke my language. When man come, that woman wash clothes down by the river. Want me stay take care baby. She go on, then this boy talk with me. He tell me: "Tomorrow, 'nother white man come, gonta take you off. Way down. Tomorrow, white man come."

So it did happen. He take me then. This boy say: "Better you stay white people, better for you. All your people killed. Nothing to come back for." . . .

He bring me back Alder Point,[23] this white man did. From there he take me down low. I ride on packsaddle. Had big blanket over me. Winter time. Get up on top of mountain, meet 'nother white man, got li'l Inyan boy with him. This boy talk my talk good. He ride packsaddle too. They take us way up Blue Rock Mountain.[24] White man live there. Dogs begin barking. We get there, ride up to gate. White man take me off. I can't walk. Ride all day. Take li'l boy off too.

I see woman come out door. I know that woman, one of my people. Bill Dobbins' mother. This one, her father's my aunt. She know me. I know her. She set down in chair, hug me, commence cry. I cry too, cause think 'about mother all time. This woman live with old white man. . . .

Then they took me to Long Valley.[25] He had 'another wife there. Next morning that other man was there, washing face. He come in, count my finger: "One, two, three, four, days you going down, close to ocean." . . .

---

22. Fort Seward, where Lucy's mother was.
23. In Humboldt County.
24. About fifty-six miles from Alder Point.
25. More than 300 miles east of Blue Rock Mountain and across the Sierra Nevada.

Lucy Young. This photograph of Lucy Young was taken on July 1, 1922, when she was in her late sixties.

Two Inyan women come in. Talk quick to me: "Poor my li'l sister, where you come from?" "I come from north. That bald-headed man bring me."

"He got wife and children," they say.

These women talk clipped my language. "That's way all Inyan children come here," they say. "He bringum all." I half cry, all time for my mother. After while, bald-headed man come back, talk women long time. Gonta have big gamble over there, they say. Men got up and left. First, they give women grub, hog backbone, ribs.

These women say: "In four days you go stay old couple close by us." One um say: "I got white man, I come see you."

They leave for home. Little ridge, over hill. I hear Inyan talking, li'l way. I stand there and think. Only show for me to run off, now. Nobody there. I run in house. Match box on shelf. I put it in dress pocket. In kitchen, I find flour sacks. Take loaf bread, take boiling meat. Take big blanket from my bed.

I went out so quick, I never shut door. Then I went out to barn, open door, let all horses out.

All day I travel on edge of valley. I forgot I gonta have to swim Eel River.[26] . . . [Lucy goes on to tell about several months on the run, including miraculously meeting up with her mother who facilitates her escape by boat across the Eel River. With a cousin's help she is eventually taken up first as a domestic laborer and later as a concubine by the twenty-seven-year-old Abraham Rogers living in the Hayfork area.]

---

26. In present-day Humboldt County, Lucy's home area.

White man name Rogers come after this. Ellen my cousin's man, went to work for him. I go with her to Hayfork, and take li'l boy too.

Rogers, my white man, took me then to take care of, that summer. Marry me bimeby when old enough . . . [27] I stay there at Hayfork long time. My mother come there, too. She die there after a while at Hayfork. . . .

Li'l sister, white man took her away. Never see her no more. If see it, maybe wouldn't know it. That's last young one tooken away. Mother lost her at Fort Seward.

I hear it, I went back, got mother, brought her to Hayfork. Lotsa Inyan there, lotsa different language, all different. Mother stay with me until she die.

You ask 'bout father. He got killed and brother in soldier war, before soldiers captured us.[28] Three days fight. Three days running. Just blood, blood, blood. Young woman cousin, run from soldier, run into our camp. Three of us girls run. . . .

We had young man cousin, got shot side of head, crease him, all covered his blood, everything. We helpum to water. Wash off. No die. That night all our women come to camp. I ask mother: "You see my father, big brother?," "Yes," she say, "both two of um dead." I want go see. Mother say "No."

Young woman been stole by white people, come back. Shot through lights[29] and liver. Front skin hang down like apron. She tie up with cotton dress. Never die, neither. Little boy, knee-pan shot off. Young man shot through thigh. Only two man of all our tribe left-that battle.

White people want our land, want destroy us. Break and burn all our basket, break our pounding rock. Destroy our ropes. No snares, no deerskin, l flint knife, nothing. . . .

All long, long ago. My white man die.[30] My children all die but one. Oldest girl, she married, went way off. Flu take restum. Oldest girl die few years ago, left girl, she married now, got li'l girl, come see me sometimes. All I got left, my descendants. . . .

---

27. Lucy was probably about fifteen years old at the time.
28. This attack happened just before Lucy, her mother, and sister were captured and taken to Fort Baker narrated at the start of testimony and excluded from this extract. If it was indeed soldiers who attacked her band, it would appear to have been during the California Volunteers' first campaign under Colonel Francis J. Lippit.
29. Lungs.
30. Census data shows that Rogers died in 1915, but Young was living with Rutledge in 1900 already. See "Lucy and Sam Young," 3.

I hear people tell 'bout what Inyan do early days to white man. Nobody ever tell it what white man do to Inyan. That's reason I tell it. That's history. That's truth. I seen it myself.

✦✦✦✦✦

A Vigilante Leader's Firsthand Account of the Three Knolls Massacre of August 1865

These excerpts are taken from the reminiscences of Robert Allen Anderson, a notorious Indian hunter who lived and operated mainly in Yana territory in the west-central Sierra Nevada region. Anderson published his memoir, *Fighting the Mill Creeks*, two years before Ishi surrendered himself to modernity, and recounts his activities as a vigilante from the late 1850s through to the mid-1860s. The Mill Creeks consisted of remnant Yana and other displaced people from surrounding groups such as Wintu, Nomlaki, and Maidu, who had taken shelter in the rugged brushland of the Mill and Deer Creek Valleys north of Chico.

Anderson was born in Missouri in 1840 and came to California as a seventeen-year-old. He started prospecting along the north fork of the Feather River for a short while before switching to growing and selling produce to miners, and soon after that, into cattle ranching in Deer Creek. Shortly after his arrival in 1857 through to 1865, when Native American resistance in the Deer-Mill Creek area was effectively broken, Anderson played a prominent role in vigilante initiatives against Native Americans. He had no compunction about describing himself and accomplices as "man hunters." A successful rancher and at one point Butte County sheriff, Anderson became a respected member of his community, unlike several of his accomplices who did not survive the turbulent frontier period. He died in 1915.[31]

The selected passages describe the Three Knolls Massacre of mid-August 1865, which Ishi as a child, together with a few family members, reputedly survived.[32] Anderson was sufficiently frank to acknowledge that: "As in almost every similar instance in American history, the first act of injustice, the first spilling of blood, must be laid at the white man's door."[33] He was nonetheless very proud of his considerable accomplishments as a vigilante and felt morally justified in visiting exterminatory violence on Indian communities.

---

31. For a short biographical sketch, see "Robert Allen Anderson (1840–1915)," WikiTree, accessed May 25, 2020, https://www.wikitree.com/wiki/Anderson-17260.

32. See Theodora Kroeber, *Ishi in Two Worlds: A Biography of the Last Wild Indian in North America* (Berkeley: University of California Press, 1961), 81.

33. Anderson, *Fighting the Mill Creeks*, 86.

The extract takes up the story after Anderson and Harmon Good, another notorious Indian hunter and close associate of Anderson's, agreed to lead a vigilante group from Concow, which had suffered a raid by Mill Creek Indians the day before in which three whites had been killed. The evening prior to the dawn attack, Anderson and Good had waded upstream to scout the location and layout of the Indian camp of about fifty people, and to position their men in readiness for the assault.

Questions for Consideration

How would you describe the tone and spirit of Anderson's writing in these extracts and how would that affect your evaluation of the manuscript as historical source material? In what ways could one counterbalance the inevitable exaggerations and distortions of Anderson's account? What offensive strategy was used and why do you think they resorted to these tactics? To what extent does Anderson evince values and behaviors that may be regarded as intrinsic to all settler societies, and to those that were part of the making of Western global domination specifically? If Anderson were to be tried in a modern-day court on a charge of genocide, what are the chances that he would be convicted?

Fighting the Mill Creeks[34]

Chapter XIV

. . . We decided to move forward just in time to get the camp surrounded before the break of day. . . .

. . . As day began to peep over the high walls of the canyon, I found myself lying about thirty feet above one of the three little knolls that had served us so well as land-marks. I had left orders for His's[35] party to lie quiet and let us make the attack. This would throw the Indians onto the [sand] bar next the open ford, where they would be completely at the mercy of both our forces.

It grew lighter and still no sound disturbed the morning excepting the incessant roar of the nearby stream. Henry Curtis[36] was close to my right. Suddenly he chirped like a bird. I glanced toward him and saw him pointing toward the top of the knoll. Turning my eyes thither I was just in time to see the half-breed, Billy Sill, lowering his rifle in a line with my head. I rolled behind a tree, and

---

34. Anderson, *Fighting the Mill Creeks*, 78–86.
35. Harmon Good.
36. Curtis, a friend of Anderson's, was the informal leader of the Concow vigilante gang.

the half-breed, knowing that he was seen, sank out of sight behind a rock. I had ample time, in the glimpse I caught of him, to see that he still wore a white shirt.

Almost on the instant that he disappeared, Good's rifle cracked, and the fight was on. We crowded forward and poured a hot fire into the Indians from upstream, while Good's men hammered them from below. Into the stream they leaped, but few got out alive. Instead, many dead bodies floated down the rapid current.

Billy Sill made a break to escape by leaping straight up the mountain-side. Several shot at him, but missed. I swung my rifle on him and cut him down just as he was about to spring into a thicket. As he rolled toward the creek he cursed me venomously with his last breath. He was known to many of us, having lived from childhood with Uncle Dan Sill. He had been herding sheep for Sill a short time before this, when one day he left the band and joined the Mill Creeks.

This battle practically ended the scourge of the Mill Creeks. I had often argued with Good regarding the disposition of the Indians. He believed in killing every man or well-grown boy, but in leaving the women unmolested in their mountain retreats. It was plain to me that we must also get rid of the women. On this occasion the Concow people were intensely wrought up over the horrible atrocities practiced by the Indians on the white women whom they killed, and I had told them that they were at liberty to deal with the Indians as they saw fit.

While ransacking the camp after the battle was over, a little child possessing six toes on each foot was found. Hi Good at once took a notion to the child and said that he wished to take it home with him. Knowing that he had odd tastes about such things, I consented, whereupon he declared that he must take along a squaw to carry the child. I asked Curtis what his pleasure was in the matter, and, after consulting with some of his own party, he grudgingly agreed. The woman selected for the purpose was slightly wounded in the heel. She packed the youngster in stolid silence up the long hill, and over its crest into Twenty-Mile Hollow. Here, however, she became sullen and refused to go a step farther. I gave her over to the Concow people and they left her to swell the number of the dead.[37] ...

---

37. Curtis and the "Concow people," enraged because two settler women had been killed in the Mill Creek raid, were bent on slaying as many of the Indians as they could. Anderson and Good thus sought their consent to spare this woman's life. After Anderson "gave her over," Curtis took the woman aside and shot her. See Sim(eon) Moak, *The Last of the Mill Creeks, and Early Life in Northern California* (Chico: no publisher, 1923), 26. Moak also provides an eyewitness account of the massacre.

Chapter XV

It was well known that several bucks and a number of squaws and children escaped during that last fight at the three knolls. . . . A remnant of the Indians who caused so much uneasiness in those early days remains hidden away in the dark caverns of the hills. They haunt that section from Deer Creek to Mill Creek, making stealthy descents upon the cabin of the white man, but committing no serious crimes. They have developed the art of hiding to a perfection greater than that of the beasts of the woods, and, while in no wise dangerous, they are probably the wildest people in America.

Chapter 4

"That Nation Must Vanish from the Face of the Earth": Genocide of the Herero People

The colonization of present-day Namibia from 1884 onward as German South West Africa (GSWA) resulted in several uprisings against German rule by Indigenous peoples. One such insurrection in 1904 by the Herero people—who numbered about 80,000 and occupied north-central Namibia, the main focus of German colonization—escalated into a bloody conflict that led to the near-complete obliteration of their society. About 80 percent of all Herero died as a result of military action or German retribution, leaving survivors scattered across the territory, most living as virtual slaves to colonists. The genocidal intentions of Lieutenant General Lothar von Trotha, appointed commander of the colonial army in Namibia in May 1904, and preeminent perpetrator of the genocide, is abundantly evident in his attitudes, utterances, and actions. On October 2, 1904, he publicly proclaimed his objective of annihilating the Herero people by issuing his infamous *vernichtungsbefehl* (extermination order) against them. At the height of his exterminatory offensive, Trotha, in a letter dated October 27, 1904 and addressed to Governor Theodor Leutwein, made plain his determination to eradicate the Herero entirely with the pronouncement: "That nation must vanish from the face of the earth."[1]

Little more than a week later in another letter to Leutwein dated November 5, Trotha sought to justify his genocidal campaign by explaining that:

> I know enough tribes in Africa. They all have the same mentality insofar as they yield only to force. It was and remains my policy to apply this force by unmitigated terrorism and even cruelty. I shall destroy the rebellious tribes by shedding streams of blood and money. Only thus will it be possible to sow the seeds of something new that will endure.[2]

Most noticeable here is the willing, even eager, use of excessive and indiscriminate force against an already defeated enemy, including women, children, and

---

1. Horst Drechsler, *"Let Us Die Fighting": The Struggle of the Herero and Nama against German Imperialism, 1884–1915* (London: Zed Press, 1980), 161.

2. Quoted in David Olusoga and Casper Erichsen, *The Kaiser's Holocaust: Germany's Forgotten Genocide and the Colonial Roots of Nazism* (London: Faber and Faber, 2010), 139.

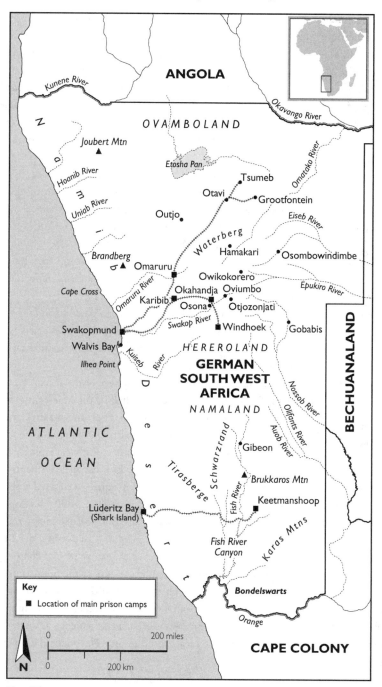

Namibia.

the aged. There is also a murderous character to the racism underlying Trotha's pronouncement in that it embraced a Social Darwinist vision of the complete destruction of Herero society and its replacement with a racially superior social order. Social Darwinists rejected the competing colonial ideology of the civilizing mission as outdated, sentimental, and unscientific. Not content to allow "nature" to take its course, Trotha wanted to hasten the process and achieve this outcome himself. His rhetoric reflects the hubris of a supreme military commander who felt that he had both the mandate and the resources to execute his policy of total annihilation.

Although Trotha's campaign against the Herero was extreme, the ideas upon which it was based were part of mainstream European and German thinking about the essence of colonialism. German imperialists generally saw their colonial project in South West Africa, their only settler colony, as part of a centuries-long global enterprise of expansion necessary for the flourishing of Western civilization and the German nation. It was envisaged that in South West Africa, Indigenous peoples would "vanish" through a combination of disease and an inability to compete for the necessities of life with superior races—or be exterminated as was happening in other parts of the world where European powers had founded settler colonies. For Social Darwinists the destruction of Indigenous society was neither a crime nor a matter of morality but the outcome of an inexorable law of nature—of the strong prevailing over the weak.

In Germany this outlook had developed in the context of the disconcerting social impact of rapid industrialization in the latter half of the nineteenth century. A population explosion, precipitate migration to cities, and massive overcrowding of the urban poor in slums led to fears that the German nation would run out of *lebensraum* (living space) in its own country, and that ongoing emigration, especially to the Americas, was draining it of its most virile elements. It was in this milieu and with the prospect of Germany acquiring a colonial empire that leading German geographer Friedrich Ratzel in the late 1890s developed his highly influential theory around *lebensraum*, based on the pseudoscientific proposal that in order to survive and thrive nations, like all species, need to expand their "living space" and control of resources at the expense of competitors. Social Darwinist reasoning formed an important part of the mindset that allowed imperialists, whether lounging in plush parlors in Berlin or roughing it in remote outposts of the Namibian frontier, to feel vindicated in their appropriation of Indigenous land and the perpetration of mass violence against the inhabitants. Four decades later these ideas would inform Nazi depredations in eastern Europe.

Precolonial Herero Society

Archaeological and linguistic evidence as well as oral tradition indicate that the forebears of the Herero people migrated onto the central plateau of Namibia as early as the twelfth century CE from the Great Lakes region of East Africa. They were seasonally nomadic pastoralists who also resorted to hunter-gathering and horticulture as supplementary forms of subsistence. Cattle were central to regulating patronage and political relations, as well as fulfilling a range of social and spiritual needs, including those relating to marriage, burial, and religious practices. That the original meaning of the word "Herero" is "possessor of cattle" signals the great economic and cultural value they placed on these animals. Through much of the nineteenth century there was also ongoing competition with Nama and other pastoral Khoikhoi-speaking groups to their south for grazing and access to water. This rivalry spilled over into cattle raids and periodically flared into sustained conflict, most notably in times of drought.

Half a century before German colonization, the peoples of central Namibia were progressively drawn into the nexus of Europe's global imperial and economic relations and rivalries that would culminate in the "scramble for Africa" from the mid-1880s onward. The impetus for these changes came mainly from the expanding trade networks of Great Britain's Cape Colony in the south, but also through Portuguese influences in Angola, as well as European traders who operated in the region from the 1860s onward. The main items of trade were cattle, ivory, hides, and skins that were exchanged for firearms, liquor, tobacco, and a range of manufactured goods. The plateau of north-central Namibia, which was controlled by between four and eight mutually competitive chiefdoms and came to be known as Hereroland, constituted the best cattle ranching land in the region. These grasslands separating the Namib and Omaheke Deserts supported herds totaling tens of thousands of cattle.

Importantly, already from the early 1840s onward, missionaries from Germany's Rhenish Missionary Society had come to live among the Herero. Although it took some time for these Protestant missionaries to win converts, mission stations from the mid-1860s onward attracted a growing number of Herero residents, who started adopting elements of European culture as well as a sedentary lifestyle. An increasing number of younger Herero, many the children of chiefs and the elite, attended missionary schools, acquiring the key skill of literacy and an understanding of Western values. A few became teachers in their turn. Mission stations achieved a significant degree of economic success, becoming centers of agricultural production and trade. Missionaries became important players in local politics not only as leaders of growing Christian communities, but also as intermediaries with the outside world and between Herero leaders as well.

On the eve of colonization, the Herero were thus well placed to withstand German incursions into their territory. The historian Gesine Krüger is at pains to point out that the Herero were not "prehistoric tribes" but ". . . groups who had lived for several generations in an increasingly militarized society, maintained economic and diplomatic exchanges with the Cape Colony and pursued their own strategies for ensuring the continuity of power, including the use of 'modern' methods such as writing and weapons [firearms]."[3]

Much of the recurrent conflict with the Nama during the latter half of the nineteenth century was led by one of the great heroes of Herero history, Maharero Tjamuaha (ca.1820–1890). It was Tjamuaha's eldest son, Samuel Maharero (1856–1923), who was to lead the war against German domination in 1904. Tjamuaha's death in 1890 sparked rivalry between potential successors through much of the 1890s for his estate, which included his cattle herds, the Okahandja chieftainship, and his status as effective paramount chief. This rivalry played an important role in the German strategy for undermining chiefly power and gaining control of Hereroland. Having converted to Christianity, Samuel Maharero could count on the support of missionaries against his rivals, and on being favored by colonial officials, despite having a weak claim to his father's estate in terms of Herero rules of inheritance.

German Colonialism 1884–1904

German colonial intervention in Namibia started in April 1884, when Otto von Bismarck, the German chancellor, in an unexpected move decided to annex parts of Namibia; and it ended in July 1915, when an invading army from the Union of South Africa took control of GSWA. South Africa effectively ruled the territory as a colony for the next seventy-five years. Bismarck's move was partly prompted by the fear that the British, who had colonized much of southern Africa—and in 1878 had already annexed Walvis Bay, the only deep-water port along the coast—would grab the territory. It was on this basis that Germany successfully laid claim to South West Africa at the Berlin Conference of 1884–1885, organized by Bismarck, and at which European colonial powers carved out spheres of influence in Africa among themselves.

For much of the first decade, German rule of the territory was nominal, as Bismarck was not prepared to commit significant resources to the venture and was hoping to run the empire on the cheap by using concession companies. In

---

3. Gesine Krüger, "The Golden Age of the Pastoralists: Namibia in the 19th Century," in *Genocide in German South-West Africa: The Colonial War of 1904–1908 and Its Aftermath*, eds. Jürgen Zimmerer and Joachim Zeller (London: Merlin Press, 2008), 14.

August 1885, three officials headed by the rather grandiosely titled imperial commissioner, Heinrich Göring,[4] were sent to GSWA in a symbolic move to strengthen German claims to the colony in the eyes of European rivals. Göring's main task was to sign treaties of protection with chiefs to extend German influence beyond Lüderitz Bay. The first German soldiers to arrive in South West Africa consisted of a tiny contingent of twenty-one troopers sent there in 1889 under Göring's successor, Curt von François, as a gesture to help forestall anticipated British interference in the colony. Significant numbers of settlers started coming only from 1892 onward, their numbers growing from a mere 1,200 in 1894 to about 2,600 in 1897, and 5,000 by 1904. In 1893, a further 250 soldiers were sent to GSWA. François immediately used these troops in a dawn stealth attack on the settlement of the charismatic Nama chief, Hendrik Witbooi. Despite eighty-eight members of his community—nearly all women and children, including his crippled teenaged son—being killed in the Hornkranz Massacre, Witbooi remained unbowed. His subsequent guerrilla attacks on François's troops and his humiliation of the German garrison by stealing nearly all its horses, leaving the cavalry immobilized for months, resulted in François's recall the following year. Thus, although Germany claimed the territory in 1884, colonial penetration was at first utterly superficial. It was not until the mid-1890s that the colonial state was able to start asserting authority over parts of the Indigenous population.

Beginning in 1894, with the appointment of the competent Theodor Leutwein as military commander and governor, German control of the territory gained momentum. Leutwein, through a deliberate strategy of divide-and-rule, methodically set about subduing the Indigenous peoples of southern and central Namibia, making land available for settlement by German immigrants, and developing an infrastructure of roads, railway lines, forts, and a centralized administration to facilitate the commercial exploitation of the colony. Leutwein's administration, drawn mainly from the military, sought to develop GSWA as a colony primarily of European farm settlement. In the decade prior to the Herero-German War (1904–1908), large swathes of land occupied by the Herero and Nama peoples were confiscated by the colonial state, bought up cheaply by speculative land companies, or purchased by settlers for cattle farming. German administrators increasingly found themselves having to mediate between raucously avaricious settlers, who continually demanded the expropriation of land and cattle from Indigenous peoples, and Herero and Nama, who were often armed with modern firearms and were militarily well organized. Many settlers found themselves in direct economic

---

4. He was the father of notorious leading Nazi Hermann Göring.

competition with Herero. They deeply resented that some Herero were wealthier than they were, and that they were often obliged to lease or purchase land from Indigenes. Leutwein tartly commented: ". . . Europeans flooding into Hereroland were inclined, with their inborn feeling of belonging to a superior race, to appear as members of a conquering army, even though we had conquered nothing."[5]

While the German administration was extremely weak when he took charge, over the next decade Leutwein inexorably extended his control over Indigenous leaders and peoples using German military superiority as well as the services of collaborators. Among the Herero, Leutwein's most dependable collaborator was Samuel Maharero himself. In 1894, Maharero, who was politically weak and relatively poor, was on the verge of a crushing defeat by his rivals for Tjamuaha's estate when he appealed to Leutwein for support. Even though he knew that Maharero's claims were weak, Leutwein saw an opportunity not only to gain an Indigenous ally but also to implement his divide-and-rule strategy in a more effective manner. Maharero got the military backing he needed to turn the tables on his rivals, but he was ultimately to pay a heavy price for his pact with Leutwein. A highly unequal but symbiotic relationship developed between the two over the following decade especially after 1896, when they used primogeniture as a legal pretext to have Maharero formally recognized as Tjamuaha's successor and paramount chief.

There was a clear pattern to Leutwein's strategy for asserting German authority that capitalized on his ability to concentrate German firepower in ways that put individual chiefs at his mercy. Leutwein visited chiefs one by one and pressured them into signing highly prejudicial "protection" treaties with the colonial government, using threats and false accusations in the menacing presence of well-armed contingents of German soldiers as well as of collaborating chiefs accompanied by their own warriors. By virtue of these ostentatious shows of force, chiefs were browbeaten into accepting German sovereignty, acknowledging Maharero as paramount chief, and pledging support against Indigenous "rebels." The treaties conscripted chiefs as German surrogates, some even being paid annual stipends for their service to Leutwein's system of indirect rule. When signatories broke the terms of their treaty, as many were bound to, Leutwein would use German military superiority and the help of strategically chosen chiefly collaborators to inflict a limited defeat on opponents and then use that opportunity to confiscate land and cattle, which would be sold to settlers. In that way Leutwein incrementally spread German control through the central and southern areas of Namibia. Early on, within the first few weeks of his governorship, Leutwein made a highly successful example of recalcitrant Khauas Khoi chief Andreas Lambert. He accused

---

5. Quoted in Helmut Bley, *Namibia under German Rule* (Hamburg: Lit Verlag, 1996), 139–40.

Samuel Maharero (left) and Hendrik Witbooi (right).

Lambert of shielding the murderers of a German trader, among other things, then arrested, tried, and had him hanged—all on the same day. For the next decade, the specter of this punishment hung over all of Leutwein's negotiations with Indigenous peoples.

In return for Leutwein's support, Maharero, among other things, allowed the establishment of German garrisons at his headquarters of Okahandja and other strategic locations, agreed to support military action against Indigenous chiefs who resisted the imposition of German control, and importantly, consented to a southern boundary line to Hereroland that dispossessed thousands of Herero of prime grazing land, including that of his main rivals, Nicodemus Kavikunua and Kahimemua. Kavikunua and Kahimemua subsequently revolted against German rule in March and April of 1896, were defeated by a German-led coalition that included both Maharero and Witbooi and were both executed with Samuel's full support in June of that year. Maharero received financial reward and gained power over his rivals through the barrels of German guns but became a pawn in Leutwein's designs for subduing Hereroland. Leutwein adroitly used Maharero both to supplement the meager military force at his disposal, as well as his status as paramount chief to legitimate and enforce his system of indirect rule. Maharero became more and more alienated from his peers and increasingly dependent on Leutwein's goodwill.

In the eleven years the pragmatic Leutwein headed the administration, he effectively brought the areas occupied by the Herero under German control.

Throughout this period, Leutwein did not hesitate to interfere in chiefly politics, using classic divide-and-rule tactics to undermine Indigenous power structures. Conscious of the limited resources at his disposal and the relative strength of Indigenous chiefdoms, Leutwein skillfully used a mix of force, bullying diplomacy, and the sowing of dissent among opponents to bring most of Hereroland under German control.

Both the Herero and Nama peoples periodically staged minor revolts from the latter half of the 1890s onward as colonial rule and the influx of settlers placed them under growing pressure. Indigenes suffered loss of land and cattle, were restricted in their access to water and grazing, were coerced into working on settler farms, and were routinely abused by colonists. What is more, during this period the political and economic independence of Herero society was critically undermined by a natural disaster in the form of an exceptionally virulent rinderpest epidemic that broke out in 1897. Rinderpest is a contagious viral disease of ruminants, including cattle. More than two-thirds of Herero herds succumbed within six months of the outbreak, with estimates of the casualty rate as high as 95 percent in some areas. A locust plague and a drought followed, intensifying the impact of the rinderpest epidemic. Not only were the economic consequences devastating to Herero, but their social order, which revolved around cattle holdings, was in disarray. It is estimated that the resultant famine and disease claimed between 10 and 15 percent of the Herero population. Being a pastoral people whose culture and self-concept revolved around the possession of cattle, this epizootic was extremely traumatic to Herero society.

This clustering of disasters made the Herero vulnerable to settler demands for their land, livestock, and labor. As a result, many Herero were forced to work for settlers or the colonial state; become migrant laborers seeking work as far afield as Cape Town and the Johannesburg goldfields; fall back on hunter-gathering; or take on debt by purchasing exorbitantly priced foodstuffs from German traders. To compensate for their loss of cattle, chiefs resorted to raiding those who still had stock and to the sale of communally owned land. Samuel Maharero was a major culprit in this regard. The rinderpest epidemic irrevocably changed the balance of power in Hereroland by profoundly weakening Herero society and strengthening the hands of both the colonial state and the settler community.

Leutwein's ultimate aims were to destroy chiefly power, confiscate Herero land and cattle, and force them onto reserves, where they would serve the colonial economy as a cheap labor force without rights—what he at one point referred to as rendering them "politically dead."[6] Suffering great turmoil and

---

6. Drechsler, *Let Us Die Fighting,* 148.

hardship in the wake of the rinderpest epidemic, it is not surprising that Indigenous groups in south and central Namibia periodically were driven to rebellion. German forces, however, always prevailed because the uprisings were localized, they had superior weapons, and Leutwein was able to rely on the support of powerful Indigenous collaborators. Having neither the military nor financial resources to implement his plans expeditiously, Leutwein was content to subdue chiefs one at a time, stamp out rebellions, and pursue his goals incrementally. Leutwein was successful in doing so to the extent that by late 1903, he had sufficient control of Hereroland to start implementing his policy of creating reserves.

Causes of the Herero-German War

Despite having collaborated extensively with German authorities to the detriment of Herero society for a decade, Samuel Maharero underwent a radical change of heart by January 1904, when he led a unified Herero uprising against German rule. This insurrection was made possible by another act of insurgency—when the Bondelswarts, a Nama group in the far south of the colony, rose up against a German initiative to have their firearms licensed with a view to eventually confiscating them.

The fundamental reason for the Herero's resort to armed resistance was that they were starting to experience colonial oppression in a way that was forcing traumatic change on their society and unraveling their way of life. By 1903, nearly a third of Herero pastures had been lost to colonists, and the pace at which they were losing choice land was accelerating. By the outbreak of war, a few hundred settler farmers already owned as many cattle—about 45,000—as the entire Herero people. As Herero herds started recovering from the rinderpest catastrophe, it was apparent to many that a land shortage was looming. Also, the German administration became ever more demanding of land, taxes, forced labor, and political subservience as it consolidated its hold on the territory. There were growing fears among the Herero about their future, and this was compounded by increasing colonial disregard for chiefly authority. As Leutwein started implementing his reserve policy in late 1903, a major step in the political emasculation of Herero chiefs, it was clear that he would soon have little need of Maharero as paramount chief.

Settler racism toward the Herero also played an important part in fomenting violence. Immigrants had an overbearing sense of racial superiority, usually regarding Africans as less than human and commonly referring to the Herero as "baboons." Colonists saw Indigenes as a source of cheap labor, there for their convenience, and demanded the right to use corporal punishment to discipline workers. Physical assault and whippings occurred frequently—sometimes for the smallest of infractions—and were at times so severe that victims were incapacitated for several days and some died of these beatings. The sexual exploitation of Herero women by settlers was another inflammatory grievance. Given a sex ratio of about 7-to-1 in the immigrant community, which consisted mainly of young, single men who were armed, consumed prodigious amounts of alcohol, and regarded Indigenes as racially inferior menials, it is not surprising that Herero women and girls were frequently raped or pressured into having sexual intercourse. While there were a few stable relationships and a handful of interracial marriages, much sex across the colonial divide was coerced and violent. Because of the colony's dual legal system that separated settler and Indigenous judicial processes, aggrieved Herero had very little recourse to redress in law as colonists could not be tried by Indigenous authorities. Few settler perpetrators of serious crimes against Indigenes, even murder, were prosecuted. Those who were arraigned either got off scot-free or received absurdly lenient sentences. Writing less than a month after the outbreak of war, missionary August Elger, commenting on the naked racism of "the average German," noted that they ". . . value their horses and oxen more highly than they do the natives. Such a mentality breeds harshness, deceit, exploitation, injustice, rape, and not infrequently, murder as well."[7]

Besides the implementation of Leutwein's reserve policy, there were two developments in 1903 that put further pressure on the Herero and influenced their decision to take up arms. Firstly, the colonial government disclosed its intention of building a new railway line from Swakopmund to the Otavi copper mine. Not only would the line run through the heart of Hereroland, but the state required unpaid labor from the Herero, and the construction company claimed all land and water for twelve and a half miles on either side of it. By opening access to markets, the railway held the prospect of a new rush of settlers into the surrounding countryside, as had happened when the line from Swakopmund to Windhoek was completed in 1902.

Secondly, Leutwein proclaimed a moratorium on all debt the Herero owed settlers. As from November 1, 1903, traders were given one year in which to collect outstanding debts, after which they would fall away. Impoverished by the Rinderpest epidemic, many Herero had been encouraged by European traders to buy exorbitantly priced goods, especially food, on credit. As their liabilities accumulated, people found themselves at the mercy of unscrupulous traders who confiscated land and cattle to settle their arrears. In addition to established traders,

---

7. Drechsler, *Let Us Die Fighting*, 167–88.

a number of poorer settlers who aspired to becoming farmers resorted to peddling goods to Indigenous peoples to accumulate capital with which they hoped to buy land and cattle. Leutwein was concerned that the unscrupulous methods of traders would result in unrest among the Herero, and that indiscriminate land seizures would frustrate his plans for creating a system of reserves for Indigenes. The moratorium led to traders pressurizing the Herero to settle their debts immediately, causing great dissatisfaction as land and cattle were confiscated across Hereroland.

The Herero Take Up Arms

The opportunity for insurrection, which started on January 12, 1904, was created by Governor Leutwein moving, together with most of his troops, to the far south to quell the Bondelswarts revolt. Historian Jan-Bart Gewald debunks conventional arguments that the uprising resulted from a strategic decision by the Herero to take advantage of the temporary troop reduction in Hereroland. He demonstrates that, with the moderating influence of Leutwein out of the way, particular settlers and officers left behind in Hereroland, principally the young, aggressive, and extremely arrogant district officer for Okahandja, *Leutnant* Ralph Zürn, tried to provoke the Herero into hostile acts. Zürn, among other things, browbeat Maharero and threatened chiefs, so that he would have an excuse to retaliate by confiscating land and cattle.

It so happened that at this very time leading Herero chiefs accompanied by several hundred armed followers gathered peacefully at Maharero's headquarters in Okahandja to discuss the succession to the recently deceased chief Kambazembi of the Waterberg region. This alarmed settlers who were prone to fears about impending Indigenous revolts. They worried that the Herero were gathering to attack them in a prelude to a mass uprising. Their panic-stricken and belligerent reactions—principally of the battle-ready Zürn, who ordered all settlers in the area to evacuate their homes and take shelter in the fort—in turn convinced the Herero that they were about to be attacked and that Zürn was planning to kill Maharero. In this atmosphere of confusion, extreme distrust, and heightened nervousness, the first shots of the Herero-German War rang out in an exchange of fire near the Okahandja fort. It is not clear who fired the first shot or for what reason, but the provocateurs got more than they bargained for as the Herero gathered at Okahandja were pushed too far. The insurrection spread rapidly in an explosion of violence that reflected pent-up Herero grievance, frustration, and fear for their future. War soon engulfed the whole of Hereroland. Maharero, fearing for his life, had earlier gone into hiding at the nearby village of Osona, so was not at the flashpoint. It would appear that Maharero had been swept up at the head of an uprising not of his making and of a war he did not want. In a subsequent letter to Leutwein, Maharero pointedly stated: "This is not my war . . . it is that of Zürn."[8]

At that point, the German army in GSWA was quite small, consisting of about 770 troops plus a small auxiliary force of African soldiers. With the greater part of the army far away in the south and unable to return immediately, the Herero had a substantial advantage in the initial stages of hostilities. For several weeks, squads of Herero fighters roamed freely about the countryside launching guerrilla raids on German targets, primarily in outlying areas. They attacked German farms, plundered traders, and overran smaller military camps, killing as many as 160 male colonists in the first few weeks of fighting. German communications were disrupted as telegraph lines were cut and railways sabotaged. Coordinated guerrilla assaults by Herero warriors inflicted startling losses on the *Schutztruppe*, or "defense force," as the colonial army was known. Settlers who survived these attacks fled to undermanned garrisons and towns for protection. Herero warriors on the order of Samuel Maharero deliberately spared women, children, Afrikaners, Britons, and missionaries. The idea behind attacking only German males was not only to target their main source of grievance, but also to try to avoid alienating other whites. It would appear that it was in particular men who had raped Herero women or otherwise severely abused Herero who were targeted. It is deeply ironic that supposed "savages" conducted war in a "civilized" manner, whereas the Germans who regarded themselves as highly "civilized" and racially superior were to conduct war in a most "savage" way. Leutwein was only able to return to central Namibia ahead of his army on February 11, 1904, after containing the Bondelswarts revolt by administering a hasty and indecisive military defeat and then negotiating a peace treaty with them.

The outbreak of war took the German administration and the settler population by complete surprise. They were shocked and frightened by the skill and doggedness of the Herero warriors and their successful attacks, even after the *Schutztruppe* returned from the south. The settler establishment could hardly believe that these "godless savages" had had the temerity to attack colonists and challenge white supremacy. There were loud demands for revenge compounded by exaggerated and fabricated stories of the slaughter of settlers, especially women and children, and the mutilation of their bodies. This is not to deny that there were acts of brutality and ritual mutilation perpetrated by the Herero. It is, however, clear

---

8. Olusoga and Erichsen, *The Kaiser's Holocaust*, 128.

that the fighting intensified the racialized anxieties and feelings of hatred that settlers felt toward Indigenous people. That propaganda demonized the Herero as animal-like sadists further inflamed these animosities. Many settlers made outright calls for the extermination of the Herero.

Although their guerrilla tactics were effective, and they enjoyed considerable success in the early stages of the war, the Herero had limited options in that they did not have the ability to defeat the Germans decisively nor expel them from the territory. The Herero campaign was of necessity fragmented and aimed at scattered and more vulnerable targets. Though causing considerable damage, the Herero did not strike at the heart of the German colonial presence and never seriously threatened any of the larger settlements, preeminently Windhoek. They also failed to rouse other Indigenous peoples to rebellion.

Despite the arrival of substantial reinforcements and equipment by March, Leutwein had little success against the Herero because his army was too small to counter the Herero's guerrilla tactics. The new troops, consisting largely of inexperienced youths drawn from German slums, struggled in the harsh, unfamiliar terrain, and their ranks were soon thinned by typhoid fever. The Herero, having guns and horses, and able to put several thousand fighters into the field, outnumbered them. Avoiding head-on confrontations, and using guerrilla tactics with skill, Maharero frustrated German attempts to engage and defeat him. Besides a few inconclusive skirmishes, Herero forces inflicted stinging defeats on German forces at Owikokorero on March 13, in which seven officers and nineteen soldiers were killed; and again at Oviumbu on April 13, when troops under the command of Leutwein were forced to retreat after a daylong battle.

This military failure by a "Great Power" against what was seen as a primitive, racially inferior people was deeply embarrassing to many Germans, above all to pro-imperialists, the German High Command, and Kaiser Wilhelm II. European rivals took great satisfaction at German discomfort, and opposition parties in the Reichstag severely criticized the government for the debacle. His superiors as well as the settler community felt that Leutwein was too soft on the Herero, blamed him for mishandling the situation, and for taking too long to reimpose full control over the territory. Leutwein's hands were effectively tied when his superiors, already on February 9, informed him that the General Staff in Berlin would dictate the conduct of the war from Berlin and ordered him to attack the Herero forthwith. He justifiably felt he was being pushed into a futile strategy by out-of-touch superiors who were blinded by vengeance and knew nothing of the realities of warfare in the colony. Leutwein's furtive attempt at negotiating

Generalleutnant Lothar von Trotha,
der neue Oberbefehlshaber der deutschen Truppen in Südwestafrika.

General Lothar von Trotha.

a truce with Maharero in late February was abandoned when it elicited furious condemnation from settlers, his flustered superiors, and the pro-imperial lobby back home.

In the face of the humiliation at Oviumbu, wanting to bring the crisis to a swift end, and restore German honor, Kaiser Wilhelm, the constitutional head of the German army, on May 9 replaced Leutwein as military commander of the colony with the experienced and tough-minded general Lothar von Trotha. Until his recall in late 1904, Leutwein remained governor, though. Born into a noble family in Magdeburg, Germany, in 1848, Trotha was the consummate professional soldier. From the age of eighteen, he had fought in the German wars of unification of 1866 and 1870–1871. In 1894, he served as military commander of German forces in East Africa and was responsible for the brutal suppression of resistance to German rule there. Trotha later saw service as commander of a German detachment that helped put down the Boxer Rebellion in China in 1900. By the time he was called upon to restore order in GSWA, Trotha had a reputation for being a ruthless commander, experienced in colonial warfare, and one who did not flinch at the use of brute force to subdue insurrection. When Trotha arrived in Swakopmund on June 11, 1904, he had been given a mandate and an effective blank check by the kaiser to defeat the rebels as decisively as possible. He was answerable only to Alfred von Schlieffen, army chief of staff, and the kaiser. And having declared martial law in the colony prior to his departure from Germany, he completely sidelined civilian authority, including the Colonial Department. GSWA was effectively under military dictatorship during Trotha's tenure. Meanwhile, reinforcements had steadily been arriving in the colony, so that by the time Trotha was ready to go into battle, he had a force well in excess of 5,000 soldiers at his disposal.

A War of Annihilation

After the battle at Oviumbu, Maharero gathered the bulk of the Herero forces as well as the greater part of the community—including women and children, an estimated 60,000 people, together with their cattle—at the Waterberg plateau to the northeast of Hereroland. About forty miles long and nine miles wide, the plateau gets its name from the large aquifers that feed the unusual number of springs, water holes, and streams that enhance this otherwise dry landscape. Although it was the dry season, Maharero calculated that the Waterberg offered enough water and grazing to see them through till the rainy season in February. And because this area was relatively remote, they gained an advantage from extending German supply lines. There was an expectation on the part of the Herero leadership that they would be able to negotiate some form of settlement with Leutwein, albeit with harsh penalties, as that was the style of warfare and diplomacy he had been conducting since his arrival in the colony. Unbeknownst to them, the game had changed irrevocably. The kaiser, the High Command, Trotha himself, most of the colonial army, as well as the greater part of the public back home required nothing less than a crushing defeat to salvage German honor.

In hindsight it seems obvious that gathering en masse at the Waterberg was a tactical error. Firstly, their presence there exerted great pressure on the natural resources, resulting in malnourishment and disease among the Herero as well as their livestock, notwithstanding recent rains. Even worse, the concentration of the greater part of the Herero people in one place gave the German army the opportunity to engage them using conventional means and to attack the community as a whole. Dispersal, with or without continuation of their guerrilla campaigns, would have been a far better option, making the task of the Germans much more difficult.

The Herero had camped at the Waterberg for about three months, during the latter half of which German forces started encircling them with troop and artillery placements and preparing for a decisive onslaught. On the one side the Germans had 4,000 well-armed soldiers, thirty-six artillery pieces, fourteen machine guns, and several thousand horses, albeit in poor condition due to a lack of fodder and water. On the other side were perhaps 6,000 Herero fighters with only about 2,500 rifles and limited ammunition among them, the rest being armed with war clubs. Trotha's strategy was to surround the Herero with six detachments and through simultaneous concentric attacks deliver a crushing defeat to Herero forces as well as visiting wholesale carnage on the community. He was not as yet contemplating extermination, as he had also made provision for mass imprisonment of war captives.

The German army moved to engage the Herero on August 11. Despite having an overwhelming technological advantage, the Battle of Waterberg—also known as the Battle of Hamakari—did not result in the overwhelming victory that Trotha had anticipated but was instead a curiously bungled affair. German soldiers suffered from a range of illnesses and had difficulty adapting to the heat. Many were ill, and supplies of food and water inadequate, as they had to be hauled over sixty miles through difficult terrain from the nearest rail point. At precisely 6:00 a.m. that morning, German artillery started pounding the Herero from a distance and also shelled the camp with women and children, killing many. Machine guns gave the Germans a huge advantage, but the Herero had the benefit of knowing the terrain, being used to the conditions, and being highly mobile. They used thorn bushes as fortification that acted as barbed wire fencing and that German soldiers later described as their "worst enemy." At closer quarters, the Herero fought fiercely causing significant enemy losses. Some commanders mistimed troop movements, botching Trotha's plans for simultaneous concentric attacks. After a day of pitched battle, the superior technology and resources of the German fighting forces began to tell, and the following day the main body of the Herero had little option but to flee in a southeasterly direction, where there were large gaps in German offensive positions. Because he did not have enough troops to effect full encirclement, Trotha had left his southeastern flank facing the Omaheke Desert undermanned.

When Trotha observed this flight into the desert, he ordered his men to allow the retreat because they were exhausted, and he figured that without provisions, the Herero would not get far. In mopping up the remaining Herero on the Waterberg, Trotha ordered his soldiers to kill all Herero men but to spare women and children. These orders were largely ignored, and many women, children, and the aged were killed; perhaps as many as 10,000 Herero were killed in the battle and directly thereafter. Allowing the Herero to bolt into the desert gave them only a temporary reprieve from pursuit. After first retreating in a southeasterly direction, the main body of the Herero people fled eastward along the dry Eiseb and Epukiro riverbeds that led to Bechuanaland. Not only did these riverbeds offer the best chance of their finding water, but they were also well-known trade routes to Bechuanaland. After allowing some time for his soldiers to rest, Trotha mobilized his troops once more for attack. It was at this point that he realized that hemming the Herero into the desert would not only rescue his botched battle plan, but also provide an opportunity for the complete destruction of the Herero. For the ensuing four months, German forces, despite suffering severely from heat, thirst, and exhaustion, continued to pursue surviving Herero relentlessly. Major Stuhlman in a diary entry noted that: "We had been explicitly told beforehand that what we were dealing with was the extermination of the whole tribe, nothing living was to be spared."[9]

Trotha set up a 155-mile-long cordon of military posts and patrols from Gobabis to Grootfontein to prevent the Herero from returning to the more hospitable areas in the west. The Germans also took control of key water holes and poisoned others. Squads of German soldiers set about hunting down surviving Herero bands with orders to kill all men and shoot over the heads of women and children so as to chase them farther into the desert. The soldiers interpreted this as an order to kill all Herero, including women and children. Very few prisoners were taken, and of those captured, many were subsequently executed. The Herero population was devastated in the following weeks as a result of what can only be described as a deliberate attempt at extermination on the part of Trotha and the colonial army. The greater part of the Herero population—an estimated 40,000 people—perished mainly of dehydration in the desert.

Scenes of horrific suffering and violence played out in the Omaheke. Some Herero were so desperate with thirst that they drank the blood of cattle or tried squeezing moisture from the stomach contents of eviscerated animals. A German soldier, Adolph Fischer, in a memoir published in 1914, provides a vivid description of the scene that greeted his pursuing detachment:

> The greater part of the Herero nation and their cattle lay dead in the bush, lining the path of their morbid march. . . . To the right and left of us were putrid, swollen cattle carcasses. Vultures and jackals had already filled themselves to their bellies' content. . . . Whenever we wanted to wet our burning palates, we had to pull our tired horses by their bridles through the swollen animal carcasses to drink a forbidding, disgusting broth from the puddles of water. Wherever we dismounted, our feet would hit against the human bodies. . . . Whoever took part in the chase through the Sandveld lost his belief in righteousness on Earth.[10]

Trotha on several occasions openly stated his intention of completely destroying the Herero people, most notoriously in his extermination order, dated October 2, 1904. Following on behind his troops chasing Herero into the desert, Trotha's convoy set up camp at Osombo-Windimbe, one of the last water holes on the edge of the Omaheke. There on October 3, 1904, he conducted a field service at which he read the following proclamation, the infamous extermination order, to the gathering:

---

9. Quoted in Olusoga and Erichsen, *The Kaiser's Holocaust*, 147.
10. Olusoga and Erichsen, *The Kaiser's Holocaust*, 146–47.

I, the great General of the German soldiers address this letter to the Herero nation. The Herero are no longer German subjects. They have murdered and stolen and cut off the ears, noses, and other body parts from wounded soldiers. Now they don't have the courage to continue the fight. I say to the people: anyone who hands over one of the captains as a captive to a military station will receive one thousand marks. The one who hands over Samuel will receive five thousand marks. The Herero people will have to leave the country. If the people refuse, I will force them with cannons to do so. Within the German boundaries, every Herero, with or without firearms, with or without cattle, will be shot. I won't accommodate women and children anymore. I shall drive them back to their people, or I shall give the order to shoot at them. This is my message to the Herero nation.[11]

For more than two months, until it was rescinded in early December, German policy toward the Herero was one of extermination.

Trotha refused to consider any offers of surrender or to take prisoners. He ignored pleas from missionaries, settlers, and even some of his most senior officers to desist from his extirpatory drive. Trotha's continued extreme stance after the defeat of the Herero at Hamakari was informed by three considerations. Firstly, prisoners would consume resources, and the communicable diseases they carried were a threat to German soldiers. Secondly, because he believed that if decisive action was not taken at that juncture, the Herero would in time regroup and pose a renewed threat to the colony, he sought a permanent solution to this "problem." Thirdly, and perhaps most importantly, he saw the conflict in Social Darwinian terms. He did not care that destroying a valuable labor resource damaged the economic prospects of the colony. His extreme racist beliefs drove him to place the extermination of the Herero above all else. That Trotha publicly stated his exterminatory intentions indicates that he felt justified in his actions, was acting within the accepted norms for warfare in the colonies, and had the authority to conduct such a campaign. In this he had the full support of his superiors, in particular Chief of Staff Schlieffen and the kaiser. In a dispatch to Chancellor Bernhard von Bülow, Schlieffen expressed the opinion that: "One can agree with his plan of annihilating the whole people or driving them from the land. . . . The only problem is that he does not have the power to carry it out."[12]

---

11. Taken from Tilman Dedering, "'A Certain Rigorous Treatment of All Parts of the Nation': The Annihilation of the Herero in German South West Africa, 1904," in *The Massacre in History*, eds. Mark Levene and Penny Roberts (New York: Berghahn Books 1999), 211.

12. Jon Bridgman and Leslie Worley, "Genocide of the Hereros," in *Century of Genocide: Eyewitness Accounts and Critical Reviews*, eds. Samuel Totten, William Parsons, and Israel Charny (New York: Garland Publishing, 1997), 17–18.

While Trotha persisted with his campaign of killing off surviving Herero through much of October and November 1904, there was growing pressure in GSWA as well as in Germany for the war to be brought to an end. Many colonists were aghast that "their" valuable labor resource was being destroyed and that Herero cattle, instead of falling into their laps, were dying in the desert. Within Germany itself, parts of the reading public were well informed about the war and Trotha's merciless tactics through press reports, accounts from soldiers, and agitation by the Rhenish Missionary Society. Many were appalled. The Social Democratic Party, trade unions, missionary societies, and other left-leaning political and humanitarian groups were highly critical of the way in which the war was being conducted. Swept along on a wave of patriotic fervor, Bülow's coalition government initially supported the war but started having misgivings when reports of mass atrocities filtered back into Germany and the costs of war, both financial and reputational, started escalating.

Growing domestic pressure as well as criticism internationally forced both the German High Command and government to reconsider their tactics. On November 23, 1904, Schlieffen wrote to Bülow suggesting that they rescind the extermination order and accept the surrender of the Herero. Bülow in turn set about persuading the kaiser to revoke the extermination order, arguing that it was unchristian, impractical, economically damaging, and undermined Germany's standing as a "civilized" nation. Wilhelm II was reluctant to intervene, and it took more than two weeks of coaxing for Bülow to get the kaiser to comply. It was only on December 9 that the kaiser finally ordered Trotha to accept the surrender of the Herero and the mediation of missionaries. Herero who sought asylum were to be detained in camps run by the military, while offensive operations to round up and imprison the rest were to continue. Trotha reportedly flew into a rage when these orders came through, refusing at first to implement them.

Concentration Camps as Instruments of Genocide

With the repeal of Trotha's extermination order, official policy changed from the extermination of the Herero to their incarceration as prisoners of war in concentration camps. This did not, however, put an end to the genocidal destruction of Herero society because the state of war in GSWA did not cease with Germany's unilateral declaration of its end on March 31, 1907, but only with the closure of concentration camps from early 1908 onward.[13] Conditions in the camps were

---

13. So argued by Jürgen Zimmerer and Jaochim Zeller, "Foreword by the German Editors," in *Genocide in German South-West Africa*, eds. Zimmerer and Zeller, xiv.

so harsh, violence so prevalent, and the neglect of prisoners' most basic needs so blatant that, in the words of Isabel Hull, "imprisonment was a continuation of annihilation by other means."[14] The more than three years the Herero spent in concentration camps meant continued suffering and implosion of their numbers.

There were five main concentration camps strategically located at Windhoek, Okahandja, Karibib, Swakopmund, and Lüderitz both for security reasons and for the efficient distribution of labor. There were a number of smaller camps housing prisoners where their labor was needed, for example, at larger towns such as Omaruru and Keetmanshoop, and at construction sites of various infrastructural projects. It was German policy to send prisoners to locales far from home both as a security measure and to sever their links to the land. Women and children formed about three-quarters of the camp population as a higher percentage of men had been killed during the war, and because men were more likely to evade capture. Men, women, and children were jam-packed into the same quarters and were subject to the same harsh regimen of atrocious living conditions, hard labor, physical abuse, and a meager diet.

Missionaries were keen to mediate between the colonial army and the Herero for humanitarian reasons and to rescue their evangelical enterprise, which had all but been destroyed by the war. They were, however, side-lined for nearly all of 1905 because of Trotha's antagonism toward and distrust of missionaries as well as his doggedly punitive attitude toward the Herero. Trotha thus conducted camp policy as harshly as his orders allowed.

While some Herero surrendered voluntarily, during 1905 most of those interned were captured by military patrols combing the countryside for Herero in what were referred to as "cleansing actions." These extensive sweeping movements by the army throughout north-central Namibia often netted hundreds of prisoners at a time. Despite the military cordon and being hunted in the Omaheke for months, thousands of Herero managed to sneak back into the more hospitable western areas of the colony. Patrols habitually resorted to violence, assaulting and killing individuals, or even massacring groups. This brutality is hardly surprising given that immediately prior to this, soldiers were engaged in an exterminatory offensive against the Herero. Captives were force marched to concentration camps, many dying of exhaustion and starvation on the way. Starving Herero also came to German towns to surrender, some dying in the streets. Over 13,000 Herero were captured by the end of 1905.

Missionaries were given a much more prominent role in mediating with the Herero by Friedrich von Lindequist, who took over the governorship in

---

14. Isabel Hull, *Absolute Destruction: Military Culture and the Practices of War in Imperial Germany* (New York: Cornell University Press, 2005), 90.

Prisoners of war in chains before being transported to concentration camps.

mid-November 1905 after the recall of Trotha, whose campaign against the Nama had gone badly awry. The new governor, being more pragmatic, was concerned with minimizing the security risk of having Herero fugitives roaming the countryside, relieving the severe labor shortage in the colony, and redirecting military resources to combating Nama guerrilla fighters who were destabilizing much of the southern areas. Lindequist thus enlisted the help of missionaries to round up free Herero. Missionaries dispatched armed collection squads of trusted Herero, incongruously referred to as "peace patrols," into the wilderness for weeks at a time to persuade Herero to surrender. The peace patrols were extremely successful in persuading frail, half-starved Herero to surrender. Within little more than a year they had induced another 12,000 Herero to leave the refuge of the bush with promises of food and fair treatment. Casper Erichsen justifiably describes the involvement of missionaries in the persuasion of Herero to give up their freedom and put themselves at the mercy of the colonial state as a "betrayal of trust" because they lured Herero into captivity with promises of food, peace, and freedom when they were well aware of the horrific conditions in the camps.[15] Peace patrollers were themselves betrayed because when their work was done, they were packed off to concentration camps.

Those brought to concentration camps were, almost without exception, debilitated through illness, malnutrition, and deep psychological trauma. Many

---

15. Casper Erichsen, *"The Angel of Death Has Descended Violently Among Them"*: *Concentration Camps and Prisoners-of-War in Namibia, 1904–1908* (Leiden: African Studies Centre, University of Leiden, 2005), 34.

died of exhaustion, starvation, or illness on their way to, or soon after reaching, the camps. As already noted, conditions in the concentration camps were appalling, resulting in a horrendously high death rate. These camps were little more than compounds of makeshift hovels surrounded by barbed wire and thorn bush fences. Some shelters consisted of nothing more than sacking, canvass, or blankets nailed onto wooden frames. Prisoners were inadequately clothed, usually dressed in rags or sack cloth, or they went half naked. Nutrition was critically deficient, especially for those tasked with manual labor. The quality of the food was exceedingly poor, consisting mainly of rice and flour, and infrequent servings of inferior grade meat. Detainees were expected to cook their own food but were not provided with enough pots or firewood to do so. The result was emaciation, weakened immune systems, dysentery, diarrhea, scurvy, and other ailments associated with chronic malnutrition. Extremely crude sanitation together with high concentrations of people, many of whom were sick, aided the spread of infectious diseases—as well as infestations of flies, fleas, maggots, lice, and rodents. Diseases such as pneumonia, tuberculosis, influenza, and typhoid took their toll.

On top of this inmates, including women and children, were expected to work, which more often than not, meant backbreaking labor for long hours under the whip of overseers. Prisoners were routinely beaten and abused by soldiers, supervisors, and employers, sometimes with extreme savagery. So many forced laborers died of exhaustion that the government issued death certificates with "death by exhaustion" preprinted on the forms. Forced labor was mostly used for the building of roads, railway lines, and harbor facilities. Victims were also deployed in the mines and by the army. The military appropriated whatever laborers, including women and children, it needed for the running of barracks and care of its cattle and horses. A significant number of adolescent male survivors were taken by German officers and soldiers as *bambusen* (personal servants). Women and children had little defense against sexual predators, resulting in the spread of sexually transmitted diseases among both detainees and colonists, with exceptionally high rates of venereal disease among soldiers guarding the prisoners. The collection and trafficking of Indigenous body parts, particularly skulls, as raw material for racial science in Germany was rife in the camps. Larger businesses such as the Woermann Shipping Line and the Lenz Company, which had been contracted to build railway embankments, ran separate camps guarded by the military. The government also hired out workers to colonists at set daily and monthly rates. Prisoners were continuously moved around depending on labor needs and occasionally for security reasons. They thus led an unsettled existence with whatever family and communal ties that remained being further sundered.

Herero prisoners in the Shark Island concentration camp in Lüderitz Bay.

In addition to the deliberate maltreatment of prisoners, the genocidal conduct of camp policy is demonstrated by the willful neglect of their most basic needs. Despite protests from missionaries and others, no serious attempt was made to improve conditions in camps, to provide medical attention, to rein in the abuse of officials, soldiers, or colonists who had contact with internees, or in any way to protect the vulnerable. Prisoners were simply allowed to die, the high death rate being accepted with complete composure by both the colonial and metropolitan governments. While inmates were used as forced labor, the squandering of this resource and the sheer cruelty with which the camps were run show that the punishment and eradication of targeted populations, rather than their exploitation, were the primary motivations. There can be little doubt that mass death was an intended outcome of concentration camp policy. In three and a half years of the camps' existence, approximately half of all detainees died.

With the closure of the camps—announced on January 27, 1908 in celebration of the kaiser's birthday—surviving Herero were distributed as forced laborers among settlers, commercial companies, and government agencies in the ensuing months. The Herero had been left leaderless, landless, had lost all their cattle, and their society was atomized. As the official German history of the war put it: "The Herero ceased to exist as a tribe."[16] By its own count in a census taken in 1911, little more than 15,000 Herero were still alive in GSWA. About a 1,000 Herero, including Samuel Maharero, managed to escape into Bechuanaland,

---

16. Bridgman and Worley, "Genocide of the Hereros," 20.

where they lived in poverty, while a similar number managed to flee to Ovambo kingdoms in the north. There was still a small number of Herero who evaded capture and preferred the precarious but independent existence as fugitives beyond the reach of colonial authority.

After the War

It was only after the concentration camps had been closed and the war against the Nama had wound down by 1908 that the colonial administration was able to start implementing in any meaningful way its utopian concept of the "model colony" of agricultural settlement, which had animated the colonial imagination in GSWA from early on. In this fantasy, colonial society would operate in terms of a strict racial hierarchy, in which a fully privileged German settler community would dominate a rightless, landless, Indigenous population living in reserves, and with these distinctions inscribed in law. The cheap, compliant workforce and exploitation of natural resources would ensure rapid economic development of the colony. The German nation would then have acquired significant new *lebensraum* as Friedrich Ratzel's theory predicted.

All land formerly occupied by the Herero was confiscated by the state, mainly to be sold off to colonists. To create the legal basis for implementing its utopian vision, the colonial administration enacted a code of "native law" regulating the lives of Indigenes in the interests of the settler establishment and to ensure that they would never become a threat to the colonial order again. At the center of this code stood three "native ordinances" passed in September 1907. According to the Control Ordinance no Herero was allowed to own land, cattle, or horses without the permission of the governor to ensure that they would not be economically independent and thus be available as cheap labor for the colonial economy. The names of all Herero were to be entered into a central register that would record their location and details of employment, so as to optimize the exploitation and control of this resource. The Pass Ordinance decreed that all Herero over the age of eight had to carry a visible pass at all times. They were to be issued with metal disks embossed with the emblem of the Reich on one side, and on the other a number that was to be used to control them as units of labor. They were required to wear their passes around their necks, without which they would not be able to obtain work, food, or lodging. Any settler could demand to see their pass and hand culprits over to police. Anyone leaving their place of residence needed a travel pass. Those without passes would be prosecuted as vagrants. The Masters and Servants Ordinance stipulated that no more than ten Indigenous families would be allowed to live on the property of their employer. This measure was meant to ensure efficient distribution of scarce labor, to promote effective surveillance, and to prevent any resurgence of organized resistance or ethnic solidarity. The main aim of these laws was to create an amorphous class of Indigenous helots that would service settler labor needs.

These laws were not effective in many respects, as the state did not have the capacity to implement the regulations to the extent it desired or to impose them in the face of mass noncompliance. The colonial bureaucracy was small and inefficient and the policing system inadequate to ensure full obedience. Some Herero absconded, preferring to live as fugitives off a combination of hunter-gathering and stock theft. Others threw away their passes and worked for employers other than those to whom they were assigned. There were also not enough metal badges to go around and maintaining the labor register posed insurmountable obstacles. Many settlers themselves undermined the regulations in the ensuing competition for labor. Earlier exterminatory policies had resulted in a severe labor shortage, and an economic boom after the war greatly compounded the problem. The opening of the Otavi copper mine after the completion of the railway line to Swakopmund in 1907, the discovery of diamonds near Lüderitz in 1908, and the more than doubling of the settler population after the war boosted economic growth—and with it, the demand for labor.

These oppressive conditions did not spell the end of Herero identity despite concerted efforts by the colonial state to erase any sense of ethnic affiliation among them. Beneath the ashes of genocide, small embers of Herero identity remained alive in four areas after the war. Firstly, in the camps many Herero converted to Christianity because missionaries alleviated some of their privations. Also, Christianity provided some spiritual sustenance and a means by which to conceptualize their predicament in affirmative ways. After their release, the converted Herero molded the belief system to their own needs and perceptions, aided by Herero proselytizers who were allowed some freedom of movement by the colonial state. The distinctive brand of Christianity that the Herero created was important in fostering a sense of community among survivors. Secondly, in the army, the *bambusen* and other forced laborers forged a sense of cultural affiliation using military precepts, practices, and insignia. This developed into the *Truppenspieler* (troop player) movement after the ending of German rule, in which members congregated regularly to perform military drills and socialize, thereby asserting their identity as Herero. The movement has endured to become a prominent part of contemporary Herero culture. Thirdly, there were the small clusters of Herero who continued to live as fugitives in the Namibian outback beyond the reach of colonial control. Finally, there were Herero living in exile in various parts of southern Africa.

Fanned by the winds of South African invasion and occupation of GSWA from July 1915 onward, the faint embers of Herero identity started glowing brightly. Many Herero, in acts of open defiance, left their masters, returned to their ancestral lands, sought out family and clan members, acquired stock, and started rebuilding their lives, increasingly as pastoralists squatting on vacant land. The South African regime did not have the administrative capacity or the political will to restrain Herero initiative in this regard, and it was not until the 1930s that it started asserting control over the community. In 1923, these coals burst into open flame when Samuel Maharero died in Bechuanaland and his body was returned to Okahandja for burial. Thousands of Herero from far and wide gathered for his funeral on August 26, 1923, reconnecting with compatriots, re-cementing long-lost ties, and reestablishing a unified sense of Herero community. This was the first time Herero had congregated en masse since the war. In the meanwhile, the *Truppenspieler* movement had expanded into an organization of perhaps as many as twenty regiments across Hereroland that met routinely to practice their drills, helping to overcome the isolation of their scattered membership. Some regiments were sufficiently organized to provide members with rudimentary welfare services, such as paying for burials and small pension grants to the destitute. These were the key catalysts for the regeneration of Herero identity and through which survivors managed to reconstitute themselves as a functional social group, albeit on a basis different to its traditional form.

Ever since Maharero's funeral, Herero people have gathered annually at Okahandja in late August for a three-day celebration known as the *Otjiserandu*[17] to commemorate those who died in the war, pay homage to their deceased chiefs, and reaffirm their identity as Herero. Today there are about 180,000 Herero people in Namibia, forming about 7 percent of the population. Since the turn of the twenty-first century, Herero leaders and activists have launched a series of court cases seeking reparation from the German government and corporations involved in the genocide. So far they have received a qualified apology from the German minister for development, Heidemarie Wieczoreck-Zeul, in 2004 at the centenary commemoration of the genocide, and in 2018 succeeded in having the German government return twenty of the reputedly several hundred skulls and other body parts of Herero and Nama people held by German museums and universities.

---

17. Otjiserandu means "red band," a reference to Samuel Maharero's practice from the 1890s already, of handing out red scarves and bands to his warriors as a symbol their loyalty and Herero unity.

A Clear Case of Genocide

The destruction of Herero society is one of the clearest examples of genocide in Western global expansion. Besides the very high proportion of Herero killed, key German players expressed an explicit intention of annihilating their society, and either pursued this goal with vigor or were complicit by encouraging or enabling the actions of perpetrators. There can also be no gainsaying that German conduct of the war, administration of concentration camps, and "model colony" policies were aimed at the entire Herero community, rather than at combatants or those posing a threat to settler security. The policy of extermination was changed to one of incarceration not so much because Trotha's superiors found it abhorrent, but because the political outfall was becoming costly. This did not represent much of a mitigation, though. Postwar policies, though not openly lethal, were patently genocidal in their intended goal of suppressing and destroying remnant Herero identity and communal life.

In assessing responsibility for the genocide, there is a need to look beyond Trotha's bloodlust and utopian racial fantasies, as there is often too much of an emphasis on the good general himself. This is especially the case among apologists who tend to heap blame on him, while denialists dismiss his genocidal utterances as mere rhetoric, the casualty figures as exaggerated, and the brutalities as typical outcomes of war. Although Trotha played a critical role in the impulse toward genocide, it must not be forgotten that he acted with the approval of both his military and political superiors, in particular the German High Command and the kaiser. For nearly ten weeks subsequent to the extermination order, when the greater part of the Herero community was annihilated, the official policy of the German government was the extermination of the Herero. And many soldiers went beyond the letter of Trotha's orders and killed women and children when they were instructed to shoot above their heads. It would appear that the greater part of German society also either favored the way in which the war was conducted or contemplated it with equanimity. When public opinion was put to the test in the so-called Hottentot election of 1906, fought primarily to decide whether to continue funding the costly war of attrition against the Nama, the jingoistic pro-war faction won a landslide victory. In a passage that confirms the genocidal intent behind German conduct of the war, the General Staff's official history of the conflict triumphantly crowed its approval of Trotha's exterminatory campaign:

> This bold operation shows in a brilliant light the reckless energy of the German leadership in pursuing the beaten enemy. No trouble, no deprivation was spared to rob the enemy of the last remnants of his capacity to resist.

He was driven from water-hole to water-hole like a beast hounded half to death, until, having lost all will, he fell victim to the natural forces of his own country. The waterless Omaheke would complete the task begun by German force, the annihilation of the Herero people.[18]

The Herero genocide, the first of the twentieth century, can be seen as occupying a pivotal position in world history. On the one hand, its exceptional brutality represents the culmination of five centuries of colonial warfare. On the other hand, as a genocide perpetrated by the leading industrial nation of the time, deploying the latest technology, as well as the modern accoutrements of racial science and concentration camps, it foreshadowed far larger catastrophes that would scar the ensuing "century of genocide."

SOURCES

Samuel Maharero's Views on the Causes of the Herero-German War

After he had returned from the far south to Swakopmund on February 11, 1904, Governor Leutwein hoped to negotiate a truce with the Herero. He thus sent Maharero a letter in which he asked him to explain why the Herero had taken up arms. In response, Maharero, who had withdrawn into the interior to the small settlement of Otjozonjati along the Swakop River, summarized what he regarded to be the reasons for the outbreak of war in the letter below.

It subsequently became known to settlers that Leutwein was corresponding with Maharero. This was leaked to the press and pro-imperialists in Germany, causing an uproar. Leutwein was ordered to break off negotiations and engage the Herero forthwith, leading to the setbacks at Owikokorero and Oviumbu.

Questions for Consideration

Specify the various causes of the war given by Samuel Maharero and compare it to a comprehensive list of your own. How would you account for the differences? Which issues are emphasized by Maharero and why? Taking into account the tone, content, and emphases of the letter, what are you able to glean from it about the mindset, expectations, and the political, diplomatic, and military strategies of

---

18. Jürgen Zimmerer, "War, Concentration Camps and Genocide in South-West Africa: The First German Genocide," in *Genocide in German South-West Africa*, Zimmerer and Zeller, 41.

Maharero? What evidence is there in this letter to support the contention that the outbreak of war was not the product of a carefully planned uprising but came about as a result of a series of misunderstandings and the arrogance of *Leutnant* Zürn and his acolytes? Would you agree that this letter is of prime historical significance?

Samuel Maharero's Letter to Governor Leutwein[19]

Otjozonjati 6/3/1904, To the Kaiser's representative Gouverneur Leutwein . . . The outbreak of this war was not initiated by me in this year, rather it was begun by the whites. How many Hereros have the whites, particularly the traders, killed? Both by guns and by locking them up in the prisons. And each time I have brought these cases to Windhoek the blood of my people always had to pay. Cattle to the amount of 50 to 15 head. Many of the traders have exacerbated the difficulties by shifting their debts onto my people. And when something like this occurred you shot us. And began making my people pay and to drive away their cattle, and the people had to pay up to 1 pound if they robbed 2–3 cows. These things have led to the outbreak of war in this country. And now in this year, when the whites saw that you had friendly intentions and love towards us, they began to say to us "Your beloved Gouverner, who loves you, has gone to a serious war and has been killed, and because he has died, so you too will die."[20] Then added to this they then killed two Hereros of Tjetjo,[21] until also *Leutnant* Zürn began killing my people in prison, up to 10 men. They claim that they died due to disease, however they were killed by their captors. Finally *Leutnant* Zürn began to mistreat me and to look for a reason with which to destroy me.[22] And it happened that he said the people of Kambazembi and Ouandja are busy with war.[23] And it

---

19. This letter is housed in the archives of the Evangelical Lutheran Church in Namibia, Windhoek, I, Konferenzprotokolle und Beilagen, 1.19 A. It is written in Otjihero, signed by Samuel Maharero, translated by Jan-Bart Gewald, and reproduced in Gewald, *Herero Heroes* (Oxford: James Currey, 1999), 167–68.

20. Rumors that Leutwein had been killed during the Bondelswarts campaign circulated among settlers in central Namibia.

21. Tjetjo was a prominent Herero chief and Maharero's stepbrother.

22. During Leutwein's absence, Zürn browbeat chiefs into signing a document delimiting the borders of the Okahandja reserve they justifiably thought to be inadequate, and forged the signature of Waterberg chiefs on another document setting the boundaries of that reserve. Zürn throughout acted in an extremely rude and aggressive manner, at one point shouting at Maharero: "Hold your mouth, you pig!" See Gewald, *Herero Heroes*, 145–56.

23. This is a reference to the delegations of Herero chiefs and their warriors who had gathered at Okahandja to discuss Kambazembi's succession with Maharero. Zürn feared that the gathering was the prelude to a revolt.

happened that he called me to him to ask me and I told him directly that this was not the case. But he did not believe me. And finally at dawn he added soldiers to the fort which he hid in chests and called me, but if I had come they would have shot me. Because I realized this I fled. Then *Leutnant* Zürn sent people of the gun on my path to follow me and shoot me this incensed me and consequently I killed the whites which had damaged us, because my death was ordered.[24] This I heard from a white man present here named M. von Michaelis. This is how the war began. It was initiated by the traders and *Leutnant* Zürn. I indicate how the war started, it is not mine. . . . The present war is that of Zürn. These are my words, I am the chief Samuel Maharero.

◆◆◆◆◆

General Lothar von Trotha Explains His Exterminatory Campaign to His Superiors

The report from which this extract is taken was written one day after Trotha issued his extermination order and was addressed to Alfred von Schlieffen, German chief of staff. Having failed to deliver the resounding victory he had promised at the Battle of Waterberg, Trotha needed to explain his new strategy to the German High Command. He saw the war as having reached a deadlock and that radical action was needed to attain the final solution to the Herero "problem" he so zealously sought. A serious complication for him was that many Herero preferred filtering back into Hereroland as opposed to fleeing to Bechuanaland as he had hoped. Trotha also sought to neutralize expected criticism of his plan of action from settlers, and especially from Leutwein, both of whom were concerned about the dire economic impact of the extermination order on the colony. He clearly did not care about the economic consequences and prioritized the destruction of the Herero above all else. Trotha got the support he needed from both the German High Command as well as the kaiser. Not only did their backing confirm that civil authorities, including the Colonial Office, had been sidelined, but also sanctioned the effective military dictatorship Trotha had put in place since mid-1904.

Questions for Consideration

Why, according to Trotha, did the Herero people need to be destroyed? What means did he propose for achieving this end? What evidence is there in this

---

24. A German patrol based at Okahandja had been ambushed and killed the night before the uprising. Maharero thought that the patrol had been sent to assassinate him and thus ordered its destruction.

extract that Trotha was a committed Social Darwinist? Explain how Trotha's assumptions underpinned his course of action and the extreme measures he took. Read this extract in conjunction with the extermination order quoted earlier in the chapter and outline how the ideas and beliefs expressed in this report are a logical extension of the tactical, moral, and ideological principles affirmed there. What credence can be given to arguments that the extermination order and other extreme utterances by Trotha were mere rhetorical flourishes and psychological warfare?

General Trotha's Justifications for His Exterminatory Offensive[25]

The crucial question for me was how to bring the war against the Herero to a close. The Governor and some other "old Africans"[26] on the one hand and myself on the other are poles apart on this issue. The former have long advocated negotiations, describing the Herero nation as a labour reservoir that will be needed in future. I take a completely different view. As I see it, the nation must be destroyed as such and, should this prove impossible to achieve by tactical moves,[27] they will have to be forced out of the country through long-term strategy. It will be possible, by occupying all sources of water supply from Grootfontein all the way to Gobabis and by maintaining high mobility of our columns, to track down and gradually obliterate the small bands of people flocking westward. To pursue the main contingents of the nation with their kapteins[28] right into the Omaheka [*sic*] sandveld and to capture and annihilate them is not feasible at the moment. On the question of provisions I have already passed the limits of what is reasonable. Only time will show to what extent it will be possible for the Estorff unit[29] left behind in Osombo-Ovondimbe to drive them back from any water-holes they may find and to force them to seek refuge in Bechuanaland. If this is impracticable, everything will depend on whether the Herero are capable of holding their own in the Omaheke sandveld[30] until the onset of the rainy season, whether they will attempt to cross into British territory, or whether they will try to regain their

---

25. This extract is reproduced in Drechsler, "*Let us Die Fighting*," 160–61. The report, dated October 4, is housed in the Federal German Archives (BAP), Potsdam, in the files of the Imperial Colonial Office (RKA), 2089, "Differences between Lieutenant-General von Trotha and Governor Leutwein over Uprisings in Ger. SWA during 1904."
26. Soldiers who had served in the colonial army before the war were referred to as "old Africans."
27. By conventional military means.
28. Captains, chiefs.
29. A field regiment commanded by Major Ludwig von Estorff.
30. Dry, sandy scrubland.

traditional grazing grounds through force or total submission. Since I neither can nor will come to terms with these people without express orders from His Majesty the Emperor and King, it is essential that all sections of the nation be subjected to rather stern treatment. I have begun to administer such treatment on my own initiative and, barring orders to the contrary, will continue to do so as long as I am in command here. My intimate knowledge of so many Central African tribes—Bantu and others—has made it abundantly plain to me that Negroes will yield only to brute force, while negotiations are quite pointless. Before my departure yesterday I ordered the warriors captured recently to be court-martialled and hanged and all women and children who sought shelter here to be driven back into the sandveld, handing them a copy of the proclamation drawn up in Othiherero. . . . To accept women and children who are for the most part sick, poses a grave risk to the force, and to feed them is out of the question. For this reason, I deem it wiser for the entire nation to perish than to infect our soldiers into the bargain and to make inroads into our water and food supplies. Over and above this, any gesture of leniency on my part would only be regarded as a sign of weakness by the Herero. They will either meet their doom in the sandveld or try to cross into Bechuanaland. This uprising is and remains the beginning of a racial struggle, which I foresaw for East Africa as early as 1897 in my reports to the Imperial Chancellor.

✦✦✦✦✦

A Description of Trotha's Campaign by a Servant Who Was Part of His Entourage

This statement comes from what is generally referred to as the *Blue Book*—a "Blue Book" being a published report produced by the British government. This particular *Blue Book*, published in August 1918, detailed the nature of German colonial rule in South West Africa. The purpose of the report was to influence the terms of the peace settlement after World War I by justifying the invasion of German South West Africa by the South African Defence Force in 1914 and incorporating it into the British Empire. The *Blue Book*, which included eyewitness reports collected in the form of affidavits, was hastily compiled by South African officials in the military administration, and was intended also to establish South African claims to rule the territory.

Despite being a work of wartime propaganda and part of a calculated diplomatic offensive, the *Blue Book* is a remarkably accurate and well-documented account of German colonialism in South West Africa. German rule was so brutal that there was little need to exaggerate or invent atrocities, and there wasn't much time for fabrication. A great advantage of the *Blue Book* is that it gives voice to eyewitnesses as well as to survivors of atrocities committed by Germans. In this case, Manuel Timbu, though not native to Namibia, had lived there for a long time, was intimately familiar with Indigenous languages and cultures, and experienced Trotha's campaign from a relatively privileged vantage point.

Questions for Consideration

Despite Manuel Timbu's being an eyewitness, one still needs to treat his testimony critically. Is there any reason to conclude that he is exaggerating or deliberately distorting evidence? Explain your reasoning and conclusion. What are you able to deduce from Timbu's account about the tactics of the German forces in the wake of the Battle of Hamakari, and what indicators are there that it was genocidal?

Manuel Timbu (Cape Bastard),[31] at present Court Interpreter in native languages at Omaruru, states under oath:—[32]

I was sent to Okahandja and appointed groom to the German commander, General von Trotha. I had to look after his horses and to do odd jobs at his headquarters. We followed the retreating Hereros from Okahandja to Waterberg, and from there to the borders of the Kalahari Desert. When leaving Okahandja, General von Trotha issued orders to his troops that no quarter was to be given to the enemy. No prisoners were to be taken, but all, regardless of age or sex, were to be killed. General von Trotha said, "We must exterminate them, so that we won't be bothered with rebellions in the future." As a result of this order the soldiers shot all natives we came across. It did not matter who they were. Some were peaceful people who had not gone into rebellion; others, such as old men and old women, had never left their homes; yet these were all shot.[33] I often saw this done. Once while on the march near Hamakari beyond the Waterberg, we came to some water-holes. It was winter time and very cold. We came on two very old Herero women. They had made a small fire and were warming themselves. They had dropped back from the main body of Hereros owing to exhaustion. Von Trotha and his staff were present. A German soldier dismounted, walked up to the

---

31. A "Cape Bastard" was understood to be a person who hailed from the Cape Province of South Africa and was of racially mixed origin, usually of a white father and a Khoikhoi mother.
32. Jeremy Silvester and Jan-Bart Gewald, *Words Cannot Be Found: German Colonial Rule in Namibia: An Annotated Reprint of the 1918 Blue Book* (Leiden: Brill, 2003), 115–16. This is an annotated reprint of *Report on the Natives of South-West Africa and Their Treatment by Germany*, Cd. 9146 (London: HMSO, 1918).
33. Large numbers of non-Herero people—especially Damara, but also San, Ovambo, and Nama—were killed in this indiscriminate way.

old women and shot them both as they lay there. Riding along we got to a vlei, [34] where we camped. While we were there a Herero woman came walking up to us from the bush I was the Herero interpreter. I was told to take the woman to the General to see if she could give information as to the whereabouts of the enemy. I took her to the General von Trotha; she was quite a young woman and looked tired and hungry. Von Trotha asked her several questions, but she did not seem inclined to give information. She said her people had all gone towards the east, but as she was a weak woman she could not keep up with them. Von Trotha then ordered that she should be taken aside and bayoneted. I took the woman away and a soldier came up with his bayonet in his hand. He offered it to me and said I had better stab the woman. I said I would never dream of doing such a thing and asked why the poor woman could not be allowed to live. The soldier laughed and said, "If you won't do it, I will show you what a German soldier can do." He took the woman aside a few paces and drove the bayonet, through her body. He then withdrew the bayonet and brought it all dripping with blood and poked it under my nose in a jeering way, saying, "You see, I have done it." Officers and soldiers were standing around looking on, but no one interfered to save the woman. Her body was not buried, but, like all others they killed. Simply allowed to lie and rot and be eaten by wild animals.

A little further ahead we came to a place where the Hereros had abandoned some goats which were too weak to go further. There was no water to be had for miles around. There we found a young Herero, a boy of about 10 years of age. He had apparently lost his people. As we passed he called out to us that he was hungry and very thirsty. I would have given him something but was forbidden to do so. The Germans discussed the advisability of killing him, and someone said that he would die of thirst in a day or so and it was not worth while bothering, so they passed on and left him there.... I was an eye-witness of everything I have related. In addition I saw the bleeding bodies of hundreds of men, women and children, old and young, lying along the roads as we passed. They had all been killed by our advance guards. I was for nearly two years with the German troops and always with General von Trotha. I know of no instance in which prisoners were spared.

◆◆◆◆◆

Inmate Perspectives on Their Concentration Camp Experiences

While there is much source material on the concentration camps, there is precious little from the perspective of prisoners themselves. The *Blue Book* preserves a few firsthand accounts of camp survivors. Two such narratives are reproduced

---

34. A small lake or water hole.

here, one describing conditions in the Shark Island camp, and the other the environment in one of the Swakopmund-Tsumeb railway construction compounds.

The first deposition is that of Samuel Kariko, son of a Herero chief, a respected and learned Herero teacher, and church elder from Omaruru. He was in the employ of Rhenish missionaries, who in mid-1905 sent him to Shark Island in Lüderitz Bay, by some measure the worst of the concentration camps. While we do have some information on the background and circumstances under which Kariko served in the camps, thanks to missionary records, we have no such contextual information about the second survivor, Traugott Tjienda, besides what can be gleaned from his statement.

Conditions were so bad and the mortality rate so high on Shark Island that soldiers stationed there referred to it as *Todesinsel*, the island of death, because most prisoners sent there were expected to die soon. Besides just about every aspect of life including quality of food, shelter, and working conditions being worse on the island, the bare granite rock was exposed to icy winds and fog from the south Atlantic. Later in 1906–1907, when Governor von Lindequist sought to liquidate sections of the Nama population, he banished them to Shark Island. Within a mere nine months about three-quarters of the approximately 2,000 Nama sent there had died.[35]

Kariko was dispatched to Shark Island, together with eight of his family members, to proselytize and to minister to the spiritual needs of prisoners. He lived with the inmates and for some months was forced to labor alongside them until relieved of this toil at the request of missionaries so that he could perform his pastoral duties. Kariko suffered ill-health, and undoubtedly psychological trauma, to the extent that after nearly six months of this wretched existence, he asked to be discharged of his obligations and, together with his family, to be removed from the island. His forlorn appeal was ignored by his employers until a replacement was found a few weeks later. Ashamed that, unlike the martyred disciple Paul and others who had suffered "to do the Lord's work," he was unable to withstand the torment of Shark Island, Kariko lamented that: "I did not have the spirit of holiness in my heart."[36] In his deposition Kariko was trying to outline the ordeal of Herero people on Shark Island as a whole rather than narrate his specific experience of it.

Clearly a figure of authority and a member of the Herero elite before the war, Traugott Tjienda confirms the atrocious conditions under which railway workers toiled and died in great numbers. The mortality rate in railway construction

---

35. For further detail about the Nama experience on Shark Island see Erichsen, *Angel of Death*, 101–45.

36. Erichsen, *Angel of Death*, 98.

camps was exceedingly high because the labor was extremely taxing, workers were continuously exposed to the elements, especially intolerable heat, and because of the deplorable living conditions they were forced to endure in mobile compounds that shifted along with the construction of the railway line.

Questions for Consideration

Mortality rates were higher in the coastal and railway construction camps. What evidence can be gleaned from these extracts to corroborate this? Compare the two testimonies and explain what their similarities and differences tell us? What do these excerpts indicate about how the camps were run and how the colonial administration viewed their purpose? Is it justifiable to conclude that for the Herero, "captivity was as deadly as war"?[37] What about the judgment that the conduct of camp policy should be construed as war by another means?[38] What indications are there in these extracts that the execution of camp policy was genocidal?

Samuel Kariko (Herero schoolmaster and son of Under-Chief Daniel Kariko) states under oath:—[39]

When von Trotha left, we were advised of a circular which the new Governor, von Lindequist, had issued, in which he promised to spare the lives of our people if we came in from the bush and mountains where we lived like hunted game. We then began to come in. I went to Okambahe, near my old home, and surrendered. We then had no cattle left, and more than three-quarters of our people had perished, far more. There were only a few thousands of us left, and we were walking skeletons, with no flesh, only skin and bones. They collected us in groups and made us work for the little food we got. I was sent down with others to an island far in the south, at Luderitzbucht. There on that island were thousands of Herero and Hottentot prisoners.[40] We had to live there. Men, women and children were all huddled together. We had no proper clothing, no blankets, and the night air on the sea was bitterly cold. The wet sea fogs drenched us and made our teeth chatter. The people died there like flies that had been poisoned. The great majority died there. The little children and the old people died first, and then the women

---

37. Hull, *Absolute Destruction*, 90.
38. See Zimmerer and Zeller, "Foreword," in *Genocide in German South-West Africa*, xiv.
39. Silvester and Gewald, *Words Cannot Be Found*, 175–77.
40. At the time Kariko was on Shark Island nearly all of the prisoners were Herero. Significant numbers of Nama were only brought in during the second half of 1906. Herero and Nama were housed in separate camps.

and the weaker men. No day passed without many deaths. We begged and prayed and appealed for leave to go back to our own country, which is warmer, but the Germans refused. Those men who were fit had to work during the day in the harbor and railway depots. The younger women were selected by the soldiers and taken to their camps as concubines.

Soon the greater majority of the prisoners had died, and then the Germans began to treat us better. A Captain von Zulow took charge. And he was more humane than the others. After being there over a year, those of us who had survived were allowed to return home.[41] After all was over, the survivors of our race were merely slaves.

Traugott Tjienda (Headman of the Hereros at
Tsumeb, who also surrendered under von Lindequist's
Amnesty Proclamation), states on oath:—[42]

I was made to work on the Otavi line which was being built. We were not paid for our work, we were regarded as prisoners. I worked for two years without pay. . . .[43] As our people came in from the bush they were made to work at once, they were merely skin and bones, they were so thin that one could see through their bones they look like broomsticks. Bad as they were, they were made to work; and whether they worked or were lazy they were repeatedly sjambokked[44] by the German overseers. The soldiers guarded us at night in big compounds made of thorn bushes. I was a kind of foreman over the laborers. I had 528 people, all Hereros, in my work party. Of these 148 died while working on the line. The Herero women were compounded with the men. They were made to do manual labor as well. They did not carry the heavy rails, but they had to load and unload wagons and trucks and to work with picks and shovels. The totals above given include women and children. . . . When our women were prisoners on the railway work they were compelled to cohabit with soldiers and white railway labourers. The fact that a woman was married was no protection. Young girls were raped and very badly used. They were taken out of the compounds into the bush and there assaulted. I don't think any of them escaped this, except the older ones.

---

41. The camp was only closed down in the early part of 1908.
42. Silvester and Gewald, *Words Cannot Be Found*, 178.
43. The ellipses are those of the compilers of the *Blue Book*.
44. Whipped.

REFLECTIONS AND CONCLUSIONS

Major General Edward Braddock, commander in chief of British forces in North America at the start of the French and Indian War (1754–1763), emphatically asserted that "no savage shall inherit the land."[1] With these words Braddock flatly rejected a proposed alliance against the French by Delaware chief Shingas, in return for being allowed to retain their land in the upper Ohio Valley. The general paid heavily for his arrogance because the Delawares and several other Native American peoples in the area sided with the French instead. This allied force, consisting overwhelmingly of Indians, routed Braddock's army and killed him early on in the war.

Although uttered by a sojourner rather than a settler, Braddock's rebuff goes to the very heart of all settler colonial projects, particularly those that were part of Western global expansion since the fifteenth century. "No savage shall inherit the land!" would have served as the perfect rallying cry for settlers around the world and perhaps throughout history, especially those prepared to commit violence against Indigenous peoples to secure personal control of acreage, or more expansively, the territory they claimed as their new homeland. Not only does Braddock's pronouncement emphasize the centrality of exclusive control of land and homeland in perpetuity to settler projects, but also the racialized contempt with which Indigenous peoples were held. These sentiments, which echoed across virtually all settler frontiers through six centuries of Western expansion and conquest and that found abundant expression in our case studies, were foundational to the violence visited upon Indigenous peoples who got in the way of settler invasions. And as anthropologist Deborah Bird Rose reminds us: "To get in the way of settler colonization, all the native has to do is stay at home."[2]

Both Braddock and Bird Rose point to the basic reason why settler colonialism tends to be so much more destructive of Indigenous societies and so much more prone to exterminatory violence than other forms of imperialism—it is a winner-takes-all contest focused on the expropriation of Indigenous land and on the elimination of an Indigenous presence from the settler homeland. Two overarching questions that arise is what our case studies reveal about the relationship

---

1. Gary Anderson, *Ethnic Cleansing and the Indian: The Crime That Should Haunt America* (Norman: University of Oklahoma Press, 2014), 74–75.
2. Quote taken from Patrick Wolfe, "Settler Colonialism and the Elimination of the Native," *Journal of Genocide Research* 8, no. 4 (2006): 388.

between settler colonialism and genocide, and how concomitant factors facilitated genocidal outcomes in settler colonial situations. Also, having established that settler colonialism is not inherently genocidal, we also need to ask why in our particular cases hostilities escalated to exterminatory levels. Although each conflict was unique, with important case-specific factors at play, they did share a core of primary facilitators.

A fundamental circumstance tipping the balance decidedly toward exterminatory violence in Western settler expansion was that access to globalizing markets and an attendant desire among colonists to accumulate wealth rapidly encouraged the intensive exploitation of natural resources for short-term gain. This spurred a resort to annihilatory practices to eliminate obstacles or threats to the colonial project or personal ambitions, be they plants, animals, or Indigenous peoples. This impulse to quick riches, though present from the start of European colonization, and very evident in the conquest of the Canary Islands, for example, intensified markedly with European industrialization and the rapid growth of world markets from the late eighteenth century onward. Settler rapacity, excited to a fever pitch by opportunities for profiteering during economic booms, invariably proved deadly for Indigenous communities. Ensuing busts and settler retreats, which were most pronounced along pastoral frontiers, seldom resulted in much of a reprieve for Indigenous communities as in many cases, severe or irreparable damage had already been inflicted on their societies. Also, frustration, fear, and desperation on the part of settlers often incited callous behavior toward Indigenes. After setbacks, it was usually only a matter of time before renewed settler expansion and attacks on Indigenous peoples occurred, as we observed in three of our case studies. In the fourth, California, the demographic swamping of Indigenous communities was so swift and overwhelming that there was little opportunity for effective or sustained Indigenous resistance.

The case studies in this volume confirm that the degree to which settler economies were integrated into the globalizing economy, together with levels of demand for the commodities they produced, had a profound influence on the probability and levels of exterminatory violence perpetrated. It was this market's ability to absorb large quantities of merchandise and create the anticipation of substantial wealth for producers that spurred immigration to colonies, and that propelled farmers, prospectors, speculators, fortune hunters, mercenaries, and other opportunists into head-on collisions with Indigenous peoples. This was what stoked ruthlessly exploitative attitudes to land and labor, a sense of settler entitlement to resources, and a determination that nothing would stand in the way of their prosperity.

Thus, in the Canary archipelago, two realities provided the principal impetus behind the destruction of all seven island societies: initially the Indigenes themselves were by far the most valuable "commodity" the islands had to offer, and there was high demand for slave labor in western Atlantic and Mediterranean markets. It nonetheless took the better part of a century to subdue all the islands because of the resolute resistance of larger island communities and logistical constraints faced by European invaders. Importantly, it was the booming sugarcane industry—of which the Canary Islands became the chief producer for the better part of the sixteenth century—that made the archipelago attractive as a settler destination. In Queensland, a major supplier of wool, among other commodities, to burgeoning British markets, settler greed ignited a series of land rushes and accompanying massacres that effectively denuded a large and densely populated swath of the Australian continent of its Aboriginal societies within half a century. Genocidal processes were much more acute in the case of California, where history's greatest gold rush brought in hundreds of thousands of marauding immigrants within a few years. As only a small minority succeeded in making a living as prospectors, most soon fanned out across the countryside to engage in other economic activities, devastating Indigenous societies in their paths. In German South West Africa economic motives were less important, as it was the hubris of the colony's supreme military commander and the wounded pride of German nationalism, embodied especially in the person of Kaiser Wilhelm II and the German High Command, which propelled the genocide. It is worth noting that, unlike most settler genocides, civilian-driven violence played little part in this case, as it was perpetrated almost entirely through military and state structures. This arid land, which produced little by way of exportable commodities before the war, nevertheless drew a significant number of land-hungry settlers who placed great pressure on Indigenous peoples in central and southern Namibia.

Settler incursions brought with them the privatization and commodification of natural resources, especially land. This defining characteristic of capitalist economies undermined Indigenous societies fundamentally. Systems of land tenure based on personal entitlement, fixed boundaries, registration of title deeds, as well as commerce in, market valuation, and transfer of land, were foreign to Indigenous worldviews and effectively excluded them from legal ownership of vital resources. Commodification—the abstraction and reduction of landholdings to ciphers that allowed transactions in them at remote distances—generally meant the permanent loss of their most basic means of subsistence and that settler claims were backed by the legal apparatus, and ultimately the armed might of the colonial as well as the metropolitan state. Their ability to claim legal title to natural resources in many instances gave settlers cause for going on the offensive against Indigenous peoples and, no doubt, reason for justifying such violence to themselves. Economic and political imperatives invariably resulted in the colonial and metropolitan states condoning settler land confiscations, even in cases where both tried to restrain settler aggression.

The nature of settler economic activity fundamentally shaped the contours of violence along particular frontiers. The three mainland-based forms of settler economic activity—crop growing, pastoralism, and mining—all had genocidal implications for Indigenous societies, though the underlying dynamic of destruction of each was different. Their impacts, which regularly overlapped and were exacerbated by commercial activity, created zones of intensified destruction. In our case studies, but also globally, commercial stock farming was the major contributor to land confiscations, and thus bloodshed, on settler frontiers. The crucial pattern at play here was the rapid occupation of sweeping expanses of land by stock farmers, especially when entering new territory. As suppliers to world markets, these farmers were generally incentivized to produce as much as possible, whatever the environmental and human cost, particularly during economic booms. Their incursions into Indigenous territories tended to be rapid, extremely damaging to the ecosystem, and uncompromising in dealing with Indigenous resistance. On frontiers, settler stock-keepers generally were not bound to ranches and, even where they laid formal claim to landholdings, were usually mobile, engaged in an ongoing search for pasture and water, particularly in drier environments. Vast stretches of countryside were treated as communal grazing or open range with dry spells and drought accelerating their dispersal beyond the fringes of colonial settlement.

Colonial crop growing had a different genocidal dynamic from that of commercial stock farming. Agriculturalists were much more sedentary, marking out longer-term occupancy of land with houses and barns, fences and hedges, and tended to expand incrementally and contiguously, leaving little or no space between landholdings. Crop farming was locally more destructive of the natural environment and Indigenous societies because it occupied land more comprehensively and permanently and supported denser populations. It, however, spread more slowly than herding, which often left large spaces and significant ecological niches intact between landholdings allowing for a degree of Indigenous subsistence, usually combined with stock pilferage. Distance from ports and markets was far less of a concern to stock farmers than their crop-growing counterparts, as in most cases their produce was capable of carrying themselves to desired destinations.

On the other hand, the discovery of minerals—most dramatically gold rushes—could extend frontiers precipitately. Explosive increases in population and the extreme ecological damage that came with mining operations spelled doom for Indigenous communities in and around prospecting areas, but sometimes also far beyond as their effects rippled outward. The attendant growth in farming, especially of stock, in response to the increased demand for foodstuffs was usually an important ingredient in the devastation of Indigenous societies far beyond the prospecting centers themselves. This was evident in the numerous gold rushes experienced in Queensland, and most spectacularly in California. Newly built infrastructure such as roads, rail, and port facilities to support the mining economy often opened up new areas for settlement previously considered too remote or hazardous. Even where mineral deposits were soon exhausted, the impact of mining operations was generally permanent.

It was particularly asymmetries in military technologies that empowered settler economic penetration of Indigenous lands, even under hostile conditions. While colonial states were often weak and had little control over frontier regions, and settlers were in many instances dispersed in small numbers across extensive landscapes, their access to superior weapons allowed them to concentrate their firepower and thus impose their will on Indigenous groups at particular times and places. This in effect ensured at least an incremental, but at times also explosive, extension of settler control over Indigenous territories. It also meant that proportionately small clusters of armed colonists could confiscate extensive areas of land, massacre large groups of Indigenes with virtual impunity, and defend strategic locales such as water sources, transport nodes, or settlements with relative ease. It gave colonial states the means to intimidate or force targeted Indigenous groups to do their bidding, such as sign detrimental treaties, relocate, or collaborate against resisters.

Although different legal regimes applied to different colonies, and conditions varied considerably across the globe, it is nonetheless possible to generalize broadly about the role of colonial law in spurring Indigenous dispossession and processes of elimination in settler societies. The law, which was instrumental to the functioning of the market economy, in general operated in ways that sanctioned the use of both civilian-driven and state-led mass violence against Indigenes. Importantly, it confirmed settler claims to the land, consolidated their control of Indigenous labor, and after the closing of the frontier, facilitated the implementation of eliminatory practices such as assimilation, expulsion, and segregation. Significantly, the absence of the rule of law on the frontier favored settlers, who had superior firepower and were generally able to confiscate land and resources as well as perpetrate violence against Indigenes with a fair degree of impunity. The absence of the rule of law also aided in the suspension of conventions, scruples, and moral codes that might otherwise have tempered settler violence. Much of this violence was committed with the knowledge and connivance of the colonial state or elements within it. And when the rule of law was eventually implemented with the closing of the frontier, it was heavily biased in favor of settlers. Not only were Indigenes routinely and explicitly disadvantaged by the legal system, but settlers also had significant sway over its institutions and day-to-day operation. This enabled settlers to perpetrate high levels of interpersonal violence against Indigenes with impunity. As Lisa Ford pithily put it, "Settler violence, then, was clothed in law."[3] It is noteworthy that in both Queensland and California, legislation deceitfully professing to protect Indigenous people intentionally did the exact opposite. In German South West Africa, "Native Ordinances" dispensed with such niceties; and in the Canaries, the privileges of conquest was in effect the law.

While the global market for commodities was in many ways the ultimate driver of genocidal violence in settler colonies, Indigenous resistance intense enough to threaten settler livelihoods was the most significant proximate factor providing it with impetus. It was when the colonial economy suffered materially or the settler project itself was seen to be under threat that social aversion radicalized into racial hatred, and tensions escalated into annihilatory rages within settler establishments. Our case studies, together with a plethora of similar examples throughout the world, confirm that where settlers producing commodities for capitalist markets invaded the territories of Indigenous peoples, the global economic system tended to bring together the practices of metropolitan and colonial governments, the interests of providers of capital and consumers of commodities, as well as the agency of colonial actors ranging from governors to graziers in remote outposts, in ways that frequently fostered exterminatory violence toward those peoples whose territories they overran.

Demographic and technological imbalances played a significant role in the genocidal destruction of Indigenous societies. Most obviously, the sheer weight of numbers and resources that settler colonial projects were able to muster, especially from the late eighteenth century onward, would in time, and with continued immigration, overwhelm Indigenous societies, which by their very nature were relatively sparsely populated. The contact that frontier communities had with world markets, their metropoles, and settled parts of colonies provided them with access to resources, technologies, institutions, and ideologies that made mass violence toward Indigenes all the easier to perpetrate and extermination all the more comfortable to contemplate. Ever larger and faster ships with which to settle and conquer; ever more accurate and rapid firing guns with which to

---

3. Lisa Ford, *Settler Sovereignty: Jurisdiction and Indigenous People in America and Australia, 1788–1836* (Cambridge, MA: Harvard University Press, 2010), 85.

kill; horses, wagons, and later, trains with which to transport goods; centralized political institutions through which to organize dispossession, mass violence, and exploitation; and an ever-growing array of tools and machines, the sophistication of which Indigenous societies could not hope to match, were among the more obvious advantages frontier settler societies derived from continued contact with their Western wellsprings. Less tangibly, such contact helped reinforce the ideological underpinnings of violence perpetrated against Indigenous peoples. Cultural and religious chauvinism, ideas of European racial superiority and entitlement, as well as jingoistic imperialism, were fortified by continued settler contact with their European and colonial hubs, and played important parts in promoting violence toward Indigenes. Where colonies gained complete independence from metropoles, even when through war and revolution, settler communities nonetheless continued to derive great sustenance from their metropolitan connections. Political separation did not mean that cultural and economic ties were cut, except in the most extreme cases.

The communicable diseases interlopers carried, to which Indigenes had low immunity, compounded the demographic disparities greatly. Even those societies with low population densities were not spared the devastating repercussions of virgin soil epidemics. Disease generally wreaked a toll greater than direct killing, and sometimes Indigenous communities were severely compromised by infections even before direct contact with newcomers was made. The impact of contagious diseases was commensurately greater in those societies suffering land confiscation, malnutrition, mass violence, forced labor, and the psychological traumas attendant upon invasion. Colonization and contagion fed off each other, a deadly pairing that buttressed racist theorizing about the inevitable demise of the "savage."

Severely skewed gender ratios, a condition almost inherent to settler frontiers, contributed to excessive sexual violence toward Indigenous women. The more remote the frontier, the greater gender disparities tended to be, with ratios between settler men and women as high as 10-to-1 on some frontiers. What is more, frontiersmen tended to be a hard, uncompromising, and rough lot who behaved in sexually predatory ways toward Indigenous women. Assault, abduction, rape, and sexual slavery of Indigenous women by settler men, who stereotyped their victims as barely human, were common on many frontiers. Sexual abuse led to the rampant spread of venereal infections, which were sometimes so prevalent that they seriously disrupted the biological reproduction of Indigenous communities. Not only were infected women often unable to conceive or bear fetuses to term, but sexually transmitted diseases in themselves sometimes killed large proportions of populations.

The nature of Indigenous society itself often contributed to genocidal outcomes when faced with an aggressive settler presence.[4] Whereas Indigenous ways of life were in many ways resilient and well adapted to their environments, they were vulnerable when under sustained attack or when faced with prolonged disruption of economic activity. None of the victim societies in our case studies produced economic surpluses large enough to sustain standing armies, conduct systematic warfare, or withstand prolonged, organized hostilities. Because of their generally smaller-scale social structures and relative lack of social differentiation, any substantial degree of organized violence against them took on the aspect of total war. Also, enslavement, child confiscation, and sexual violence to any appreciable extent assumed genocidal proportions at localized levels. This was especially true of hunter-gatherer societies, but also very much the case with pastoralists such as the Herero and agropastoralists such as Indigenous Canarians.

That there was likely to be a blurring of distinctions between warriors and noncombatants in Indigenous society, and that settler violence was often indiscriminate rather than targeted at fighters or adult males, made this doubly so. As we have seen, it was not unusual for entire Indigenous communities to be held responsible for the actions of a few individuals, for one community to pay for the acts of another, and for collective punishments in the form of massacres and random killings to be meted out to people known to be innocent. All of this meant that women and children usually found themselves in the frontline of attack and thus extremely vulnerable to being slaughtered or captured. A common pattern in settler mass violence toward Indigenous communities was to slay the men, take those women not killed as domestic and sexual drudges, and to value children as sufficiently malleable to be trained for a life of servitude. Being taken captive, which in most cases meant serving as forced labor, was integral to the genocidal process because it was in effect as destructive of Indigenous society as killing those members. It may even be argued that being taken captive was worse than being killed as survivors continued to suffer and were used to buttress settler power. Smaller scale social structures, traditional rivalries, and flat political hierarchies made it difficult for Indigenous fighting forces to amalgamate against common enemies. Again, this was especially true of hunter-gatherer societies where individual bands were able to generate no more than a handful of fighters.

The collaboration of elements within Indigenous societies with colonial authorities also contributed to settler genocides, as our case studies attest.

---

4. The observation that the nature of Indigenous society itself contributed to genocidal outcomes in conflict with settlers is not in the least meant to put blame on the victims, nor to diminish their agency. It is intended rather to indicate that such struggles were inherently uneven.

Whereas in colonies of occupation Indigenous collaboration was in most cases central to the colonial enterprise, settler colonies were less dependent on such assistance because the primary goal was not the exploitation but the displacement and elimination of native societies. Instead, Indigenous resistance tends to loom larger in settler colonial situations because the very existence of native societies was at stake. Also, the much larger numbers of colonists and other immigrants that were usually present in settler colonies reduced the need for Indigenous collaborators. Some Indigenes nonetheless collaborated with settler establishments for a wide variety of reasons, and the process was fraught with ambiguities.

In the Canary Islands case, whereas the cooperation of Tenesor Semidan seems to have been motivated by his awe at the affluence and might of European society as well as perhaps a desire to shield his people from complete obliteration, that of the chiefdom of Guimar was driven by political pragmatism derived from both internal Guanche rivalries and the need to adapt as advantageously as possible to the presence of the Spaniards. Christianity happened to serve as a handy facilitator in this regard. On the other hand, Ben Como, after long and spirited resistance, made common cause with the invaders only when the alternative he faced was annihilation. In Queensland recruitment of Indigenes to serve in the Native Police depended on a combination of divide-and-rule tactics and the presence of a pool of deeply traumatized male survivors of earlier settler exterminatory violence that existed on the periphery of settler society—people who were prepared to do this dirty work for whatever preferment it offered. As is common in similar situations, it would appear that the license to commit unrestrained violence also attracted psychopaths, both to the white officer as well as the black trooper ranks. In contrast, collaboration on any scale was hardly evident in California because the extremely rapid demographic swamping of Native Americans and the unassailable military advantages settlers enjoyed largely erased the need. As Lucy Young's testimony indicates, however, a number of Indigenes were complicit in sex and child trafficking through force of circumstance. German South West Africa prior to the genocide provides a classic example of a colonial power deploying a divide-and-rule strategy to effect piecemeal conquest. Leutwein deftly exploited the immediate and urgent needs of co-opted Herero chiefs as well as rifts in Herero society to achieve his longer-term goal of turning GSWA into a colony of agricultural settlement. That his plan, which had worked well for about a decade, ultimately backfired and that his two closest collaborators, Samuel Maharero and Hendrik Witbooi, revolted against German rule, demonstrate the deep equivocation that often underpins such relationships.

While opportunism and self-interest are the most common motivations for collaboration in settler colonial situations, some Indigenous accomplices had little choice in the matter. It also needs to be recognized that collaborators, especially in the earlier stages of colonization, may have seen traditional rivals as greater threats than European colonists, and as possible allies against local adversaries. From the point of view of conquerors, collaboration with Indigenes could help contain costs, both financial and human, and enhance the efficiency of colonial rule. At other times, colonial authorities refused to consider collaboration with Indigenes because they regarded it as compromising the settler project of gaining total control of their prospective homeland, as Braddock's rejection of Shingas's proposal makes clear.

An obvious question to ask of perpetrating groups is what shared frames of reference, ideas, and values animated their communally held animosities toward Indigenes? Or more pointedly, what were the common ideological foundations of civilian-driven violence against Indigenes in settler colonial situations? It would be no exaggeration to claim that ideology was the glue that held imperial ventures together and that helped solidify settler societies. Ideology—commonly understood as a coherent system of ideas, values, beliefs, assumptions, and other attitudinal and normative components shared by a social group and that informs their understanding of the world—is of fundamental importance for its influence on how individuals, leaders, communities, institutions, and state structures frame goals, perceive threats, devise solutions to problems, and deploy violence. Shared ideas and frameworks of meaning among perpetrators are critical in first making exterminatory violence imaginable, and then actionable.

Ideologies play a central role in genocide, as perpetrators do not kill or seek to harm targeted social groups mindlessly. They kill for a reason or a set of reasons, and at the very least with intentions they justify to themselves, and that cast victims as deserving of violence, suffering, or death. Perpetrators of exterminatory violence generally act in groups and usually with the sanction of their broader societies or sections of it. As such they share ideas about their motives and the necessity for resorting to final solutions to a perceived social or political problem. Ideologies, moreover, are important enablers of mass violence to the extent that they help perpetrators overcome taboos against taking human life, help mobilize sympathizers to their cause, and provide ready-made justifications for violence.

There were two centrally important and related ideological components that were common to settler genocides, as abundantly manifested in our case studies. The first was settler beliefs about their entitlement to Indigenous land and their right to seize it by force if necessary. In the case of the Canary Islands, Indigenous lands were taken by right of conquest, a principle regarded as lawful at the time and that remained so well into the twentieth century, though with waning legitimacy. While this precept underpinned settler claims to Indigenous land in the other cases, they were additionally buttressed by ideas of terra nullius in Australia, Manifest Destiny in the United States, and *lebensraum* in GSWA. There was another powerful ideological factor at play that encouraged settler predaciousness and that they used to justify the violent seizure of Indigenous land. Europe has had a long-standing intellectual tradition of linking agriculture with land ownership and "civilization," and the idea that individual property rights in land accrued from the improvement of allotments through the application of labor and capital in ways that enhanced their productivity. This principle, usually referred to as the doctrine of improvement, found its most famous expression in the writing of John Locke, English philosopher and political theorist.[5] Half a century before Locke published this work, John Cotton, leading theologian of the Massachusetts Bay Colony, exemplified this outlook by insisting that: "In a vacant soyle, hee that taketh possession of it, and bestoweth culture and husbandry upon it, his Right it is."[6]

In terms of this deeply rooted conviction, many land-hungry settlers believed that they had a right, even an obligation, to appropriate Indigenous land because they were supposedly able to make better use of it. In 1802, John Quincy Adams rhetorically asked if "the lordly savage" should be allowed to "forbid the wilderness to bloom like roses . . . and rise again transformed into the habitations of ease and elegance?"[7] Theodore Roosevelt, another vocal advocate of settler entitlement at the expense of Indigenous peoples, furnished the basic reasoning behind such thinking: "The settler and pioneer have at bottom had justice on their side; this great continent could not have been kept as nothing but a game preserve for squalid savages."[8] Walter Hixson explains that the unspoken corollary to this kind of reasoning is that when Indigenes "resisted giving up colonial space, 'justice' was on the side of military aggression and ethnic cleansing."[9] I would add genocide and extermination to Hixson's list and note that a great deal of this violence was committed by civilians, both in their individual capacities and in groups organized specifically to perpetrate mass violence against Indigenes.

---

5. These ideas were outlined in his book, *Two Treatises of Government* (London: Awnsham Churchill, 1689).

6. Quoted in Carla Corbin, "Vacancy and the Landscape: Cultural Context and Design Response," *Landscape Journal* 22, no. 1 (2003): 15.

7. Quoted in John Weaver, *The Great Land Rush and the Making of the Modern World, 1650–1900* (Montreal: McGill-Queen's University Press, 2003), 82.

8. Theodore Roosevelt, *The Winning of the West: From the Alleghenies to the Mississippi, 1769–1776* (New York: G. P. Putnam's Sons, 1889), 90.

9. Walter Hixson, *American Settler Colonialism: A History* (Houndmills: Palgrave Macmillan, 2013), 70.

The second ideological component relates to settler assumptions around Indigenous racial inferiority. As we have seen, Western racist thinking that dehumanized Indigenous ways of life as utterly debased was a principal contributor to exterminatory violence. Lockean ideas were most powerfully linked to racist ideologies through assertions that "savages" were incapable of practicing agriculture, or where they did cultivate the land, that they were innately inferior farmers. Settlers were often willfully blind to the extent or proficiency of Indigenous agriculture. And when Indigenous farmers proved to be skilled enough to compete with white farmers, that acted as a strong spur to violence.

It was especially in the case of hunter-gatherers, as in Queensland and California, that Lockean arguments were most effective as justification for expropriation. Because hunter-gatherers were thin on the ground and lived migratory lifestyles, their territories were much more easily imagined as empty, and their habitation of them as temporary, both in the sense that they were not sedentary and that they were seen as a "dying race."[10] The lifestyles of foraging communities were perceived as essentially feral, and that they thus did not own land but merely inhabited or ranged over it much as animals do. Though modulated by local imperatives, the generalized image of un- or under-used land occupied by dangerous, godless savages bereft of morality, reason, or any form of refinement and, most seriously, obstructing the advance of "civilization" and economic development usually underlay settler rationales for both land confiscation and accompanying mass violence. Stereotyped as immune to "civilizing" influences, and their labor unsuited to settler needs, colonists generally regarded Indigenous populations as expendable and often imported laborers from elsewhere— African slaves into the Canary Islands; convicts, Chinese, and Melanesians into Queensland; Chinese and Hispanic workers into California; and Ovambos from the north into the rest of GSWA.

Blanket racial condemnation of "the savage" helped foster indiscriminate violence and collective punishment, which easily escalated to exterminatory levels. Settlers across the globe, and very often the colonial establishments that supported them, had little difficulty justifying the killing of Indigenous women and children as well, and did so in remarkably similar fashion, claiming that the women bred bandits and that children grew up to become enemies. Notorious Californian Indian hunter H. L. Hall, for example, justified his killing of Native American children by claiming that "... a knit [sic] would make a louse." Similarly, Carl Lumholtz, a Norwegian ethnographer who traveled extensively through Queensland in the early 1880s, recounts that a Queensland farmer found it

---

10. For a penetrating analysis of the "myth of the vanishing Indian," see Jentz, *Seven Myths of Native American History* (Indianapolis, IN: Hackett Publishing, 2018), ch. 4.

"severe but necessary" to shoot "all the men he discovered on his run, because they were cattle killers; the women because they gave birth to cattle killers; and the children because they would in time become cattle killers." Nits-make-lice reasoning was an inexorable part of racist discourse and exterminatory actions on settler frontiers.[11]

Although often cast in racial terms and shot through with racist rhetoric, genocidal struggles between settlers and Indigenes were not fundamentally racial in character. They were essentially about incompatible ways of life vying for the same scarce resources, especially the right to occupy particular territories. Racism provided a rationale for dispossessing Indigenes, and their dehumanization made it easier to ignore their suffering, and to exploit, kill, or exterminate them. That irreconcilable economic competition rather than race was at the heart of these conflicts is deftly demonstrated by Edward Cavanagh's study of how the Griqua, an Indigenous, mainly Khoikhoi-speaking, group to the north of the Cape Colony exterminated aboriginal San hunter-gatherer bands in the Transorangia region. The Griqua successfully turned from subsistence to commercial pastoralism in the 1810s and 1820s as a result of market opportunities opened up by the British occupation of the Cape Colony, and became settlers in their own right with their occupation of the Transorangia region. It is no surprise that the Griqua turned into as enthusiastic and deadly slaughterers of San as European colonists who were in the process of exterminating San hunter-gatherer bands in the Cape Colony itself. Significantly, Willem Barend, a citizen of the Griqua state of Philippolis, some decades before Hall and Lumholtz aired their comments, in authentic settler style expressed his determination to exterminate all San as ". . . the children grow up to mischief [of cattle rustling] and the women breed them."[12]

A generalization I feel one can make with some degree of confidence about the mindset of death-dealing colonists in settler colonial situations is that they

---

11. Lynwood Carranco and Estle Beard, *Genocide and Vendetta: The Round Valley Wars of Northern California* (Norman: University of Oklahoma Press, 1981), 62–63; Carl Lumholtz, *Among Cannibals: Account of Four Years Travels in Australia, and Camp Life with the Aborigines of Australia* (Cambridge: Cambridge University Press, 2009; first published London: C. Scribner's Sons, 1889), 347.

12. Edward Cavanagh, "'We Exterminated Them, and Dr. Philip Gave the Country': The Griqua People and the Elimination of San from South Africa's Transorangia Region," in *Genocide on Settler Frontiers: When Hunter-gatherers and Commercial Stock Farmers Clash*, ed. Mohamed Adhikari (New York: Berghahn Books, 2015), 88–107. See 103 for the quotation, and Mohamed Adhikari, "'The Bushman Is a Wild Animal to Be Shot at Sight': Annihilation of the Cape Colony's Foraging Societies by Stock Farming Settlers in the 18th and 19th Centuries," 32–59, in the same volume.

have by and large felt that their actions were morally sanctioned. Writing about violence in general, Alan Fiske and Tage Rai in their book, *Virtuous Violence*, present a persuasive argument that a great deal of violence, if not most, is morally motivated *from the perspective of perpetrators*, rather than the product of psychological or social pathology or genetic defect, as popularly assumed. They explain that: "Morality is about regulating social relationships and violence is one way to regulate relationships."[13] Violence and threats of violence were the most important ways in which relationships between colonists and Indigenous peoples were regulated in settler colonial situations, even where ambivalent relations or middle grounds may have existed for substantial periods. Murder, massacre, and abuse of Indigenous peoples in settler colonies were therefore largely the product of what I term righteous violence, where perpetrators believed themselves to have had some moral or principled justification for using force.[14] Whether killing for God, country, religion, honor, revenge, liberty, some utopian future, to make a fortune, or simply to make a living, righteous violence is particularly pernicious as perpetrators feel little, if any, remorse and are motivated by what they regard to be honorable goals. This is amply reflected in the mythologies and manifest destinies that settler societies have constructed to justify their existence, their acquisition of the land, and treatment of Indigenous peoples.

In our case studies, as in many other examples, the destruction of Indigenous societies was not simply the unintended consequence of land alienation and the blind pursuit of selfish economic motives by colonists, but a consciously desired outcome integral to each society's vision of itself, its future, and the nature of humanity. Establishing that genocide was committed in particular cases of settler colonialism is significant, as such findings are not only of historical or intellectual interest, but also have legal, ethical, and political implications for contemporary society. Genocide is a crime in international law, and while prosecution of long-dead perpetrators is not possible, issues of apology, memorialization, recompense, and restitution come to the fore. Contemporary society too often compartmentalizes settler colonialism and its effects on Indigenous peoples as a matter to be consigned to the past, something that ended with the closing of the frontier or the ceasing of massacres. Peter Kulchyski, Canadian Native studies scholar, reminds us that settler colonialism, together with its

---

13. See Alan Fiske and Tage Rai, *Virtuous Violence: Hurting and Killing to Create, Sustain, End, and Honor Social Relationships* (Cambridge: Cambridge University Press, 2015), xxii, 15–16, 136.
14. By "moral" in this context I mean a set of subjective and culturally based evaluations of human behavior, beliefs, attitudes, and intentions.

panoply of eliminatory practices, continues to exert its baneful influence on the lives of Indigenous survivors:

> In the minutiae of quotidian life, in the presuppositions of service providers, in the structures of State actions and inactions, in the continuing struggles over land use, in a whole trajectory of policies and plans, the work of the conquest is being completed here and now.[15]

An important reason for contemporaries, especially those of us who live in settler societies, to recognize the destruction of Indigenous societies across the globe for what it was and continues to be, and to acknowledge cases of genocide, was neatly articulated by Tessa Morris-Suzuki, professor of Japanese history at the Australian National University:

> We who live in the present did not create the violence and hatred of the past. But the violence and hatred of the past, to some degree created us. It formed the material world and the ideas with which we live, and will continue to do so unless we take active steps to unmake their consequences.[16]

---

15. Peter Kulchyski, *Like the Sound of a Drum: Aboriginal Cultural Politics in Denendeh and Nunavut* (Winnipeg: University of Manitoba Press, 2005), 3. See Lorenzo Veracini, *The Settler Colonial Present* (Basingstoke: Palgrave Macmillan, 2015), especially chapter 4 for a detailed exposition of the issue.

16. Quoted in Ann Curthoys and John Docker, *Is History Fiction?* (Ann Arbor: University of Michigan Press, 2006), 220.

FURTHER READING

Introduction

Adam Jones's *Genocide: A Comprehensive Introduction* (Abingdon: Routledge, 3rd ed., 2017) provides an excellent single-volume introduction to the field of genocide studies. For a detailed analysis of the concept, read Martin Shaw, *What Is Genocide?* (Cambridge: Polity Press, 2015), which delivers insightful discussion throughout, whether or not one agrees with his central contention that genocide is a form of war. Though a little dated, Mark Levene's *The Meaning of Genocide* (London: I.B. Taurus, 2005) has much to offer. Benjamin Meiches, *The Politics of Annihilation: A Genealogy of Genocide* (Minneapolis: University of Minnesota Press, 2019), presents a detailed and theoretically informed analysis of the concept. For an expanded range of essays on the historiography of major themes and case studies, consult Dan Stone, ed., *The Historiography of Genocide* (Houndmills: Palgrave Macmillan, 2008). The title of William Schabas's *Genocide in International Law: The Crime of Crimes* (Cambridge: Cambridge University Press, 2009) is self-explanatory.

Two global histories of genocide that encompass overviews of settler genocides and contextualize them in world history are worthy of note. The first is Norman Naimark's compact *Genocide: A World History* (Oxford: Oxford University Press, 2017). The second is the majestic 700-plus-page study by Ben Kiernan, *Blood and Soil: A World History of Genocide and Extermination from Sparta to Darfur* (New Haven: Yale University Press, 2007). Mark Levene's wide-ranging *Genocide in the Age of the Nation State: The Rise of the West and the Coming of Genocide* (New York: I.B. Taurus, 2005) is a useful offering.

On Lemkin's writing consult Raphael Lemkin, *Axis Rule in Occupied Europe: Laws of Occupation, Analysis of Government, Proposals for Redress* (New York: Columbia University Press, 1944), and Raphael Lemkin and Donna-Lee Frieze, ed., *Totally Unofficial: The Autobiography of Raphael Lemkin* (New Haven: Yale University Press, 2013). For biographical studies of Lemkin see John Cooper, *Raphael Lemkin and the Struggle for the Genocide Convention* (New York: Palgrave Macmillan, 2008), and for a more rounded account, Douglas Irvin-Erickson, *Raphael Lemkin and the Concept of Genocide* (Philadelphia: University of Pennsylvania Press, 2017).

Lorenzo Veracini and Patrick Wolfe are generally accepted as the leading theorists on settler colonialism. Veracini's key work, *Settler Colonialism: A Theoretical*

Overview (Houndmills: Palgrave, Macmillan, 2010), explores settler colonialism as a global historical phenomenon. His subsequent volume, *The Settler Colonial Present* (Houndmills: Palgrave Macmillan, 2015), focuses on its contemporary significance. The publication of Patrick Wolfe's *Settler Colonialism and the Transformation of Anthropology: The Politics and Poetics of an Ethnographic Event* (London: Cassell, 1999) is broadly accepted as a pivotal moment in the emergence of settler colonial studies as an independent field. Wolfe's most cited piece, "Settler Colonialism and the Elimination of the Native," *Journal of Genocide Research* 8, no. 4 (2006), provides a good entry point to his theorizing around the concept. His most recent volume, *Traces of History: Elementary Structures of Race* (London: Verso, 2016), explores the functioning of racial oppression in settler colonial situations globally.

For studies on the history of settler colonialism or significant aspects thereof, see James Belich, *Replenishing the Earth: The Settler Revolution and the Rise of the Anglo-World, 1783–1939* (Oxford: Oxford University Press, 2009); John Weaver, *The Great Land Rush and the Making of the Modern World, 1650–1900* (Montreal: McGill-Queens University Press, 2003); Stuart Banner, *Possessing the Pacific: Land, Settlers and Indigenous People from Australia to Alaska* (Cambridge: Harvard University Press, 2007); and Walter Hixson, *American Settler Colonialism: A History* (New York: Palgrave Macmillan, 2013). A global survey of case studies from ancient times to the present is available in Edward Cavanagh and Lorenzo Veracini, eds., *The Routledge Handbook of the History of Settler Colonialism* (Abingdon: Routledge, 2017).

Chapter 1: Conquest, Enslavement, Deportation: The Erasure of Aboriginal Canarian Societies

The literature in English on the conquest of the Canary Islands is limited, and no other author I know of interprets it as genocide. John Mercer, *The Canary Islanders: Their Prehistory, Conquest and Survival* (London: Rex Collings, 1980), though dated, is an extremely informative source for the history, archaeology, and ethnography of Indigenous Canarian society. David Abulafia's *Discovery of Mankind: Atlantic Encounters in the Age of Columbus* (New Haven: Yale University Press, 2008), which investigates the early interactions between European explorers and Indigenous societies in the Atlantic world, devotes several chapters to the Canary Islands. In *Ecological Imperialism*, Alfred Crosby presents a misguided interpretation of the destruction of their Indigenous societies as the result mainly of an epidemiological disaster.

A few contemporary sources that have been translated into English and published are of inestimable value in assessing the nature of the various conflicts that constituted the conquest of the archipelago. The most important of these are Jean de Bethencourt, *The Canarian, or Book of the Conquest and Conversion of the Canarians in the Year 1402* (New York: Burt Franklin, 1970; first published London: Hakluyt Society 1872, translated by Richard Major); Alonso de Espinosa, *The Guanches of Tenerife: The Holy Image of Our Lady of Candelaria and the Spanish Conquest and Settlement* (London: Hakluyt Society, 1907, translated by Clement Markham); and George Glas, trans., *The History of the Discovery and Conquest of the Canary Islands* (London: Adamantine Media Corporation, 2006; first published London: R. & J. Dodsley, 1764).

Chapter 2: "*Improved from the Face of the Earth*": *The Destruction of Queensland's Aboriginal Peoples*

For a succinct, single-chapter introduction to the subject consult Raymond Evans, "'Plenty Shoot 'Em': The Destruction of Aboriginal Societies Along the Queensland Frontier," in Dirk Moses, *Genocide and Settler Society: Frontier Violence and Stolen Indigenous Children in Australian History* (New York: Berghahn Books, 2004). This chapter is neatly complemented by Pamela Lukin Watson's microstudy, "Passed Away? The Fate of the Karuwali," which appears in the same volume and examines the genocidal destruction of the Karuwali people, who lived in the far southwestern corner of Queensland.

Political scientist Charles Rowley was one of the first academics to document violence on the Queensland frontier in the chapter "The Queensland Frontier," which appeared in his groundbreaking study, *The Destruction of Aboriginal Society* (Harmondsworth: Penguin Books, 1970). This was followed a few years later by a more detailed examination of the subject in *Race Relations in Colonial Queensland: A History of Exclusion, Exploitation and Extermination* (St. Lucia: University of Queensland Press, 1975), a collaborative effort by Raymond Evans, Kay Saunders, and Kathryn Cronin. Two subsequent volumes, though dated, are nonetheless useful, as they document frontier violence against Aborigines in some detail. The first, Rosalind Kidd's *The Way We Civilize* (St. Lucia: University of Queensland Press, 1997), focuses on state and administrative abuses of Aborigines, while the second, Alison Palmer's *Colonial Genocide* (Adelaide: Crawford House, 2000), compares the Queensland Aboriginal experience of colonization with that of the Herero.

More recently, Robert Ørsted-Jensen, an independent researcher, privately published *Frontier History Revisited: Colonial Queensland and the "History War"* (Brisbane: Lux Mundi Publishing, 2011) to refute apologist and denialist interpretations. Timothy Bottoms's *Conspiracy of Silence: Queensland's Frontier Killing Times* (Sydney: Allen & Unwin, 2013) sets out to dispel the pioneering myth of Queensland as having been peacefully settled through the courage, enterprise, and hard work of British settlers. In the process, Bottoms details every frontier massacre he was able to corroborate in the historical record. Leslie Skinner's *Police of the Pastoral Frontier: Native Police, 1849–1859* (St. Lucia: University of Queensland Press, 1975) details the early history of the Queensland Native Police before the colony was separated from New South Wales, while Indigenous scholar Jonathan Richards has produced a comprehensive account, *The Secret War: A True History of Queensland's Native Police* (St. Lucia: University of Queensland Press, 2008).

Chapter 3: "Not a Bad Indian to Be Found": The Annihilation of Native American Societies in California

Benjamin Madley's *An American Genocide: The United States and the California Indian Catastrophe* (New Haven: Yale University Press, 2016) is by some measure the most detailed and authoritative study on the subject. I strongly recommend Madley's excellent essays focused on the calamities that befell specific groups. See, in particular, his "California's Yuki Indians: Defining Genocide in Native American History," *The Western Historical Quarterly* 39, no. 3 (2008): 303–32; and "The Genocide of California's Yana Indians," in Samuel Totten and William Parsons, *Centuries of Genocide: Essays and Eyewitness Accounts*, 4th ed. (New York: Routledge, 2013).

For colonization during the Spanish and Mexican periods, examine Rupert Costo and Jeanette Costo, *Missions of California: A Legacy of Genocide* (San Francisco: Indian Historian Press, 1987); and Robert Jackson and Edward Castillo, *Indians, Franciscans, and Spanish Colonization: The Impact of the Mission System on California Indians* (Albuquerque: University of New Mexico Press, 1995). Among the more useful accounts of US conquest and settlement of California are James Rawls, *Indians of California: The Changing Image* (Norman: University of Oklahoma Press, 1984); Albert Hurtado, *Indian Survival on the California Frontier* (New Haven: Yale University Press, 1988); and Brendan Lindsay, *Murder State: California's Native American Genocide, 1846–1873* (Lincoln: University of Nebraska Press, 2012).

Serviceable regional studies are also available. See, for example, Jack Norton, *Genocide in Northwestern California: When Our World Cried* (San Francisco: Indian Historian Press, 1979); Lynwood Carranco and Estle Beard, *Genocide and Vendetta: The Round Valley Wars of Northern California* (Norman: University of Oklahoma Press, 1981); and Frank Baumgardner, *Killing for Land in Early California: Indian Blood at Round Valley, 1856–1863* (New York: Algora Publishing, 2005).

Works on Ishi include Theodora Kroeber, *Ishi in Two Worlds: A Biography of the Last Wild Indian in North America* (Berkeley: University of California Press, 1961); Alfred Kroeber, *The Mill Creek Indians and Ishi* (Berkeley: University of California Press, 1972); and Orin Starn, *Ishi's Brain: In Search of America's Last Wild Indian* (New York: W. W. Norton & Company, 2004). Two useful contemporary accounts by participants that shed light on settler violence against the Yahi and Yana are Sim Moak, *The Last of the Mill Creeks and Early Life in Northern California* (Chico: no publisher, 1923), and Robert Allen Anderson, *Fighting the Mill Creeks: Being a Personal Account of Campaigns against Indians of the Northern Sierras* (Chico: The Chico Record Press, 1909).

Chapter 4: "That Nation Must Vanish from the Face of the Earth": Genocide of the Herero People

Though aimed largely at a popular readership, David Olusoga and Casper Erichsen, *The Kaiser's Holocaust: Germany's Forgotten Genocide and the Colonial Roots of Nazism* (London: Faber and Faber, 2010), serves as a well-researched, highly readable, and informative single-volume introduction to the genocide of the Herero people, even though it is on an unsure footing when it comes to links and continuities with the Holocaust. Together, two chapters by Jürgen Zimmerer provide a succinct survey of key themes relating to the genocide. They are "The Model Colony? Racial Segregation, Forced Labour and Total Control in German South-West Africa" and "War, Concentration Camps and Genocide in South-West Africa: The First German Genocide," both in Jürgen Zimmerer and Joachim Zeller, eds., *Genocide in German South-West Africa: The Colonial War of 1904–1908 and Its Aftermath* (London: Merlin Press, 2008). The rest of the book consists of essays by specialists on a wide range of aspects relating to the colonial wars of 1904–1908. For a historiography of the case study see Jürgen Zimmerer, "Colonial Genocide: The Herero and Nama War (1904–1908) in German South West Africa and Its Significance," in *The Historiography of Genocide*, edited by Dan Stone.

For nearly half a century, the only critical account of German colonial rule in Namibia was the notorious *Blue Book* published in August 1918 by the British government. A reprint of the *Blue Book* is available as Jeremy Silvester and Jan-Bart Gewald, eds., *Words Cannot Be Found: German Colonial Rule in Namibia: An Annotated Reprint of the 1918 Blue Book* (Leiden: Brill, 2003). It was only in the latter half of the 1960s that the first academic studies of any substance were published in the form of two ideologically opposed volumes—one emanating from East Germany and the other from West Germany. The former, Horst Drechsler's *"Let Us Die Fighting": The Struggle of the Herero and Nama against*

German Imperialism, 1884–1915 (London: Zed Press, 1980; first published in German in 1966), was written from a Marxist and anti-colonial perspective and informed by a critique of capitalism and imperial Germany. The latter by Helmut Bley, *Namibia under German Rule* (Hamburg: Lit Verlag, 1996; first published in German in 1968), and written from a liberal perspective, focused mainly on the German colonial administration and how the agendas of competing interest groups affected policy and the outcome of the conflict. These two books, which complement each other in many ways, effectively defined the level of scholarly knowledge on the matter until the latter half of the 1990s. It was only in 1996 with the appearance of Jan-Bart Gewald's *Towards Redemption: A Socio-political History of the Herero of Namibia Between 1890 and 1923* (Leiden: Research School CNWS, 1996)—republished as *Herero Heroes* (Oxford: James Currey, 1999)—that the boundaries of scholarly knowledge on the subject shifted significantly beyond those set by Drechsler and Bley.

After this, a surge of scholarly writing came with the attention brought by the centenary of the wars as well as Herero activism for redress. In addition to works already mentioned, notable contributions from mid-2000 onward include Casper Erichsen, *"The Angel of Death Has Descended Violently among Them": Concentration Camps and Prisoners-of-War in Namibia, 1904–1908* (Leiden: African Studies Centre, University of Leiden, 2005); and Isabel Hull, *Absolute Destruction: Military Culture and the Practices of War in Imperial Germany* (Ithaca: Cornell University Press, 2005).

For the post-genocidal history of the Herero people and demands for reparation see Jan-Bart Gewald, *"We Thought We Would Be Free . . .": Socio-Cultural Aspects of Herero History in Namibia, 1915–1940* (Köln: Rüdiger Köppe Verlag, 2000); Jeremy Sarkin, *Colonial Genocide and Reparations Claims in the 21st Century: The Socio-legal Context of Claims under International Law by the Herero against Germany for Genocide in Namibia, 1904–1908* (Westport: Praeger Security International, 2009); Reinhart Kössler, *Namibia and Germany: Negotiating the Past* (Windhoek: UNAM Press, 2015); and Henning Melber, "Germany and Namibia: Negotiating Genocide," *Journal of Genocide Research* 22, no. 4 (2020): 502–14.

Reflections and Conclusions

There are many books that provide interesting and varied perspectives on genocidal violence that have a bearing on the content and conclusions of this volume. A small selection includes John Docker, *The Origins of Violence: Religion, History and Genocide* (London: Pluto, 2008); David Livingstone Smith, *Less Than Human: Why We Demean, Enslave, and Exterminate Others* (New York: St. Martin's

Press, 2011); and Alan Fiske and Tage Rai, *Virtuous Violence: Hurting and Killing to Create, Sustain, End, and Honor Social Relationships* (Cambridge: Cambridge University Press, 2015).

In addition to books by Belich, Banner, Weaver, and Kiernan mentioned under Introduction, there is a very wide range of sources available on the central issue of Indigenous dispossession, sovereignty, and matters relating to land, space, and place. Significant works include Stuart Banner, *How the Indians Lost Their Land: Law and the Power on the Frontier* (Cambridge: Harvard University Press, 2005); Annie Coombes, ed., *Rethinking Settler Colonialism: History and Memory in Australia, Canada, New Zealand and South Africa* (Manchester: Manchester University Press, 2007); Lisa Ford, *Settler Sovereignty: Jurisdiction and Indigenous People in America and Australia, 1788–1836* (Cambridge, MA: Harvard University Press, 2010); Tracey Banivanua-Mar and Penelope Edwards, eds., *Making Settler Colonial Space: Perspectives on Race, Place, and Identity* (New York: Palgrave Macmillan, 2010); Aileen Moreton-Robinson, ed., *Sovereign Subjects: Indigenous Sovereignty Matters* (Crows Nest, NSW: Allen & Unwin, 2007); Zoë Laidlaw and Alan Lester, eds., *Indigenous Communities and Settler Colonialism: Land Holding, Loss, and Survival in an Interconnected World* (New York: Palgrave Macmillan, 2015); Jodi Byrd, *The Transit of Empire: Indigenous Critiques of Colonialism* (Minneapolis: University of Minnesota Press, 2011); and Andrew Woolford, Jeff Benvenuto, and Alexander Hinton, eds., *Colonial Genocide in Indigenous North America* (Durham: Duke University Press, 2014).

A major theme that permeates the entire study is that of racism. General studies that will prove useful are George Fredrickson, *Racism: A Short History* (Princeton: Princeton University Press, 2002); Ivan Hannaford, *Race: The History of an Idea in the West* (Washington, DC: Woodrow Wilson Center Press, 1996); and that of evolutionary biologist, Steven Jay Gould, *The Mismeasure of Man* (New York: W. W. Norton & Company, 1981). Studies more closely focused on racism in colonial settings include, Patrick Brantlinger, *Dark Vanishings: Discourses on the Extinction of Primitive Races, 1800–1930* (Ithaca: Cornell University Press, 2003); Gustav Jahoda, *Images of Savages: Ancient Roots of Modern Prejudice in Western Culture* (London: Routledge, 1999); and Jan Nederveen Pieterse, *White on Black: Images of Africa and Blacks in Western Popular Culture* (New Haven: Yale University Press, 1992), all of which will make better sense when viewed in the context of the analysis presented in Wolfe's *Traces of History*.

INDEX

Bold page numbers indicate an image or image caption.